To My number One

Fore

and

Until Eternity

Book Eight

The Quest

Lots of Love

Angela

By

Angela Halliday

xxxx

ISBN-13: 978-1539426882 (bk 1)
ISBN-10: 1539426882
ISBN-13: 978-1539435210 (bk 2)
ISBN-10: 1539435211
ISBN-13: 978-1539435266 (bk 3)
ISBN-10: 1539435261
ISBN-13: 978-1539454489 (bk 4)
ISBN-10: 1539454487
ISBN-13: 978-1542751308 (bk 5)
ISBN-10:   1542751306
ISBN-13: 978-1547021345 (bk 6)
ISBN-10: 1547021349
ISBN-13: 978-1548297503 (bk 7)
ISBN-10: 15482975X
ISBN-13: 978-1987791686 (bk 8)
ISBN-10: 1987791681

Fiction Historical/Action-Adventure. Feminism. Historical Female Heroes
1 Title. The Hill Fort. II Title. Bravery of the Soul. III Title. Proof of Innocence.
IV Title. Into Destiny. V Title. Tragedy of the Heart. VI6 Title. Visitors.
VII Title. Freedom Fighters. VIII Title. The Quest

Cover by GoodCoverDesign
Jacqueline Abroveit

Cover Picture: The Sword
Published by Angela Halliday

Acknowledgements

How lucky I have been to find women who were willing to spend a great deal of time helping me with this work, even though as has been mentioned, I seem unstoppable.

At times, they must have thought me completely mad, but supported me throughout without a murmur and even with some far-fetched ideas. And a word of praise to those who read this in draft form many times, thank you for your patience.

My sister Sheila for her helpful advice and corrections, especially with the Roman era, Jude Doyle-Lawson and Carol Ann Fell for helpful suggestions or checking my work so diligently. Thank you all, from the bottom of my heart.

Contents

Forward

Most things mentioned in these books, the animals of the period, the way people dressed, lived and weapons used, apart from Cross and Long Bows, are period correct. As are the herbal remedies, locations such as Stonehenge, Mai-Dun Fort (Maiden Castle), Hod Hill, the flora and fauna. The names of Romans are as accurate as possible, as are the British Queens (except Alyssa, Lauren and Sheelan that are fictional) and other characters, as well as some of the Chiefs and tribes mentioned. To be sure I understood how period weapons felt and worked I have tested and used them, I own two English Longbows, have personally tackled many of the antics quoted within the pages to gain first-hand experience so that I may write better and more accurately about them. However, I drew the line at fighting bears, lynx cats and wolves. Hopefully, I have instilled my characters with personalities that either touch your heart and induce fondness or love towards them, or cause hate, jealousy or even envy, that has been my intention. In the end and to survive, they had to get on and support each other and, in some cases, that loyalty is taken to extremes due to love of a sovereign. Although I have enjoyed researching and writing this series, some events described within them manifest from my own pain at loss and it hurt to bring them to mind once more. But life needs to be shown as it is, not through rose-tinted glasses in an idealistic way. Thank you all for reading my work. In a way I am sad to leave this era, I virtually lived in it for a couple of years. But Queens are immortal, so who knows…

If you enjoy my books, perhaps you would add a review?

Forever, and Until Eternity

Book VIII : The Quest

Chapter One

A Great Loss

Before moving across the river and into the safety of the trees, Alyssa, Sheelan and I sat quietly on our horses for a few moments looking up at the fort in the near distance perched proudly on its hill, slightly obscured by a slight evening haze. It looked magical, as a fairy-tale castle might in a storybook. My heart ached to be there, as I was sure Alyssa's did.

Poor Alyssa looked so sad: I knew from her thoughts she yearned to be dispensing judgements and fairness to her subjects. It had been our home for so long, hers for far longer, had saved us from wolves, bears and the marauding wild clans and tribes that abounded in southern Britannia and had protected our people superbly during those times of crisis. It had a hospital we were now unable to access and the lovely palace which we both missed. Worse still, our family was split asunder, our daughters out of our reach. That broke our hearts more than anything.

I realised at the same time though, that since the invaders had landed the fort was an outdated mode of life. It was no longer a fort, more like a prison now that the invaders controlled the land by military might. Its wooden walls could no longer withstand the weapons that were4 be ranged against them anymore, they were too powerful. While our walls were not flimsy and weak, Roman siege artillery would eventually break them. But I had loved it there, right from the start of this crazy journey I had begun when stepping into that strange mist and was time-shifted from the early twenty-first century right back to the Iron Age, fifty something years after the break of the millennium to an era diametrically opposed to the one I knew during the lifespan I had spent in the future. Timing the period depended on who was the Roman Governor now, and that was the brutal Quintus Veranius, which in turn meant Nero was the Roman Emperor. Time had moved on, it must be around fifty-six to fifty-eight Anno Domini. All those studies at college that gave me this information seemed a thousand years ago. Now I think about it, it was two thousand years ago! *"My oh my, how time had flown,"* I muttered to myself ruefully. Most people here never understood the ages, stone, bronze and iron, each was a vast period of time. Now I lived in the Romano-Iron Age, the age when the Roman Empire had invaded Britain, naming it Britannia and the world was changing fast. The invaders had better swords than us, made of the first signs of steel by the addition of carbon which gave the metal greater strength and kept a better edge. However, although ours were still the iron Celtic long sword, the weapon gave us greater reach and a heavier hitting force than the Roman gladius, a fact that helped us in close combat and made the Romans fearful of us.

My beloved Alyssa didn't understand any of the things that were going on around her, although she tried. She had lost everything her life had stood for during the years she had ruled her land. Now all that was gone in the blink of an eye, possibly forever, the people she loved and her hill fort wrested out of her control by a brutal foreign army. And to add insult to injury, she had been tied onto a frame by her wrists, left for her full weight to dangle on her shoulder joints and flogged within its palisades in front of her populace, suffering pain and humiliation into the bargain for no justifiable reason, other than Legate thought it a good idea to display his power over us.

I snorted. "Some bloody bargain. How dare they punish such a noble Queen for trying to stand her rightful ground, we were a Client-Queendom allied to Rome, that should never have happened," I muttered angrily.

Now we were unable to enter it, the result of doing so would be capture, another flogging if we were lucky, then thrown into the cell and left to die of starvation and our corpses to rot. However, the worst thing and what really irked me, was we had done nothing to warrant this kind of treatment. So far only Vespasian had allowed us to live as we had before the Romans came. He asked for nothing, other than a little help with their wounded and sick, which we willingly gave. The two governors that followed him only wanted to plunder our riches and crush us and were incredibly brutal if they didn't get what they desired immediately. Artorius Maximus and a few other young Romans had been friendly and even risked severe punishment or possible death by helping me free Alyssa from the dreadful cell. So, they weren't all bad, that behaviour seemed to be confined to some of the Commanders who liked to throw their weight around.

"Are they making a town not far away?" Alyssa's question broke into my thoughts.

"According to Aulus, my love," I nodded. "It's to be called Sarum. It won't be a fort, more a collection of houses around the junction of their roads. Villages will spring up between towns though, so our people will fare well enough once they start to mingle and learn the invader's ways so they can begin trading. Let's get out of sight, please, I feel uncomfortable in full view of the sentries."

Our horses drank as they stepped into the river, causing yet another pause and the ever-increasing danger of challenge from the Roman guards at the fort's south gate. I nudged my heels into its flanks to move it forward, knowing there is a stream further in the trees that would be safer to stop at. This was an open forest, open enough to drive a wagon through as we had often done in the past on sad occasions such as interments in the barrow by the sacred Standing Stones.

Eva gave the halt once at the stream. We dismounted,

wandering around looking for any sign of the swords as this was where we had left them, but our search revealed nothing. That only increased Alyssa's and my low moods and our worry of their whereabouts.

As usual with her curiosity, Sheelan had gone farther away and had become isolated.

I was about to call her back when a large stag came out of the trees and bushes only about twenty feet from her.

It bellowed annoyance at her intrusion into its world.

Fortunately, and having learned lessons the hard way in the past, she had taken her longbow and had a quiver on her back, so in this instance she was armed.

It didn't mess about as stags had previously done when Brevit and me had confronted them and after snorting down its nostrils, its breath drifting slowly through the trees as a white thin vaporous cloud. It followed that with a couple of scrapes of a hoof on the ground it began a charge without further ado.

She was in terrible danger and I was under no allusions as to the outcome of such a fight, having seen it twice before, so started running to give aid, although goodness knows what that would be, I had no weapon.

Then, to my utter surprise, Sheelan started running towards the beast with all the power in her body, her arms swinging wildly, matching the speed of her feet as they pounded across the ground. They were about to meet in one horribly violent collision, the thought of which caused me to screw my face up at the injury an impact of this magnitude would inflict upon her and offered a quick prayer to the Gods for her safety. Within the last few feet she amazed us all by springing upwards, using the energy and velocity of her sprint as her feet hit the ground again to become airborne, spinning into a somersault over the beast's head to land squarely on the its back. She stood, knees a little bent, arms outstretched either side in an attempt to balance herself in that precarious position, wobbled slightly as she turned her head to see the stag's reaction, but remained upright.

The stag had halted once its target had so suddenly vanished right in front of it, swinging its head up to follow Sheelan's direction as she flipped over its head to stare over its shoulder. I think it had a look of disbelief on its face and didn't seem to know what to do, so stood stock still. I don't suppose it had ever been ridden bareback before.

But Sheelan was only there momentarily, she whipped the bow off her body, jumped up into another somersault, landing on her feet directly behind the animal allowing her legs to fold into a squat, spun on her feet, nocked an arrow, drew the bow and as the stag turned to charge again, released her right index and second fingers. All this she achieved in one beautiful fluid motion, almost a ballet of action, and the missile went whizzing off to hit the luckless beast squarely in its chest.

Its legs buckled under it as the animal fell with a thud, to lie very still and dead.

She calmly stood, as if she did acrobatics with irate stags every day of the week, went to it to pull the arrow out, looked over at us and said, "Dinner?"

Our whole band had stood mesmerised all through this amazing performance, even I had halted from my cross-country sprint so not a soul had had time to think about getting a bow. Yet Sheelan had executed a wonderful jump, managed two beautiful somersaults, had a momentary ride on a very startled stag, executed some amazing acrobatics and killed her quarry in a few seconds.

Clapping erupted.

Sheelan looked puzzled at the outburst. "What?" was all she said, looking from one to the other, bemused by our cheering.

"I've said it before and I'll say it again, Sheelan, you are totally amazing. You didn't even think about what you should do, you simply did it. Well done, sweetheart."

Eva couldn't stop laughing. "She is, isn't she? That was very athletic and impressive, I doubt I could have done it. What have you done to her, Lauren?"

Eva had a valid point. I had done nothing to her, plainly the Stones had endowed her with extra physical and mental powers of some kind with a brain that could make lightning fast decisions.

Sheelan shrugged her shoulders as if it was nothing at all, bent down and proceeded to clean the carcass ready for cooking There was plenty of suitable wood in here and we were shielded from prying eyes from both the track outside or the fort, so by common agreement it was decided to stay here overnight and continue our search in the morning.

We were few, so had to work as a team with everyone needing to pull their weight. Lalena and Merial helped Sheelan with the stag, Taal and Verna got the fire going while the rest of us pitched the tents ready for later. Nianda checked our arrows and bolts, we had to keep numbers of those up and the ones we had in good condition. Juna and Freda, aided by Addani were set to guard us while this work was undertaken which meant patrolling around the perimeter, we were short of guards.

Verna even volunteered to get water, although she never had far to go, just a few feet so hardly overstrained herself.

We dined well that evening and kept the fire high for as long as we could, now evenings were drawing in earlier a night chill set in. A relaxing chat around its flickering flames was also good, we needed to discuss our predicament and what we should do.

Our objectives were still the swords, they were the whole point of coming here in the first place. Once found, to try and discover what we should use them for.

"The Gods must have empowered them for a reason," Alyssa pointed out.

"But who could have taken them?" Bran put in. "And do they know their power? According to you, Lauren, they each have amazing strength. What if the person finds that out?"

"I think whatever extra powers were imbued upon them only manifests when held by the rightful, true owner, as it did when I took a swipe at the tree. When I went to pick Alyssa's up it caused pain in my fingers. But that might only be for the first time. It's the jewels I'm more concerned about. Whoever has them may try to prise them out of the settings and that would ruin the weapons completely."

"I don't think they will be able to," Alyssa said. "They come from our dimension, so have very special properties, darling."

I nodded slowly. "There's sense in that, they are not of this earth and in that case, it may not be possible to steal them."

"What, even my one?" Sheelan asked, surprised.

"That's possible, after what happened, I wouldn't be surprised. That's why it's so important we find out where they are," I replied.

"It's getting late," Eva broke in. "We had better decide who's on guard tonight. Don't stay on too long, change as soon as you feel weary. So Lalena and Merial first. Then Freda and Juna, followed by Taal and Verna and after them, if necessary, Lauren and Sheelan and again if it's required, Bran and me. In an emergency one of you call Nianda and Squirrel. That should give us all some sleep."

That agreed, we went to our tents, paired off in that way so the change of guard didn't disturb anybody else.

"I'll miss you tonight," Alyssa said, sadly.

"There's no reason you can't come in with us as normal, my love, Sheelan's as warm as me."

Sheelan grinned. "Yes, I am, Alyssa. We'll be okay."

"Highness, Highness." An urgent voice called out of the darkness, at the same time a hand began shaking my shoulder.

"Don't call me that." I snapped it out sharply, I hadn't meant to, but people knew how dangerous it was if that was overheard. "Who is it?"

"It's Verna, um, err, Lauren. Taal sent me to wake you, she said there are people in the wood."

"Okay, I'm coming," I replied through a yawn. "I hope it isn't Damarion wandering about again, I thought he said he was going to the fort to mingle with his family. But it could be, he might have taken refuge in here before going in."

Sheelan got up. "I'll get Eva and Bran," she muttered, she sounded only half awake.

It was a half-moon tonight, so it was lighter than the last time Verna had woken me in the southern forest, which meant I could see Taal crouching behind a bush. "Any idea who it might be?" I whispered.

The movement she gave told me she had shaken her head, so no, she didn't. "Over there, Lauren, I think whoever it is, camped during the night, they weren't there when we went to bed, they would have seen our fire."

"In that case it's most likely strangers, our people never do that unless unavoidable, and it wasn't last night."

Eva and Bran crept up to us. Eva asked the question I just had.

"No, Leader I've no idea yet. I wonder what time it is?"

"We were the watch after Freda and Juna, so it must be nearly morning, Lauren," Taal replied.

"Still too dark to see much. Verna, go back quietly and wake everybody else, then bring two crossbows and four long ones with the right quivers, please. Oh, and my firestick from my horse," I added.

She looked blankly at me.

I did the fingers thing. "That many long bows, Verna. Taal, have you any idea how many camped?"

"A lot I think, by the noise they were making, about two patrols perhaps."

Twenty then, I thought, or about that many. We wouldn't know until it got lighter.

Verna arrived back and gave the bows out. We agreed to settle down to await the dawn and keep an eye on their camp. They had no idea we were here, coming in very late as they had so I didn't want to make any loud noise. If we met carefully in daylight it could be done peacefully. While we

16

had been camped in the southern forest I had asked Shaila to dye our tents green, now that paid off, otherwise white would have shown up brightly in the moonlight, even in here among the trees.

Alyssa squeezed in beside me, slipping her arm around my waist.

I smiled back at her. Even with the worry of late she looked remarkable. Rich red hair, a flush on her cheeks and reddened lips. There were no lines on her face that I could see, she was delightful. Leaning her way, I stole a kiss.

She smiled back.

This had taken but a few minutes, but now we were all in position and the other camp none the wiser of our proximity.

There was such an almighty racket beside me, I nearly jumped out of my skin. It could have been the *RMS Queen Mary* docking sounding her horn, it's said that was audible for over seven miles!

Verna had sneezed!

Only it wasn't just a sneeze as any normal person would have, there was so much force in it I half expected her brains to come flying out.

In an instant everything changed and all hell broke loose!

People in the other camp went all ways grabbing weapons which was bad news, it's much better if you know where each person is, not have them dash off like loose cannons.

I could cheerfully have taken my rifle and hit Verna over the head very hard with it, but she was so stupid I didn't want to break the rifle. And that was a point, the silly bitch had forgotten to bring it. I fled to my horse, whipped it out of its sheath, grabbed ammo from the straddle bag, loaded, and began hurrying back.

By then Alyssa and Sheelan had split up, I don't know why, they should have stayed together for support. It meant Alyssa was fighting someone on my right alone, while Sheelan was engaging a person way over on the left. In that case, we were partially surrounded.

I was almost to Alyssa when I heard the sound of an arrow

in flight, exactly the same moment she did.

She had half turned when it hit her in her back. Her eyes opened wide in total surprise, those lovely blue eyes I adored so much. She gasped "Aahh," as air rushed out of her lungs with the force of impact. Then she fell.

I threw the rifle down and slid my arms under her. I felt the arrow, it was in her left side. "Lay still, darling," I choked out the words, tears streamed down my face. The battle faded into obscurity as I held her. I wanted an arrow too, into my own heart. I would have stood and let it happen but I couldn't let her go, I needed to hold her, she should not be alone now.

A soft smile flitted across her face. "I love you, I'll wait while you fight, darling." There was a softness in her voice. She knew she was seriously injured, possibly dying.

"I can't leave you, my love," I replied through tears. "I love you too, so very much and will until eternity ends."

Her smile faded as her body sunk closely into mine. I held her tight, her head on my breast so to keep it from rolling sideways. I felt her warmness, fingers touched my hand as she tried to show her love.

Then my anger came, a red mist descending before my eyes. How dare they hurt my wonderful Alyssa? What right had they to attack us and do this vile deed? We had not threatened them, only watched.

Carefully lying Alyssa down, I whispered in her ear. "I have to help them, I shall kill them all for hurting you, my love." Snatching up the rifle, it was quickly fully cocked, a round pushed into the chamber by my acting on the under lever, brought it to my shoulder and I began blazing away as quickly and as accurately as I could.

The gun was empty, I knelt and reloaded, then was up again. An arrow slipped passed my left ear, I cared nothing about arrows, they were of no consequence. Clack, click, bang, clack, click, bang, the gun kept firing. I was out again, it just clicked when I pulled the trigger. More cartridges came into my hand, they slipped into the magazine and the rifle was cocked and ready for action. The bangs deafened my ears once more, again and again, as the enemy came before my eyes, until a hand held my arm to stop me. I turned to find Sheelan staring at me.

"They are all dead, Lauren, you're shooting dead bodies, my darling. Give me the firestick, please. Come, let us go see Alyssa,"

Slowly the red curtain began to fade as my dreadful anger left me to see Sheelan's concerned face, then to dissipate into a hurting heart. I burst into a never-ending flood of tears while trying to speak but no words came, so I pointed at Alyssa lying a few feet away. My knees gave out and I was beside her, stroking her beautiful red hair.

Sheelan asked someone to bring a knife. She knelt beside me and cut the shaft of the arrow off a few inches from Alyssa's body.

I tried to speak again, but my mouth just hung open in despair, something inside me had turned to a cold granite boulder, I knew it was my heart.

Sheelan's arms held me tightly. "We must get the arrow out, Lauren, you should have stayed with her while we fought. Let's make her more comfortable, then you must work your magic and get her well."

I nodded, pulling myself together. Crying my heart out wasn't going to help Alyssa, it had been a tremendous shock seeing it happen before my eyes.

"Bring some furs to lie her on. Get the medications from the straddle bags and some linen to wrap around my hand. Are there tips on the arrows?"

Taal brought one. "Highness, they have plain shafts."

Sheelan cleaned the broken end of the arrow, ready for it to be pushed through and out. "Will it hurt her?" she asked worriedly.

"A little, I'll be as quick as I can. When I push you pull in a straight line, it must be straight, Sheelan. Ready?"

Her head nodded.

My hand went in fast, pushing the arrow shaft hard. Sheelan snatched the tip and out it came.

Alyssa gasped.

"I'm sorry if I hurt you, my love. It had to be done."

She smiled in that amazing way and nodded. "I know, my dear Lauren."

I cleaned the wound and dressed it. "You should be okay, sweet one, it missed vital organs but it was very close, so please rest and be still. Sheelan, help me hold her up so Alyssa can take a couple of painkillers."

"Your tent is cosy and warm, Highness," Bran said. "We should get the Queen into it quickly."

Alyssa was lifted on the fur and carefully carried to it. She winced a couple of times but didn't cry out.

"Thank you, my lovely Lauren. Will I survive?" The only fear in her voice was of leaving me if she died, of the memory of my pain after Madeil passed away; she didn't want to put me through that agony again.

"I hope so, it is a nasty wound but never bled as much as a vital one would, like a kidney or lung. But you must rest, listen to what Sheelan and I say. We'll get you well, my love." I bent and kissed her.

"Thank you, darling," Alyssa said in a hushed tone.

"Why did you leave her?" I asked Sheelan.

"I was going to stay with her, it's my duty, Lauren. But Verna was cut off and in trouble, she cried out for help. They got around behind us so Taal was fighting two and was unable to disengage. I failed her, Lauren, I am so sorry."

She was sorry! Sheelan must feel the same as me, the poor darling. I leant into her, she held me again.

I felt her tears hit my cheek, so looked up and kissed her. "Alyssa's alive, that's the main thing. Situations develop in a fight, we can't help our reactions, it wasn't your fault."

"I should have stayed, Lauren," she repeated, shaking her head.

"Don't feel guilty, you did what needed doing, that's all. I would probably have done the same thing. You had to leave your post to rescue Verna. Now we are stuck here with a badly injured Alyssa, unable to move if any Romans come looking. And we need food, vegetables and bread, we can hunt the meat, but grain and veg must come from the fort."

Chapter Two

Verna

In truth, I could cheerfully have brained Verna with something very heavy and solid. Why was she way over there with a bow, she's not a warrior? She should have been with Taal instead of splitting our defence line up.

Alyssa moved, her hand gripped my wrist. "We'll need coins to get those things, darling. It means going to the Stones to retrieve them."

I looked at her, lying there, the poor darling, worrying about problems that she shouldn't. She had aged. "How is the pain, sweet one?"

"Hurting, but it's bound to. A dreadful ache in my side."

"I'll get some antibiotics, arrows aren't the cleanest of things." At my horse my eyes were full of tears, I was fumbling around in the straddle bags.

Nianda touched my arm. "What do you need, Highness?"

"A needle and a small phial. But you can't read, Nianda, I must look."

She held me and smiled. "Let me wipe your eyes so you can see better. I'll hold the bag open, that might be easier."

It was, and she did. She used the back of her hand tenderly, then cuddled me. I soon found what I needed and thanked her.

Loading the syringe, I looked into Alyssa's lovely, yet pained face. "This might hurt a little, just try to stay relaxed."

"I won't feel a thing, darling, do it, please."

Her side was badly bruised, there was swelling. I hoped it wasn't internal bleeding. I leant back and wiped the injection clean. "There, that should help."

"Thank you," Alyssa said. "You have a wonderfully soft

touch, Lauren."

I had to go outside for a few moments. Sobbing racked my whole body as hands and arms took me in comfort.

"She will be alright, won't she?" Taal said, uncertainty in her voice, her eyes wide and bright.

Nodding, I tried to smile and look confident. "Yes, I hope so, as long as we can keep infection at bay. The Queen said we must get coins, so I need Eva. Have you seen her? I haven't for a while."

Taal cast around. "I don't know, Highness, I haven't seen her either since the battle."

Something horrible and cold ran across my shoulders and back. It was the grip of fear. "Search for her, everyone, quickly."

Within a few moments Bran yelled out. "I've found her, over here, quickly Lauren." There was an urgency in her voice that bade ill.

Dropping to her side, I could see why. An arrow protruded from the centre of her chest. There was a lot of blood over her and she was panting hard.

Eva's eyes seemed to melt into mine. "I'm dying, aren't I Highness?"

"Let me look at you." I tore her tunic open but knew immediately it was a fatal wound. I looked back at her, she smiled through her pain. "Yes, I am afraid so Eva, there is nothing I can do my dear sweet woman."

Tears took my eyes yet again. In a few minutes of madness, we had Alyssa badly injured and Eva in her death throes. And all because of bloody Verna and her stupid sneeze, that female was a menace. I was beginning to wonder if she could do anything right at all, she didn't have a very good track record.

Eva gripped my wrist. "Hold me, Highness. I don't want to go to Otherworld alone."

I stooped to collect her in my arms. "Of course you don't, Eva, my love. I have you and we are all here, you're tightly in my arms, I'll not let you go. Have no fear, brave warrior."

Bran wiped her forehead. "We are all beside you, Eva."

"Call me Lauren, please, we are closer than the Highness thing, you and me. Remember when we first met, how you held your bow at me and brought me to the fort as a prisoner?" I gulped, my eyes were filling again and voice choking up.

A weak smile took her lips. "Yes, I do, Lauren. I wish I had trusted you more then, forgive me. I can hear you, but can't see very well, it's misty and getting dark. Why is that, Lauren?"

"It's because you're slipping away, my wonderful warrior. I am here with you, show no fear, we'll meet in Otherworld one day, maybe sooner than we expect with our lifestyles. I love you, sweet Eva."

Her reply was very faint. "And I you, thank you for coming to us, I am glad you did and I lov..."

Her head rolled to one side. I checked for a pulse but it was over, Eva had gone. I held her to me still, how could I put her down on the earth, she deserved better than that. I lifted her, carrying her still form to a tent. "Get a fur, please, someone."

Bran did. "Here, Highness, lay her on this."

She helped me put her gently down. My head dropped forward as I knelt beside her, the back of my right hand barely touched the side of her pretty face as I stroked it.

"Go, my brave woman, to be with all the other courageous warriors that await you now. They will take you into their arms, as I held you as you left us, they will care for you, Madeil, Brevit, Teal, Sorel and many more." I looked up. "By the Gods, this is awful, Bran."

She put an arm around my shoulders. "We'll all miss her badly. Eva was a wonderful woman and a pillar of our community. You look angry, Lauren."

My face hardened. "Bring me Verna." I shouted loudly, suddenly standing up. "Get that wretch of a woman here. Please cover Eva with a fur, she must be sent to Otherworld properly."

"I can't find her," Taal wailed, desperation in her voice.

"Go look for her then, don't stand there staring at me, go woman! I don't care how, just find her and bring her before me!"

Taal backed away. "Yer... yes Highness, I will." Her eyes were wide with fear of my actions.

Bran's hand came on my sleeve. "Nobody can help sneezing, Highness."

"She could have gone away when she felt it coming, put a finger under her nose, a hand over her face to smother it, something, instead of standing up and letting it out like that as if it was midday on the lower field. She's caused a death and a serious injury by her stupidity. There might have been no need for that fight if she hadn't been such an idiot. I don't blame the enemy from reacting that way, I would have done exactly the same."

Sheelan's arm came around my shoulders. "Don't be too hard on her, please darling. I know she's a bloody nuisance but she does respect you, it's why she keeps calling you Highness when she shouldn't."

"And that's another thing. It isn't just me she puts in danger, it's everybody here. She disobeys commands, look at the horse businesses, that damn near got us all slaughtered. It was just luck Wolfy and his pack were nearby. One would think she had learned a lesson when Alyssa had her flogged, it seems not."

After half an hour's searching, there was no sign of Verna. Goodness knows where she had run to, but she was away from me for the moment, so she kept her life.

Taal was crying.

"What's the matter with you?" I asked abruptly.

"She's lost, Lauren. There are wild animals here. I'll go have another look, if I may?" she asked, from her position on the ground where she had collapsed in desperation.

Taal's distress touched me, I knew that feeling only too well, I had been there a few times and it damn-well hurt. She was plainly very upset. I squatted beside her.

"I'm sorry I shouted at you Taal, it was my anger,

26

something I rarely show or feel. She has to learn, that's twice she's nearly caused all our deaths. She's a liability to this group. Look at that tent, there is poor Eva, having to go to Otherworld and in ours, the Queen badly hurt, it was just luck she isn't dead, too, all because of her. How many more must die or suffer as is Alyssa and Eva, because of Verna's inability to think? Dead warriors of that calibre cannot be replaced."

Taal's head slumped forwards on her shoulders.

I sighed and softened. "Very well, Taal, go and look. But we have all looked and she's missing. Where might she have gone to?"

"Perhaps to the fort, Lauren?"

"Mmm," I mused. "That's possible. But none of us can go there and if she has, she's taking terrible risks and again placing us in danger having to go search. Everything she does seems to put people in jeopardy, Taal. She's plainly not thought about the consequences of hiding in a place full of Romans."

"It's the way she is, Lauren. Irrational, but I love her for all her faults." Emotion bubbled through her voice.

"As far as I have seen, she treats you with indifference. Why do you put up with it?"

Taal shrugged her shoulders. "Because I fell in love. I couldn't help it, I just did."

I nodded. From experience I knew only too well how easy it is to fall for a person, I have, three times. "Very well. Go up towards the fort. You're not well known, take Merial with you. Have a look, call her, she may come."

"But you'll punish her, Lauren, may even banish her."

"I'll speak to the Queen, see what she says. Alyssa will have the final say."

Taal rose, stood silently looking very glum. She knew what Alyssa had said last time, so it didn't look good.

Merial came and took her hand and the pair walked slowly off.

I went to Alyssa. "How are you, darling?"

"It's hurting again. Poor Eva is dead?"

"Yes, I am afraid so. What do you want to do about Verna? It was her stupid sneeze that started the fight."

Alyssa sighed. "She couldn't help a sneeze. Bring her before me, please."

"She's vanished. Taal's going to the fort to see if she ran away there."

"That's dangerous, Lauren. If she's recognised it may cost all of us our lives if she lets on where we are under torture."

"So, she's putting us all in danger again!" I couldn't help the sarcastic comment. "She's terrified I might have her flogged and banished."

"Verna does very silly things. She doesn't seem to think. How is Taal?"

"Upset. She says she loves her, that's why she's risking going to the fort. But I'm not sure that love is returned, Verna seems to use Taal as she sees fit. Is she worth pursuing?"

A cry went up. Bran stuck her head in the tent. "They're coming down the track, Lauren, in full view of the fort. If they turn off into here the Romans will know where we are."

"By the bloody Gods!" I couldn't help the outburst, it just ripped out. "Get to the edge of the trees and tell Taal to go on along the track until she's well out of sight of the sentries. They can come in through the trees farther back from the south."

"I feel too ill to judge her, darling and you might make a hasty decision, so it must be me when I'm better. Put her under arrest, Taal and Bran. She is not to leave the camp or do anything without express permission from you, Sheelan, me, or her guards." She winced with the effort of speaking.

"I must look at that wound, sweet one."

"*Sweet one,*" she repeatedly softly.

It was angry and showing signs of infection, no wonder Alyssa didn't feel well and it pained her, she had the beginnings of blood poisoning. They could have used contaminated arrows, nothing was easier than doing that here, pushing the tips into the ground was all it needed. "I'll wash it again, I'll go get some medications, be still, please."

As I arrived at my horse, Bran came running up. "They went as you said, Lauren, but have somehow got trapped by a bear as they came back in the wood. What shall I do?"

"Oh hell! I can't come, take Nianda, Freda, Juna and Eva... oh no, you can't. Take Lalena instead, arm them with longbows. I think you know how to approach a bear, go and prove you can."

Bran called names. The group left.

Sheelan and I washed Alyssa's side, I put some antiseptic cream on and covered it again. We were getting low on the field dressings Stan had kindly sent, we needed more. But the portal was the other side of the fort and near the Roman camp, asking Stan would have to wait for a better moment.

"There, darling, take a couple of these, Sheelan will help you sit up."

Alyssa smiled in her enchanting way. "How lucky I am to have you beside me, Lauren. I know I can die, but you'll do your best."

"Don't talk like that, Alyssa, you won't die if you think positively about the future. There's a lot to do once your side is better. Our swords must be found, and we should gain more knowledge of them."

"Yes, Alyssa," Sheelan cut in. "You'll be up and about before you know it and we can all see the lovely way you walk again."

A roar came from further down.

"Stay with Alyssa, Sheelan. I'm going to see what's happened." I kissed Alyssa before I left.

"What's going on?" Alyssa asked. "Why must you leave me?"

"Bloody Verna's got herself into difficulties again down by the river. Is there no end to her idiocy?" Grabbing a longbow and slipping a quiver over my shoulder, I sprinted through the trees as fast as my legs would carry me. The road was very close, they weren't far in. Where was everybody else?

"Over here, Lauren," Bran called.

I flitted the two trees between us, but still couldn't see a bear. "Where are Taal and Verna?"

"Down the drop to the river, I think they had decided to use that to get back. There are two bears drinking and they stumbled on them, now they're trapped between the two."

"Where are Freda and the others?"

"We split up as we approached. One group is that side, I don't know where the others are."

"We must get closer. At least you have a longbow."

Another tree forward, no sign. I motioned on again, putting one finger up, meaning a tree at a time.

Another roar tore through the trees.

"Save me Taal," Verna cried loudly. "I don't want to die."

Taal must have been annoyed. "Shut up!" she snapped. "Yelling will attract the bears more and endanger us both."

Bran and I moved another tree. Then I saw Taal standing in front of Verna, protectively screening the woman from the animal with her body and arms spread either side of her. She was being incredibly brave. The bear was only a few feet away, standing on its hind legs, its front ones open.

"Shall we loose?" Bran whispered.

I nodded, drew my bow and let fly. The bear moved forwards a step or two at that instant, so our arrows went behind its back and on into the forest beyond. I quickly nocked another as did Bran, there was little time to take careful aim, we loosed at the same moment.

Shwoosh, thud, thud.

The bear fell at Taal's feet.

I searched around. Where was the other one?

Bran motioned to my right.

I slipped on another tree. Then I saw it, walking along on all fours behind Taal. It got to within five feet and stood.

Taal partially obscured my target and as Bran was even farther left, she had no shot at all. I nocked and drew, hoping my aim was exceptionally good on this occasion.

At that instant the bear staggered a few steps, then fell forwards flat on its face. Two arrows stuck up in the air from its back.

"Come on Bran," I shouted. We dashed to Taal. "Are you well?" I asked, taking her into my arms.

She was as white as a sheet and I could feel her trembling inside. "Ye... yes, thank you, Highness. It was so close," she stammered, "so very close." Her head dropped to my shoulder.

"You are both safe now, we're all here. You were incredibly brave, Taal."

She gave a weak smile.

Juna, Freda and the others appeared.

"Is it dead?" Merial asked. "Lalena and me took the shots."

"Very, thank you, and well done everybody. Come on, let's go back to camp," I said, giving Taal and encouraging peck on the cheek. "I have only seen an act as brave as that once before and Brevit gave her life doing it."

Taal tried to smile again. "Thank you, Lauren, that is very kind of you."

Verna was crouching down behind Taal, too terrified to move.

Taal bent, took her arm and gently spoke. "Let's go back, now, my love. They are both dead. Lauren helped us."

Verna slowly nodded, looking warily at the bears sprawled out on the ground. She didn't speak but was unsteady on her feet from the fear that still held her heart in an icy vice-like grip.

It was a solemn arrival back with the pair. Sheelan came out of our tent. "Alyssa's having a nap."

"Good, that will keep her resting. I haven't the faintest idea what should be done about Verna. Placing her under guard as Alyssa said, doesn't seem enough for the chaos she has caused. But it's Alyssa's wish, so ask Taal to bring Verna before me, please, Sheelan."

It was plain that there was a strong feeling for Verna from Taal to have tried to protect her that way, and the woman was a steady member of the group so I didn't want to distance her from us. Loyalty is hard to come by.

Verna's eyes goggled in fear as she half staggered towards me, urinating herself with the thought of her punishment. She was plainly terrified and expected a flogging and banishment followed by an awful death of some kind, alone. It was the worst thing that could befall anyone. She clung to Taal's arm. I stood silently looking at her, my mind going over the punishment I would have meted out, but surprisingly, Verna had been spared any of those by Alyssa, a person who I had expected to come down on her like a ten-ton weight. But instead, she had shown clemency even though her injury had been partly caused by Verna, so I decided to follow her example.

Verna dropped to the ground and grovelled. "Please spare me, Highness, it was an accident. Don't beat me again like last time, it hurt so much."

"How much do you think Alyssa is hurting right now because of your stupid sneeze? You suffered nothing compared to her pain. In future you stay with Taal during fights and only take a bow if she tells you to. Do not go wandering of alone, as you did, that split our forces and caused the Queen to be shot and Eva to be killed, both injuries emanating directly from your action. And you didn't bring my bloody firestick either, I had to leave Alyssa to get it, so you didn't fulfil instructions. In my opinion, you're a menace, disobey or ignore directives and do the most idiotic things that places everybody in danger. You are lucky this time, Verna, the Queen has asked me to go easy on you. Had she not, I would have had you flogged and ejected from this band, outcast, to fend for yourself. You are under the charge of Taal and Bran. Do nothing unless either one tells you, or you are instructed to by Sheelan, Alyssa or me. Think of it as a loose arrest and we'll see how you go. You can thank the Gods I never judged you. Now leave me, keep out of my way and stay with Taal. You should thank her for her amazing bravery, too, she stood in front protecting you from a bear risking her life. She must think an awful lot of you to do that."

"Yes, Highness, I will, I promise. Thank you for not punishing me." She stood, turned to Taal and kissed her. "Thank you as well, Taal, you're much braver than me."

Chapter Three

A Royal Farewell

Sheelan turned to Bran. "Would you try to find out who that tribe was, please, although I doubt any will have lived after Lauren shot them so many times."

Bran's face came close. She kissed my cheek. "I'll do my best, Lauren, I know it means a lot to you. We need to get their bodies away as well, they'll attract predators here. I'll get a work group together."

"Eva gone. I can hardly believe it," I muttered with a slight shaking of my head, I sighed. Tears welled up again. "She was the first person I spoke to when I came here and I've known and admired her ever since. She was lovely, another good friend lost to me and us all."

Sheelan held me, so we cried together at my dreadful loss and distress.

Bran squatted beside Sheelan and me, kissed us with a hug. "No idea who they were, I'm afraid. And I hate to say this, Lauren, but we need to get Eva into the barrow as soon as possible. She was the Queen's Guard Commander, closer to the Queen than our Fighting Leader, so should have a full interment, but we are only few and have no regalia. It will be hard getting the stone open, that takes several people, we haven't the power."

I gulped back my grief. "There is reg... reg... regalia," I stammered. "Sheelan knows where it is. Eva must be sent to Otherworld properly with the weapons she used during her life and any other worldly goods for her to use in the Beyond. I'll not allow her to be just interred. And as Alyssa said, we need currency to survive in this new world, the barter system is ending. The Romans have the grain pits, although they are hidden so they may not have found them yet?"

35

"If it's in the southern forest we can't get it, Lauren. That will take too many moons."

I shook my head. "It's not far, very near here."

"Not in the fort?" Bran replied, aghast. "We cannot go there, Lauren, pulling the palace apart looking for it would be too obvious, you would be taken."

"No," Sheelan cut in. "It's even nearer than that. But only us two can get it, nobody else must know where the jewellery is hidden."

"Bran must know, Sheelan, as must Freda and Juna," I said. "The rest must stay and guard our lovely Alyssa."

Sheelan hesitated, but quickly nodded agreement, she could see the sense of that arrangement. They are all trustworthy Royal Guard members. "Very well, Lauren. We'll go now."

"But you'll need something to dig with and we have nothing," Bran put in.

It dawned on me then, that we should carry an entrenching tool for such occasions. It had occurred several times when someone had been killed, like the tinkers, and we were stuck with nothing to dig with. I was about to say *"I'll get Toler to make one,"* but realised he wasn't with us at the moment.

"We'll have to get into the fort to get one," Bran muttered, despair in her voice. "That's very risky."

"We've done it before," I explained. "At Gaelich's fort. It's thinking of a different method, we can't go in as slaves as we did then, there are no slaves here."

"Perhaps some travellers?" Bran suggested.

"We'll be searched in that case," I pointed out. "Then they would recognise us."

"It needs to be something that a guard would pass over without too much attention," Freda put in. "Like a pregnant woman."

"Yes," Bran declared. "That's perfect. They'll be on the lookout for Lauren, they wouldn't suspect her if she was with child."

"How can she be with child," Sheelan stated rather

indignantly. There was disdain in her tone at the thought.

"Not really, silly thing, Sheelan," Bran replied. "Just to look like it. We could stuff a tunic inside hers. But Lauren, you'll have to walk convincingly."

I gaped at her. "Me? I haven't any idea how a pregnant woman walks, I won't be able to pull it off."

"It's for Alyssa and Eva," Bran pointed out. "And all of us, we'll all need food. I think they kind of waddle a bit, lay back to balance the weight."

Sheelan stood, hands on hips. "We're a fine lot trying to work that out, none of us like men!"

Finally, we found a way, and after a practice and helpful or comical hints from all and sundry, we agreed I looked the part.

Bran felt a small group was best and those of us less likely to be recognised. Even then we knew it was risky and of course, we would need to be unarmed. Women with child don't carry swords, daggers or bows. So, after discussion we decided Bran, me and Leilan. Three was enough, but not too many.

Sheelan didn't want to be left out, but she was well known there now and I wanted someone caring to stay with Alyssa, and there was nobody more caring than her. She eventually saw the wisdom of it and agreed.

"I just hope Toler has got back to the fort. If not, we'll have to raid his workshop for a spade," I said as we walked.

"How are we going to get a spade out?" Leilan asked. "It will look odd."

"Maybe say her sister had a stillborn and we need to bury it?" Bran offered.

My heart wasn't in this and it must have shown, but they were doing their best. I hated lying because it's so easy to get caught out in one but again, it was necessary and I would do anything for Eva. I rubbed dirt on my face to help my disguise.

Bran stopped us and took me in her arms. "I'm sorry, Lauren. You must feel terrible. But we have to do this, it's the only way." She cuddled me tightly. "Be brave."

A heavy sigh emitted from me. "Yes, I know, and I will. I just wish we didn't have to do any of it, but it's happened and that can't be undone. Did I look that miserable?"

Bran gave me a weak smile. "I am afraid so, Lauren. Just remember why and who this is for, two of our group, my Queen," she whispered close to my ear.

"We're nearly at the gates and there's a Roman guard there. I need to look as though my back is aching. Better to stop close to him, it will look natural and that we have nothing to hide."

Leilan held my left arm as though supporting me. "I'll put your hood up, that will help keep the sun off your face, Leina."

Within feet of the legionary we stopped again. I put my hand into the small of my back and squirmed, as if trying to get comfortable.

"Come on Leina," Bran said loudly. "Not far now."

The guard gave us a cursory glance and waved us in.

We were through and as easy as that, I couldn't believe it. But it meant keeping our act up until well into the fort. I got several sympathetic looks from women as we struggled along and I felt a terrible fraud, but it had to be done. Then we were at the palace.

It looked deserted, a sorry sight now, doors open to swing freely, the wind having blown dust and loose dirt inside. I went and peered in. It hadn't been touched, everything was just as we had left it, except there was no hearth fire to warm the room. Memories of Alyssa and how we had shared her home, our lives and our family in here came flooding back, of the girls in the annex, how Alegia loved dancing with Selene and of us all singing together. It was too much, I broke down.

Hands took me away. "Let's go find Shaila, see if the women are back yet," Bran said softly.

I nodded, my voice had left me once more, I was choked up inside so let them lead me to the north gate.

The women's house was empty, too. It had only been a few days since we left them in the southern forest and we were a small group on horseback, so had travelled faster.

"To Toler's forge," I muttered. "He must have a spade or something there."

He was absent as well, having to return with an oxen drawn wagon laden with the tools of his trade, so that was understandable. We searched and found what we needed, a small hand spade.

"Now all we have to get out again," Leilan said, concern in her voice.

Haff was walking towards us as we approached the gate. I gave Bran a nudge and indicated with my head.

She took the hint and cut her off. "Lauren is with us, Haff, but she's going under another name, Leina. For goodness sake don't use her right one."

Haff looked me over, noting my supposedly swollen tummy. "Would you take tea, Leina? You look as though you need a rest."

A Centurion and legionary were walking past as she said it. He came over, taking one of my arms. "Allow me to aid you to her home, good lady. Which way?"

As we were only yards away from her house, we accepted. It would look convincing and what anybody would have done under our assumed circumstances.

"Over here, Centurion," Haff replied quickly. "She can rest a short while."

He smiled. "I have a son I am proud of. I pray to Jupiter he will be a Centurion one day. I hope your child is a boy, too." He saluted and the pair left, going to the sentry by the gate, where the legionary was changed.

I grinned at Haff. "I have a male tunic."

"What are you all doing here!" she exclaimed, once inside. "They've been searching for you, patrols going out almost daily. Where is everybody?"

Bran explained what had occurred. "We've seen no patrols though."

"Oh, by the Gods," Haff muttered half under her breath. "That's terrible. You poor thing, Lauren, you must be heartbroken."

"We need to send Eva to Otherworld," Leilan said. "That's why we had to come here, to get a spade."

A look of horror lit Haff's face. "You're never going to bury her!"

"No, Haff," I assured, patting her hand. "Eva will be interred in the long barrow. We need to uncover her special regalia used on formal occasions so she can go properly dressed, as a Queen's Guard Commander should be, and with her weapons."

"Thank the Gods for that," Haff replied, heaving a sigh of relief. "Have you food, like grain and vegetables?"

Bran shook her head. "No, just meat from a stag Sheelan killed."

"Then take this," Haff said, producing a bag of stuff. "Don't you carry it, Lauren, you're with child, so wouldn't. Let Leilan take it. Now go, before anybody recognises any of you. The less time you're all in here, the better."

We hugged each other and left the sanctuary of her home.

The guard stopped us. "What's in that bag?" he snapped.

Leilan showed him. "Can we go, please, my friend needs to get home," she said, indicating me.

"Very well. You're the woman my Centurion helped, aren't you? Go on your way."

He gave Leilan a cursory glance. "Why the spade?"

"To dig our plot with," Bran stated.

He seemed satisfied and we passed. It had to be done slowly, no rushing, a steady walk down the gradient to the river and track, where we paused while I sat on a boulder. Bran watched until the sentry was busy, then the tunic was quickly removed and we hurriedly made our way back to the others.

"You've been ages," Sheelan complained as she rushed to me. "I was getting worried." Her arms took me in an embrace.

"A woman in Lauren's condition has to walk slowly," Bran said, with a grin on her face. "Here, Leilan has some oats and vegetables from Haff."

'I don't feel much like eating," Sheelan replied, glumly.

I took her in my arms. "Neither do I, darling, but we need food to keep us going so we can care for Alyssa and send Eva to Otherworld. Let's get to the Stones and retrieve what is needed."

Bran chose Sheelan, me and Freda. "I want the rest of you here to guard the Queen. We won't be long. Keep hidden."

Out the other side of the trees and onto verdant green grass of the plain. Ahead stood the Stones. They looked sullen, unhappy, perhaps angry somehow. Although it was a sunny day the air was cold, yet no wind blew and there was a dreadful, heavy stillness and even though late in the day, a mist swirled a foot or so above the ground snatching at our ankles.

"Over here," Sheelan said, pointing.

To our horror, the place had been dug open.

"By the Gods," Bran shouted. "Who else knows of this secret place that they should come and desecrate it?"

I squatted to examine the contents of the hole. "But it's all here, Bran, look. The bags with Alyssa's robes and her crowns and daggers, and here's Eva's bag. It's as if this place was opened up for us." I looked up at her in amazement.

She stood agape. "But.. but... who..." she stammered.

"I have no idea who, Bran, but some powerful being has had a hand in this, more powerful than us feeble humans. Let's take what we need, some of the gold and silver for our journey, place the planks over it again and close this up."

The hole was in-filled and smoothed over. Grass would soon grow and cover its bareness.

As I leant onto a Stone it shook beneath me and a great rumble of thunder rolled across the sky.

Bran grabbed my arm to pull me away. "Be careful, Lauren, mysterious and powerful forces are at work here."

I patted her arm that held mine. "I think I know who it is."

I walked to the altar, placing both my palms down on it. That strange vibration began, gradually increasing until it got almost too painful to bear. I knew I dare not let go, so gritted my teeth.

A streak of blue lighting shot down, engulfing the Altar Stone and stayed on it, pulsing rhythmically. I gasped in air, it was such a shock. For some reason I glanced up along its length and there, way up in the sky, a pure beam of light began slowly descending, twisting round and around the lightning in a spiral until it reached the Stone where it glittered and danced as if in joy, pleased at something I had no knowledge of. To say I wasn't frightened would be lying, I was, my knees were shaking and weak. This was a phenomenon I had never experienced before, perhaps nobody ever had. Although some strange things had occurred since coming to this land, this one must take the biscuit. But I felt that whatever force or power was causing this was a friendly one, so would not harm me. 'Is that you, Maddy?" I ventured, nervously.

"Hello Lauren," a soft voice said. *"This is Evelyn, please don't be afraid, I can sense your concern. Thank you for taking the trouble to look after Alyssa for me, she needs your love and attention now, as well as Sheelan's. It shows how much you do love her to risk your life at the fort. Send Eva's mortal remains to me, please, so she may become whole again here in Otherworld. Try not to be too upset, she is safe here in spirit and misses you very much. I am sure Eva will see you soon in your world but because she died so violently, it will take a short while for her to recover, as it did for Madeil. Be patient, my dearest Lauren. Place her in the long barrow, I have made a place for her there. The stone will move easily but replace it afterwards. Thank all the others, too. Alyssa will get worse soon, be prepared for that, be vigilant and on your guard. Goodbye for now. I send you a gentle kiss."*

The pulsing vibration within the Stone ended, but I kept my hands firmly planted on it for several seconds until I felt able to remove them safely and without offending the Spirits. On turning, the others stood with their mouths wide open gaping at me. "What?" I asked.

"We heard and saw it all," Bran said. "How incredible. It shall be done as Evelyn wishes. Come, let us return."

I turned to give the Stones a wave just before we entered the trees, hoping, I suppose, either Evelyn or Madeil's spirits were there still, perhaps Eva's too, watching us depart.

The others rushed and held each of us as soon as we appeared. "We heard," Juna explained. "Every word. How is that possible?"

I shrugged my shoulders. "Who knows what the spirits and Gods can do, wish to do or are even capable of doing when they have an inclination. They have powers we barely understand. Let's dress Eva in her best clothes and regalia for festivals."

Bran got water from the stream so we could wash her to purity. After that her clothes were changed to her best Royal Red tunic and trousers, her shield and ceremonial sword, a dagger put on her right hip and the sword returned to its scabbard across her back. A low crown of laurel leaves was placed on her head, denoting her status as a brave warrior.

"I wish Addani were here, she would have highlighted her face as she did for Madeil and Brevit." I stopped and sighed.

"What's the matter?" Bran asked.

"So many, Bran, so many good souls." Tears filled my eyes again, I couldn't help it. "They will all be together soon."

Many arms enfolded me. "You've suffered many such events, Lauren," Freda said. "I do hope there are no more."

Wiping my eyes with my tunic sleeve, I tried to smile back. "Thanks, all of you. We must do this deed now, let's carry her to the barrow in the lower field. I shall create an air shield between us and the fort, the sentries won't look this way and even if they do, they'll see nothing."

We used the fur we had laid her on to carry her body. Out of the trees, across the shallow river and over the field to where the barrow mound stood.

"Evelyn said the stone would move easily," Bran muttered. "I wonder how easily? Shall we try rolling it to one side?"

I nodded, then put my shoulder against its edge.

Bran leant over me and pushed with her hands.

It moved, almost too smoothly and there it was, that black hole to Otherworld and the caverns. Yet there was light inside. How could that be?

I ventured warily in. It was very cool, as it always had been on my previous visits to this sad place of repose. Flickering by a gap surrounded with flowers was a wick in a dish of oil. As Evelyn had promised, she had prepared Eva's place in here ready for her to occupy forever, as was her right as the Queen's protector.

Bran called in. "May we enter?"

"Yes, of course. Look, isn't it amazing. A perfect place for her to remain until we join her. I know Evelyn and Brevit will care for her here, Eva will be safe whatever happens. We should bring her in."

I carefully placed her sword behind her, arranging her black hair around her in a sort of halo and once done, to finally bent and kiss her lips. "Goodbye my friend, my warrior, our Guardian. I shall miss you so very much. Farewell until we meet in that other world once more, go to safety. There will be more of us there then, most of your friends here, they all respect you, then our hearts will be mended."

Sheelan did the same, telling Eva how fair she was in her handling of people, patiently and with care, kissing her gently on her cheek.

Outside, the stone began to roll back as soon as we touched it as if a giant hand was pushing with us.

At the instant it closed a massive thunder clap ripped across the sky.

My shoulders sagged in a sigh. "Goodbye my dear Eva, and thank you, Gods of the skies and Otherworld. Care for her with all the power at your disposal."

We staggered back to the wood, our hearts grieving for our friend and carer. Eva had been special, a good companion, fair and gentle, always there when needed. I knew we would all miss her terribly.

Sheelan sat next to me. "Keep her in our hearts, Lauren, my love. She'll stay there anyway, in her own way, to help us."

She looked worn out. "You've had the pain as much as me, sweetheart. Your heart's breaking, too, the same as mine is for Alyssa. I feel completely empty inside, especially as Evelyn said Alyssa would get worse. I don't know what she meant by that? There's no way we can go searching for swords now, not with Alyssa so hurt."

She looked blankly back. Then, her face changed. "Because there is a reason, darling, a very important one. We haven't seen or been told it yet, but we will. Perhaps we should go back to the Stones?"

I huffed out. "I can't at the moment, it's all too raw."

"Then what should we do, my love? You have always led us, now we seem to be lost."

How could I think of anything right now, least of all what our futures were? I just wanted to care for Alyssa, make sure she pulled through her wound and this infection. But there were others here, Sheelan for a start, who must feel exactly as I do. She needs support; we both needed it. And thinking of Sheelan; what would I do if anything happened to her? I couldn't bear another loss, that would be too much for me to deal with. Then there was Betany and Alegia. I needed to see them again, they were also a huge part of my life.

"What are you thinking about, Lauren?" Sheelan asked.

I told her. "We need to let the others know of events and see our children."

Sheelan looked horrified. "But that means going back into the fort. Is that wise? It might be pushing your luck doing that again."

Chapter Four

Addani

We stayed in the forest for about a week. Alyssa got worse, as Evelyn had forecast, with a higher temperature which I found hard to control. During this she was only partly cognitive, lapsing in and out of consciousness continually, often muttering to herself, although we never found out what she said.

"Why isn't Alyssa getting better?" Sheelan asked.

"I think she has blood poisoning from the arrow shaft so it's taking longer. Eva had it once when her and Brevit came back after a row, it took a while for her to recover."

"She will, though, won't she?" She was uncertain, a tremor of panic in her voice.

I detected her fear. My arms pulled her close. "I hope so, sweetheart. I've beaten this before."

Her green eyes opened wide. "You're not sure, are you, Lauren? There is doubt in your voice."

"No, Sheelan, I am not. But Evelyn didn't say she would die and we are doing all we can, someone is with her all the time to talk to her, I think that helps."

She looked downcast. "I don't want her to go to Otherworld, my love."

"Neither do I, and I promise I'll do my very best."

She sighed. "I know you will, Lauren. There is another matter. We're getting low on food, I need to hunt. Maybe Freda will come."

"That's a good idea, keep busy. We should make a horse cradle as well in case we have to move quickly."

"What's a horse cradle?"

"It's like a seat made out of twigs and branches that will fit

47

over the rump of a horse. If we are discovered Alyssa will have to be tied into it and the seat strapped onto the horse. I'll get our band onto that right now."

Bran listened carefully. "I understand, Lauren, that can be made in a day, today in fact," she ended with a grin. She had organised well, setting watches along the track to the fort in case a patrol came this way so we would get an early warning.

On this day, Leilan was on duty and I was tending Alyssa, dabbing her brow with cool water and chatting to her, hoping that my voice would penetrate the haze her mind was in, or if she could hear at all, although sometimes she would smile a little and move her head. Her temperature had dropped slightly at last, so maybe she was recovering. I fervently hoped so.

Suddenly, Leilan was yelling. I looked out of the tent to see her dashing into camp waving her arms in a flap.

"There's someone coming this way," she gabbled.

"Slow down, Leilan," Bran snapped, taking her by the shoulders to shake her. "Stop it. How many?"

"Oh, sorry, Bran. But we've seen nobody at all before, not since we set the watches up. Just one woman by the look of it."

Bran frowned at her. "You must make reports properly, Leilan. One woman is hardly going to be a threat to us, is she?"

"Um... no, Bran," she said, subdued. "Sorry."

"Let's go and see who it is, shall we, but we don't reveal ourselves," Bran pointed out.

I kissed Alyssa's cheek. "I won't be long, sweet one." Whether she heard me or not, I wasn't sure, yet I believed her face lit with a light smile.

They disappeared, to return within minutes calling excitedly.

"Look who it is," Bran shouted. "Haff is paying us a visit."

"Hello Lauren. Oh dear, I find it hard just calling you that, it doesn't seem right, you're our Queen, but I understand it's for your safety." She kissed my cheeks.

"Thank you, Haff. I hope you weren't followed?"

"No, Highness, I made sure by going to the river to sit for a while and pretended to pick herbs at the edge of this wood, 'How is Queen Alyssa?"

"Not very good, she has an infection I'm having a problem curing. Have you any news from the fort?"

"Some of the people came back yesterday. Toler, and Shaila with your daughters. They've moved back into their old houses. Nobody's questioned them but the guards are still at both gates and searched the wagons thoroughly. I expect they're looking for you, Highness, I mean, Lauren."

"That makes sense, I guessed they would post sentries. But I would love to see my daughters, I miss them so much. That means coming into the fort soon and requires me getting pregnant again, of course."

Sheelan giggled. "I can't imagine that, darling."

Casting her a glance, I replied, "Neither can I, but needs must. I'll make myself dirty, too."

"All those that go should, Lauren," Haff nodded in agreement. "The scruffier the better. People seem to have given up the will to keep tidy and clean, some don't have the interest to live even, and the fields have been allowed to get run down and unattended. They all miss you and Queen Alyssa so much and hate the invaders."

"Tell them tomorrow, Haff," Sheelan said. "They'll know what to expect and warn them that the Queen is only to be called by her temporary name, Leina, please," she ended.

"Here, take this," Haff said, holding out a bundle. "Some more oats and vegetables, you must be getting low by now."

I embraced her. "You're so thoughtful and kind, Haff, thank you. Remember, I am Leina in the fort."

"You have tears in your eyes, my Queen, from the terrible worry you suffer every day and the trials you have been put through. But the others know nothing of the tragedy and loss yet. Everybody loved Eva, she was kind and caring, it's very sad." She kissed my cheeks again. "I had better go back. See you soon. Take care, Lauren, and all of you," she called to the rest of the group.

Bran looked at me sternly. "You're going to risk it again? It's very dangerous going into the fort. Legate must have given orders for your capture, that's why they're guarding the gates. If they discover who you are they'll probably kill you, Lauren."

"It went fine last time, the guard barely looked at me," I pointed out. "Why should it be any different? He may even remember me from the last visit and take less notice."

"It's not the guard that concerns me, Lauren, what if somebody recognises you and shouts out Highness or Majesty, that would put the wolf among the hens."

I knew she was right. But I wanted to see Alegia more than anything, even life itself. Shaila would update me on what had been going on since we left them in the southern forest. "We'll just have to make sure our act is very good then, won't we, Bran," I replied with a confident smile.

She sighed and gave in, knowing I was determined to go. "Okay then, but we'll need to be extra careful."

I cuddled Alyssa. I never knew if she realised it or not, but I did in case anything went awry. "I'm going to see our daughters, my love, I *so* wish you could come as well. I shall pass a kiss and cuddle on from you. I hope you'll be able to hold them yourself soon. I love you so much, please get well."

The tunic was duly placed in an appropriate position, it felt very awkward and my heart went out to any women who was really pregnant.

Sheelan looked me over. "Mmm, you seem to be convincing. I hope you're not going to get used to this," she said, with a light smile.

"Not likely, I'm a dedicated lesbian and dedicated to Alyssa and you, my love."

She blushed. Something she hadn't done for a long time.

It suited her, so I gave her a cuddle.

"Thank you, Lauren. I know you are and the feelings are mutual, it's so wonderful. Be careful at the fort, Romans aren't fools. I couldn't bear losing you, darling." She clasped me to her.

"Most men are funny about pregnant women, they don't know how to act so they'll leave me alone, especially being about eight months gone, that makes them warier," I replied, looking down at my substantial lump, "In case anything suddenly happens right in front of them. Look after Alyssa while I'm away, please, my love."

"I will, don't worry. I'll bathe her forehead like you do and talk to her all the time. Do you think she hears us?"

"I've no idea, but the subconscious is a strange thing and even while in a coma, can receive sound messages, so it's important to keep trying."

The same team accompanied me, dirtying their faces as I had. We paused at the wood's edge, pretending to look for herbs to disguise the fact we had just come out of it. Our progress up the slope was slow and halting, stopping every now and then to rest. The sentry watched as we approached, gave my dirty face a quick glance and waved us in.

We had done it again!

I relaxed a little. We didn't stop at the palace this time, continuing past and on to the women's house near the north gate. There was another sentry there who looked us over, but as we weren't going out, he turned away to check others.

Shaila stood watching our approach. She was plainly unsure, walking forward to give a hand and bringing a stool with her in her kindness. "Here, my dear, rest for a moment."

"I will my dear Shaila, thank you."

"Your Majesty!" she exclaimed.

"Shhhs," snapped Bran. "Call her Leina, she mustn't be recognised. Didn't Haff warn you?" She looked over at the sentry to see if he had heard, but he was checking through somebody's bags, so didn't react.

"Oh, yes, she did. Forgive me, it was such a surprise hearing your voice, Leina. Come in and meet Alegia and Betany, they're both here and are well."

Alegia knew me straight away. "Mummy Lauren," she cried out excitedly. "How is mummy Alyssa?"

I sighed. "I am afraid she was badly injured in a fight, sweetheart. She's still ill and not conscious yet. I'm sorry to have to tell you, but you needed to know and it was best coming from me. I'm hoping she'll get better soon, Sheelan and me are doing our best."

"The Queen is ill," Shaila said, stunned. "How terrible for you and Sheelan, Highn.... I mean Leina."

"Why did Shaila call you Leina, mummy?" Alegia asked.

"Because we had to come here secretly, sweetheart. Have you seen Madeil?"

"No mummy. Why do you ask?"

I nodded satisfaction. "Then she left it for me to tell you. Mummy Alyssa's in the forest now," I said. "She'll be safe there and when she gets better, will sing and dance just like she used to, sweetheart. I'm afraid Eva got killed, we're all upset about that, she was very special." There must have been something about my face.

"You look older," Alegia said. "Please try not to grieve, mummy, Eva wouldn't want that. She was a wonderful guard, I liked her, too." She carefully placed her little arms around my neck and kissed me. "We'll all be with her one day, it's not as if she's gone forever, is it?"

I cuddled her right back. "No darling, it isn't, and thank you for reminding me. You're such a sensible Princess."

Alegia wiped a tear from my eyes. "Poor mummy. It's hard losing a person you feel for, and I know you did."

We embraced a long time. How lovely it was to feel Alegia's little body tight into mine, I had missed holding her terribly. "How is Betany, Shaila?"

"Sleeping at the moment, Leina, we had a disturbed night

with her. I think she was upset with moving about so much. She'll settle now we're back." Shaila had tears running down her cheeks. "Yes, it is hard, young Princess. But you must do as Mummy Lauren does and not use the title of Princess, otherwise your lives will be in great danger."

"Shaila is right, sweetheart. Just be Alegia and Betany from now on until I say you can again. Promise me? One day it might change and we'll all be happy again." I asked earnestly, searching her face for an answer.

Alegia nodded. "We will then, as you wish it, mummy Lauren. I guess it must be hard living ordinary lives?"

"Yes, look at me, I had to become pregnant to come here."

"You haven't, have you?" Alegia asked uncertainly, a degree of horror in her face.

"No sweetheart, it's just a pregnant tunic."

Everybody laughed at that, and the sombre atmosphere lifted.

"Addani was here yesterday," Shaila said. "She was looking for you, Leina."

"Addani?" It was a self-question. "Why would she be here? She has a farm to run with Falcon. Was she well, Shaila?" I asked. "Did Falcon come with her?"

"She was alone and seemed as fit as ever, didn't say why she had come, just asked after you. She was very surprised when I told her what had gone on here, then said, in that case she needed to find you as quickly as possible."

"If she comes again, ask her to go and talk to Haff, please, Shaila. She knows our location, but I don't want anyone else to in case they get taken and tortured."

"Would they do that, Lauren?" Shaila asked.

"They would do anything to get their hands on us. I wonder where Addani went?"

Shaila shrugged her shoulders. "She never said, Leina. Just went striding off in that way of hers."

"Have you a spare tent? We have one with a patch in it, not sure how long that will last."

Shaila nodded and got it. "How will you get it out?"

"We'll think of something," I replied with a laugh. Leilan is very inventive."

We bid our goodbyes to them all, hugging and kissing, especially Alegia, it was hard leaving her behind and my heart broke. Then I got with child again ready to make our awkward way towards the south gate.

We were within a few yards of the sentry when Damarion's wife, Rheanna and their son Fane, came around the edge of the palisade into full view. "Highness," she said loudly. "How wonderful to see you again."

The sentry stiffened, drew his sword and began moving towards us. "Just a minute, you, stop where you are. She called you Highness, exactly who are you?"

"RUN!" I yelled, drew the tunic out and went belting down the slope towards the river. The rest followed hotly on my heels.

Behind us I heard the guard yelling blue murder that a Queen had been in the fort and for a search group to come out immediately.

We had little time. Our lookouts had seen the rumpus and us running down the slope, so warned the rest of our group. By the time we arrived, things were packed. Alyssa was lifted into the horse chair behind me and secured. We mounted up went out the wood slowly on the Standing Stones side, turned south and finally back into the next wood, through that, using the river for a while to cover our tracks, over the rutted track to the east at an angle to try and disguise our hoof prints among all the others on it, up over a grassy hill and again into a large stand of trees over the top of a high rise in the ground. That position afforded us a good field of view and cover. All through, Sheelan had ridden one side of Alyssa, Bran the other. We couldn't ride fast, just a steady plod in case Alyssa slipped.

Taal and Verna were posted as lookouts while we got Alyssa down, the tent pitched and her comfortably in it on furs. I knew it would take a while for the Romans to get organised and on the road to search and even then, they would be on foot, so we had put distance between us. Our constantly changing directions and along the river bed would take some tracking, too.

I suddenly realised I had never been in this wood before, so goodness knows what was in it.

"I need to hunt, my love," Sheelan said as she sat beside me. "The rest of the meat was left behind at the camp in the rush. I thought I would take Merial. Is she reliable?"

"As far as I know, she is. But I've never known her hunt at all. I know Nianda and Juna can, why not take one of them?"

She nodded. "Okay, Nianda then. See you soon." She kissed my cheek. "Rest a while, until we're back, you look weary. Care for Alyssa, darling."

"And you two take care, this is a new forest. The one the other side of the track is where we met bears, you remember the bears?" I said, nodding meaningfully.

Sheelan grinned. "Yes, only too well, how could I ever forget that, Lauren. Bye."

The pair waved as they set off. I knew Sheelan was an excellent hunter and was constantly aware of the space about her and what was in it, so wasn't worried about them but a reminder didn't hurt, it's always best to be on your guard when in unknown territory.

I took the opportunity to spend time with Alyssa, she needed a lot of attention and I loved giving it. I found her temperature had dropped a little more and the flush of the fever in her face had subsided. I asked Bran to bring some cool water so I could dab her forehead with it. To my delight, after a while her eyes opened.

"Lauren," she uttered. "How wonderful to see you again. Are we still near the fort?"

"We had to move, sweet one. We're farther away now on top of a hill. I'm so pleased to see you awake." Tears of joy ran down my face, I took one of her hands and kissed it tenderly. "How do you feel?"

"My side doesn't hurt as much now, those pills I took yesterday must be good."

I smiled softly at her. "That was several moons ago, darling. We've been so worried. But you have pulled through, thank the Gods for that."

She looked stunned. "Several moons? All that time? Where is Sheelan?"

"Out hunting, my love, she'll be so thrilled you're back with us, she's been worried for you, too."

"I can't wait to see her, send her in when they get back, please, Lauren."

I sat with her, checked her wound, which had begun healing already, Alyssa was an incredible woman.

I told her about the strange experience at the Stones and of talking to Evelyn.

"Really, how amazing. You'll like her, Lauren, such a gentle woman."

The hunters were gone a long time. I was about to suggest a couple went after them when Bran called out they had emerged much farther along the edge of the treeline.

I left Alyssa to watch, smiling and patting her hand. Nianda waved. Sheelan had a deer across her shoulders.

She grinned as she approached. "Remember that bear I hit with one?" she said as she stood grinning.

I sighed. "Yes, we were all together then," I mused. "Alyssa is awake, she asked after you."

Sheelan dropped the deer and dashed into the tent. I heard her crying with relief. She was some time, I left them to cuddle. She finally left Alyssa and came to me.

"Darling, you did it, brought her back to us." Her arms encircled my neck, soft lips planted a kiss on mine. "Thank you, my love, you are a Goddess still. It's just the black cloud of losing Eva that's burdening our hearts and group now. There's nothing any of us can do about that though, we sent her to Otherworld properly with full honours, she'll like that."

I knew my heart would always ache, as it had and still did for Madeil and Brevit. It was a pain I would have to get used to bearing and if possible, push to the back of the emotional queue, send it to those shadowy places in my heart and soul, out of my mind, yet at the same time keep their wonderful memories alive. They had both given their lives for me, a knowledge that made me feel very humble, so it still hurt deeply, Eva had been special to me as well, so gentle and warm. Sadly, I knew there would be more yet, dying somehow in this wild environment. I had suffered much recently, as had poor Sheelan, what with the concerns over Alyssa and me. I was probably feeling sorry for myself and selfish. I kissed her.

"Thank you, my love, that's a kind thing to say. And what of you, your heart must be aching as mine is, yet you comfort me so bravely?"

"You have suffered much more than I, darling, that's why it hurts you more. Yes, my heart aches as you say, but Alyssa is getting better so my pain will ease and go. I don't know how you cope with all the sadness. Madeil, Brevit and Crenn all passing in your arms, and now Eva, it must weigh heavily on you and worse still, we lost our home and family and can't see them anymore." At that moment the most wonderful sweet smell of Honeysuckle arose from her. She smiled gently. "To comfort you, my love."

"Thank you Sheelan, you're very thoughtful."

She had never done that before, produce an aroma to comfort or seduce, this gift must have been bestowed during the strange ceremony at the Stones. How wonderful.

Bran, who had become our Leader, got Merial, Freda and Nianda to start a fire for cooking a meal. She made a frame out of stout branches held high above the flames. Everyone was busy, even Sheelan processing her kill.

I looked in at Alyssa, quietly lifting a tent flap; she was sleeping peacefully, a smile of contentment on her face. I left her, wandering to a small group of trees and bushes to mull over my thoughts. I knew it was a bad idea to keep thinking over events, it made me feel even lower, but I was drawn to it like a moth to a flame. Perhaps I could puzzle a way out of this mess?

The night was fairly dark, only half a moon and a few

stars, cloud covered the rest, but it was pleasantly mild.

Yet another sigh left me, I seemed to be sighing more than ever lately, I mused. "There was a time when a sigh would have been out of place, Madeil would have wondered why, we were so happy. But Alyssa is recovering, that's a bright light on my deep mood," I said, softly.

"You look very sad," Madeil said from behind me. "And what of sighs, we are all entitled to them."

I spun and there she was, as lovely as ever. "My darling, how wonderful to see you."

"You would rather see Eva at this moment," she replied. "She's hurting still, but will come soon, she asked me to tell you to be patient." Madeil came closer and embracing me. "Eva loves you like a sister still, I love you a whole lot more," she kissed me lightly on my lips. "Eva said to thank you for taking such terrible risks to send her to Otherworld, although thought it funny you were with child to do it." The light smile that hovered on Madeil's lips made me smile with her.

"It was the only thing we could think of."

Madeil laughed loudly at that. "She thought it very inventive. But go back to the fire, my love, it's not safe here alone."

I felt a kiss on my cheek, then she was gone.

Turning to take Madeil's advice, I had taken but two steps when a hand come over my mouth from behind. It was so swift and silent I hadn't time to shout. My body was bent backwards as another arm swung around my middle. Mad thoughts raced through my mind. Was it those Burga clan people exacting revenge or some new tribe pushed out of their homelands by the Romans, and had come to settle here and resented our presence?

"That's how Brevit did it, isn't it?" a voice said. I was released.

Swinging on my attacker, I found Addani right behind me, or rather right in front, because I had turned around to see who it was.

She grinned.

Anger flared within me and I snorted. "You scared the life out of me, you... you... "I pursed my lips and shook my head rapidly, trying to think of a word to call her that vented my feelings. At that instant my inclination to call her all the idiots under the sun evaporated and I fell into those long arms and cried on her shoulder.

"If I had just walked towards you, you may have thought me a ghost," she retorted. She held me for a while, then took my shoulders to look into my eyes and smiled. But soon her face dropped. "I'm so sorry about Alyssa and Eva. I went back to the fort and Haff told me." Her arms enfolded and tightened once more. "Come on, let's go to the fire, there's a chill here," she whispered.

I was too choked up to speak, so nodded my head.

She took a hand to lead us back. "It's wonderful to see you again, Highness. Why were you in the trees?"

Shaking my head, all I could do was look at her, that beautiful face marred only by a band of red across her eyes and her wonderful chestnut hair flowing out behind her as we moved. The others came into view.

"Look who attacked me," I called croakily. "My favourite warrior after Brevit."

Everybody fussed over her. She was a sight for sore eyes, that was certain, unexpected and very welcome.

I took her to see Alyssa, but she was still sleeping so we didn't disturb her.

"How did you find us? Haff didn't know we moved."

"I went to where Haff told me the camp was but it was gone. I reasoned it must have been something urgent and that you would have put the forest between you and the fort so tracked you along to here. I had a real job, you covered your movements very well and the stupid Romans destroyed a lot of tracks blundering about in the woods looking for you."

"You're a good tracker then, Addani."

She smiled. "Have to be on a farm, Highness, I often need to find cows when they go missing. You seem to be okay out

here, I thought I would join you. May I?"
  A shout went up, "Yes!"

Chapter Five

Hints of Happiness

"Tell me," Addani asked, "Why are you all camping out? You could go to the town called Sarum and live better lives, they don't know you there, do they?"

"When Legate changed after Vespasian left, we were called to the Standing Stones and our swords were transformed with a special power. But we had to hide them from the new Governor quickly as we returned, he was after our blood and would have taken them for sure. They were the jewelled ones Alyssa has for special ceremonies. However, when we went to get them we discovered they'd been taken and we need them back. But we have no idea where to start looking."

"I see, I'll go back into the fort tomorrow and ask about, see if I can find out anything. I'll get my horse, it's in the trees."

"But what are you doing over here, and where's Falcon?" I asked, casting around for him. "I thought you two were farming at your house?"

It was her turn to sigh. "Falcon died in the late spring with a winter illness, Majesty," Addani said in a quiet voice.

I stared at her, it was such a shock. "I... I'm so terribly sorry for you, Addani," I stammered. "You two were made for each other, you got on so well straight away. It must be hard to bear." It was my turn to cuddle her. "You should have come and asked for help, why didn't you?" I whispered in her ear. "I would have come immediately."

"I couldn't leave him, he got ill so quickly. Thank you for that, though, I know you would have journeyed over, Highness, as fast as you could have. If only it had been different." Her eyes showed of her sorrow, those deep brown soft eyes that had tears in them now.

I put a hand over hers. "We've both suffered such loss, my brave warrior, it's so sad. And I'm not a Highness any more, nor is the Queen, please call me Lauren. A queenly title is far too dangerous for us to use at the moment."

"Why is that, it is your right, Highness?"

Sheelan cut in to explain about the Legate Scapula, our adventures in the other forest and meeting Caractacus, which led to the massacre of the two cohorts, then how we had fled across country to Mai-Dun, of Shoelr's death and our hazardous journey back into the southern forest to defeat the pig Quintus Veranius and his cohorts and won the aquila.

Addani looked dumbfounded. "You've had a whole load of adventures and took their eagle, too. Wow! I wish I'd been there at your side, Majesty."

"Sadly, Vespasian was called back to Rome, so we got this violent barbarian instead," Sheelan ended.

"That's awful, Highness. What a load of cruel bastards they are."

I gave a low snort of disgust. "That's what they call us, barbarians. At least we're civilised, Addani. We have respect for people, their feelings and property."

"I see it all now. Glad you slaughtered a whole mass of them though, well done. I would have loved to have fought by your side, Lauren. I can call you that, can't I?"

I burst out laughing.

"What's so funny," Addani asked, looking around our group, a puzzled expression on her face.

"When Alyssa gave Sheelan that odd vow, that I'm sure she made up for convenience by the way, every time Sheelan kissed me, that's exactly what she said, *"I can, can't I?"*"

"Sheelan will look after you more intently than me, it's plain she loves you dearly. We all knew she did a long time ago, that's why Alyssa made up that Vow. I'm surprised it took so long for you to realise it, Lauren. And I can call you that, can't I," she ended, with a deadpan face.

We all laughed then. Addani had brought a hint of

happiness back into our midst.

She made a pack up and left at dawn. "I've a lot to do, many people to ask, so will be away a while. Which means you must try and stay put until I get back." She hugged me. "I'll do my best, Lauren." Addani shook her head. "That seems so wrong, Highness, but it's your wish, so I'll use your given name." She waved, turned her horse's head north, and slowly disappeared over the brow of the hill.

One had to wonder if we would ever see her again, things in this bad era were very uncertain.

I was getting worried; she was ages. Four moons had passed and the fort was only half a day away and half a day back, meaning three moons for Addani to make her enquiries. But I knew she would be thorough, so hardened my heart and waited a little longer.

In the meantime, Alyssa was sitting up and chatting, her strange powers having helped her over the awful wound. But I kept her in bed most of the time, letting her up for a walk around and to see where we were. She did what I told her, although I teased her a little about it.

"You're worried, aren't you?" Sheelan chided as she sat next to me. "You shouldn't be, Addani is clever, she can look after herself."

"Does it show that much?"

"You have lines on that lovely face of yours, that's how I know, darling. It's only been a few days, try to perk up."

"I find it hard to do that, sweetheart, after all that's happened. I could cheerfully have had Verna flogged for sneezing like that, she gave us all away and that's the second time. Alyssa would have banished her had she had all her faculties and had been fit enough."

"People can't help sneezing, Lauren, she didn't do it on purpose."

I gave her a long, hard look. "She makes too many

mistakes of that nature. She forgot my rifle when she brought the bows, too, it might have saved Alyssa from injury. She's a walking disaster area."

"I'll have a quiet word, my love. Please don't do anything hasty."

Sheelan had barely got the last word out, when Verna came tearing into the camp shouting at the top of her voice.

"Highness, Highness, there's the sound of a horse coming along the track."

I was furious. "**Verna**, how many more times have I got to correct you about calling me that. Do it once more and I'll have you flogged and banished, is that quite clear?" It tore out of me, venomously.

All heads turned. Most knew me well enough that if pushed, I would carry out a threat I made, I had done it before and making idle threats undermined authority, they had to be fulfilled.

She cringed down, fear on her face. "I... I... I am so sorry, it just popped out. I was so used to calling you that."

"Everybody here was used to calling Alyssa and me that title, and for much longer than you have, yet they think first before opening their mouths. Had any Romans been near or us at the fort and you had blurted that out we would all be arrested and killed. There will NOT be another chance, Verna, use my given name, that's an order."

The woman was visibly quaking in her shoes and a trickle of urine ran down her legs in fear. She dropped to her knees and kissed my feet. "I'm sorry, Lauren, it won't happen again, I promise, I promise. Please don't beat me again and send me away, I beg you."

"It had better not, else you'll find I keep my word about such things. Get out of my sight before I have you flogged now anyway. Go to Taal."

I sat, still fuming inside. Yes, it was extremely dangerous to me, but also to every person here. If the Romans thought for an instant we were together as a group, there would be no mercy.

Sheelan squatted. "Taal's taken her to see who it is, my love. You went bright red, I've never seen you so angry with one of our own before."

"She's a liability, makes mistakes all the time, doesn't think things through and fails to consider how much danger she places us all in referring to me as Royalty. What about Alyssa when she's up and about, too? We are not Royalty for now, not until the Romans change their attitude towards us. Until then, we *must* be Alyssa and Lauren, there are no options. Sheelan, my love, it's hard being at the top, as Brevit always said, one has to lead so must make such decisions and harden your heart. I *would* carry out my threat."

Taal approached. "I apologise, Lauren. She feels that you should use your title, it's your right. I have explained why she mustn't say it and that you mean what you say. I beg you not to, please. The horse is Addani's, she'll be here soon." Taal gave a very slight bow of her head and tried to smile.

I nodded. "Very well Taal, I accept your apology. Do your best to cool her silly attitude down, I meant what I said, she'll be flogged and banished, as much as I abhor such things, it would be for all our safety." I stood and walked to the brow of the hill.

Addani waved, a grin on her face. There was someone sitting behind her, I wondered who it was. She jumped off her mount, pausing to help the woman down.

I wondered who it might be, not Haff, I could see that. Then she walked forward.

"Fran!" I exclaimed. "What on earth are you doing back here?"

She grinned madly. "I missed you all and this beautiful land. I've come to stay, may I, Highness?"

"I don't know what to say. If you wish to, you know what it's like here so have no allusions about it. I see you're wearing the sword and other things you took with you."

"Thank you, Majesty. I hope I'll fit in?" She came and gave me a cuddle.

"Don't call us by our titles for now, Fran. We're hunted by

65

the Romans."

Addani nodded approval. "I heard you shouting, Lauren. I've hardly ever heard you scream at a person like that, you must be very angry. We've all had to bury our feelings about titles and names, but it doesn't mean we lose our respect for you both. Come here, Verna, and stand before me."

Verna looked very crestfallen and slowly walked to her.

"You heard what I just said, we still respect Lauren and Alyssa as our Queens, but just don't call them that. Both Lauren and Alyssa are Queenly names, so when we use them we are still saying Highness or your Majesty. Can you think of it like that?"

She gaped at Addani, an intimidating woman over six feet tall with that mass of chestnut hair and painted face.

"Ye... yes, Addani, I see what you mean. That will be a great help, I will feel as if I am respecting them more now. Thank you." The pair returned to their watch.

"What news, my brave fighter?" I asked.

"None of the Romans there have them as far as I can make out. Haff saw Fran wandering around the fort looking for you. She took her home out of the way in case Romans began asking questions. Haff told me they had seen no strange tribes, not until the time you fought that bunch, so she doubts any of those people have them either. Shaila was out of the fort when they must have been taken and in the southern forest so knows nothing, nor does Toler. While it doesn't cut the field down, it's not expanded it either. By the way, two Roman soldiers have been asking after you. They called you Queen Lauren, said their names were Artorius and Aulus Maximus. They wanted to know where you were but I didn't tell them. Was that right?"

"For now, yes. But they are safe young men, they helped us free Alyssa from the cell when it could have cost them their lives had they been found out. I trust them. Why did they ask?"

"They are willing to leave the legion and join you, help in any way they can, Lauren. Artorius seemed furious about the floggings."

I smiled. "He's a nice young man. But I thought Artorius is vowed to one of our women. Didn't he leave and move here with Gweneth?" The memory returned of his fresh cheery face in the hospital. "He said the whole legion had fallen in love with me, how sweet. When Veranius had us tied to the flogging frames he questioned his right. Veranius refused to listen and threatened him to, a Centurion. Artorius rode and got Vespasian back to stop it. The General put Scapula under arrest. I wouldn't mind meeting them again."

Addani gave me an odd look. "I didn't think you were that way inclined," she said, a grin spreading across her face and a tease in her voice.

I laughed. "I'm not, but they are handsome, you might fall for one," I countered.

A roar of a laugh came from Addani as she bent backwards and held her sides. "Maybe, maybe... How tall are they?"

"Not as tall as you, my friend. They'll have to grow or you shrink. Now, you need a tent to sleep in so had better settle in with Leilan, all other tents are paired off. It will give you a roof over your head." I sat on the grass and huffed out.

Sheelan sat beside me. "Why the huff?" she asked.

"Why? Because we're no nearer our objective than we were before, despite Addani's efforts. Maybe the only way is to journey around all the farms asking. Somebody may know something, they can't just have disappeared into thin air."

"I have often wondered that, Lauren, since we began looking there have been strange things going on."

"But not against us, sweetheart. Spirit helped when things happened. No, there has to be another explanation. We'll start as soon as Alyssa is well enough. It means going back towards the fort, then turning right in full view of it onto the eastern track. Let's hope the Roman guards aren't curious and call out a section."

We camped for two weeks. Alyssa got steadily better and took greater interest in our situation. She went for short walks with either me or Sheelan, although she refused to be aided, saying she needed to strengthen her body after being in bed for so long. The wound had healed, leaving not a scratch on her flesh, she was amazing.

The weather changed the day it was decided to move; Rain filtered down from a grey sullen sky driven sideways by a fresh north easterly wind, which meant we would have it in our faces until we turned by the river boulders; it rapidly made us wet through. After breakfast, we packed camp, our horses were loaded, we mounted and huddled in our tunics to start down the hill and track. Fran had to double up, which meant Bran taking an extra straddle bag.

Alyssa rode between Sheelan and me, glancing each way every now and then smile with her eyes. "If it gets worse and colder, we shall have to use the furs off the mounts backs, Lauren," she called.

I guessed she was feeling it after being dry and mild for some time. But I expect the farmers were probably clapping their hands. The last chance for grass to grow before the cold time set in.

Soon, the eastern track was in sight. We turned right onto it keeping our faces in hoods or the tops of our tunics.

A shout for us to stop went up from the gates of the fort.

"Ignore it," I said. "But think of a plan if anybody comes out."

"The best plan is to keep going," Sheelan said. "They'll be on foot."

I reined my horse in by the short line of houses where I had first met Alegia. People stood looking at us in some kind of awe.

"Your Highness," a man said. "I remember you from little Alegia, you took her under your wing after the attack."

"Thank you. We are looking for our ceremonial swords that we had to hide from the Romans recently. Have you any idea of their whereabouts." I saw doubt in their eyes. "We think somebody may have taken them into safety. We need them back, that's all."

Heads shook along with blank faces. It was plain they hadn't the faintest idea what might have happened to them.

The man pointed behind us. "Look, the Romans are sending a large column out of the fort. You had better get going, my Queens. We'll all listen out for information for you and tell the Romans you were just travellers looking for somewhere to stay. Go, Majesty, quickly."

"Thank you, my good man, we're in your debt. Lead on Bran," I called to her.

Chapter Six

The Quest Begins

Someone yelled from behind. Whoever it was had the dickens of a voice, it was a real bellow. "YOU THERE, STOP IMMEDIATELY."

"Canter," Bran shouted, thus speeding us up with the intention of opening a gap.

A soft, caring voice in my head told me to look back at that moment.

What I saw sent shivers down my spine. From the rear of their unit at least a dozen horses swung out at full gallop.

"They have cavalry, Bran. We must move faster."

"Gallop," she yelled.

I wondered who the horsemen were, the Romans didn't use them normally, only officers. Had they enlisted some of our own people against us? We rode on quickly until level with the forest on the right and were not outpacing our followers, who continued the pursuit.

"Into the trees and dismount. Get longbows ready," Addani, shouted.

Bran was quick to get her gist. Her arm shot out to the right and soon the cloak of the forest took us into its protection as we jumped off our horses.

"Set up a line abreast," I shouted. "Verna, take the horses back farther and stay with them, you know how to whisper to them now. Do exactly what you're told." I said it with menace in my voice and a threatening glower in my eyes.

"Yes, Lauren, I learned that." She went farther back and was quickly hidden from view.

With her out of the way it gave us a line of twelve and I didn't have to worry about stupendous sneezes or horses whinnying.

"Fran, stay by me and use Verna's bow, share my quiver."
Sheelan squatted one side of me, Alyssa the other. Each
smiled reassuringly.

We only had to wait a few moments before hooves
sounded on the track. Orders were shouted in some odd
language, not Latin nor ours. In that case they must be
mercenaries. Swords began slashing at undergrowth as the
enemy advanced.

I caught movements slightly right, gave Bran's arm a tap
and pointed.

She nodded and adjusted our line of fire.

At about eighteen yards I stood and loosed at the leader,
my arrow shwooshing through the air with deadly accuracy.

My sudden appearance with a bow, a type he had never
seen before, stopped him in his tracks. Within a split second
he was lifted off his feet to fall about a yard or so back. All
our other arrows were in the air smashing into humans who,
at this close range, were thrown physically about.

Swords were drawn as we rushed them, but all apart from
one was dead.

I pushed my sword point into his throat just enough to
cause a slight trickle of blood. "Who are you?" I demanded.

He had dark skin and hair, his overall appearance swarthy,
deep brown eyes glared back, but didn't reply.

"They are dressed in a strange way, Lauren," Bran noted.
"They have light baggy trousers on, fastened at the ankles."

"From the east, I would guess. One of the Roman's
subjugated peoples now brought into their army. Look at
their small bows, better for use on a horse. We need to
remount and move in this forest far as we can. The Romans
won't follow us in once they see this."

Addani walked to him and thrust her sword into his chest.

I stared at her. There must have been surprise and shock on
my face.

"It needed doing, Lauren. We can't take prisoners. They
are our attackers, we have the right to send them to
Otherworld if we beat them in combat, as they have that right

on us if we had attacked them and lost."

"Yes," I replied, nodding. "I suppose it did, and you do. Retrieve our arrows."

"You've hardened against our enemies, my love," Alyssa said. "I'm pleased, they deserve no sympathy. They are a brutal race and allied to the Romans."

I smiled back at her. "It's put the lid on us being travellers looking for lodgings. At a trot through the trees, please, Bran, let's get away from here."

We rode on.It was starting to get dark.

Bran called a halt in the trees by a river. "I'll send Lalena and Merial out onto the track to see if anybody is following. Do Romans march at night, Lauren?"

"I haven't the foggiest idea. Set a changing watch on all night, but exclude Verna, I don't trust her to be responsible for our safety. Sheelan and me will take a turn, we are all equal now. The Queen can rest."

"You'll never be that, Lauren." Bran replied. "You're a Queen in my heart and always will be."

I smiled back at her. "Thank you, Bran. Give Fran the spare tent please, lucky we got it."

Time dragged. Eventually Lalena and Merial came back. "Couldn't see anything at all, Lauren," Lalena called as they walked towards us. "Do you think we'll ever find your swords, it's a big country and they could be anywhere."

"We have to try. Magical swords are few and far between. A King called Arthur in the not very distant future had one, but after he was mortally wounded in battle ordered one of his knights to hurl it into the magic lake from whence it originated."

"Really," Lalena gasped. "What happened?"

A chorus of voices came. "Yes, what happened, Lauren?"

That made me smile. A good tale is always a very welcome diversion. "Get a dinner cooking, then settle around the fire and I'll tell you."

"What has happened to your swords?" Fran asked.

"We're not sure, the Stones seem to have empowered

them. I cut a small tree down with one swipe."

"Wow, that's impressive. As an archaeologist, I have always suspected Standing Stones of having spiritual powers, or powers of some kind. You would believe that came from the Gods, I expect."

"There was a Voice," I replied.

"A voice?"

"Yes, deep and booming. It said I was a Goddess."

"From the Fairymounds probably," Fran said, thoughtfully.

The camp and dinner were quickly organised. I watched them getting it done as fast as possible and smiled secretly, it surprised me how keen they were to hear my tale.

Bran stood in front of me. "All done, Lauren. You promised to tell us of that king. Will you, please?"

"Come in a circle around me and close, I don't want to be shouting and lose my voice."

Sheelan was right at the front, her crossed legs touching mine, eyes wide open in anticipation.

"It's a tale of legend and according to it, a King named Uther Pendragon asked Merlin the great wizard, how he could protect his infant son, Arthur. He was next in line for the throne but was only a baby, so needed to grow true and strong and away from the dangers of greed and envy at Uther's court and the many battles fought between rival tribes at that time. Merlin took him away to a secret cave where Arthur grew into a strong and brave youth yet knowing nothing of his origins. In the meantime, wars in the land threatened the crown and as King Uther grew older he once more asked Merlin for a way that only his son would become the true and rightful King without challenge after his own death.

Merlin thought deeply about this, it was a tricky request from his sovereign, so needed fulfilling.

The wizard knew of an enchanted lake where a beautiful Guardian known as the Lady was supposed to live. He stood beside the water's edge and called a Celtic incantation clear and loud.

"Oh, beautiful Lady of the Lake, I, Merlin the great wizard, summon you before me."

Nothing seemed to happen until he looked down into its crystal-clear water. There began a shimmering, a bubbling, effervescing haziness spoiling his view. Faster and faster the water seemed to boil but when it eased and stopped, the outline of the Lady lay a short way beneath the surface, eyes closed in a deep sleep with the sword held in her hands along her body from head to toe pointing down at her feet.

"Our Lady of the Lake, I demand the sword Excalibur from you to be used in the selection and safety of the future King of this great realm, it to be used only for righteous and noble purpose."

At Merlin's calling her eyes slowly opened as she awoke; her hand moved to grip the sword's hilt, holding it in her right hand. Swiftly the vision raised it upwards out of the surface, scattering water with the force of her thrust. As her fingers opened to release her grip, the sword magically transported itself to the wizard, who quickly clasped it in his hand. He held it high and proclaimed a vow.

"Behold, the sword Excalibur lies within my grasp. It will be used wisely, my Lady, be assured. I, and the nation to be, thank you." He bowed his head as the Lady's arm disappeared back under the water and she vanished.

Merlin presented Uther with this beautiful weapon. "We must go to the village centre," he said. "Bring the court and summon the people so they may witness the deed that is about to take place."

A large curious crowd gathered around the granite boulder in the village square.

"Now hear this proclamation," Merlin boomed. "This is the sword Excalibur, the great mystery sword from the Lady of the Lake. Your great King has asked my help in creating a method whereby only the true King of this realm can be chosen. I shall bury this magical sword into this rock."

Without another word the wizard rested the point upon the granite and thrust with all his might.

A great shower of sparks flew into the air alikened to a rainbow, cascading and glistening as diamonds might arch out and down falling invisibly upon the ground.

People fled for their lives in terror, nobody had ever seen such a feat enacted before.

` Merlin cast his eyes around those assembled. "Now let you all take note, only the hand of the true King of the country will ever withdraw this great sword from its stony prison." Merlin turned and walked away.

Years went past and after the King's death the country fell in chaos. Many tried to extricate the weapon but all failed.

By this time Arthur had left the cave and Merlin's tuition and protection, although the wizard continued to watch over the teenager. Arthur had become the servant of a knight, what was known as a Squire.

On this particular day there was to be a joust and great festivities in which his master was taking part. But Arthur, in his excitement at going and seeing the pageantry, had forgotten to bring his master's sword to the field of contest and in a panic and fear of punishment, went running to fetch it. On his way through the deserted village he saw the wonderfully untarnished sword sticking out of the stone and guessing it belonged to nobody, reasoned it might save his master discovering his mistake. He took a hold of the hilt and withdrew it.

The knight was amazed when Arthur presented him with the famous sword that so many had tried yet failed, to withdraw from the stone. "Where did you get this?" he demanded.

"I'm sorry Sire," the young Squire replied. "I saw it in the stone and thought it would save me going all the way back to the fort. I confess master, I forgot your sword." He went on one knee expecting a rebuke.

Instead, the knight went on his knee to bow before his sovereign and Arthur became a great King of this land."

"How did he do that?" Sheelan said, squeezing closer cross-legged, just as Madeil had done when I told her the tale of Jack and the Beanstalk.

A smiled flitted across my face. "It was Merlin's magic and that of the Lady of the Lake, that only the true King could take it from the boulder, so again, it was a very magical sword, much like ours."

Alyssa had sat and listened as intently as Sheelan. "Oh, they gave metal to the water Gods in the future, too. How did Merlin know of the water lady in the first place, though?"

"He was a great wizard so just knew all the mysteries of this land, I suppose. King Arthur fought many battles and slew all those that rose against him and his people using Excalibur, it was a very troubled time. But Excalibur only worked for the King, much as ours only seem to respond to us. After Arthur was mortally wounded in battle and lay dying, he told a knight to throw it back into the same magical lake, returning it from whence it came and back to the Lady of the Lake.

Twice the knight's willpower failed him, not having the strength of mind to hurl the beautiful object out into the water believing it too valuable and powerful to throw away, so failing his King. On the third attempt he obeyed Arthur's wish and threw with all his might. As it twisted and revolved in the air the jewels inset in it glinted like a thousand stars flashing wonderfully in flight just above the water's surface and a strange noise filled the air.

Suddenly, a woman's hand shot out of the lake, water cascading off it as it waited, erect with spread fingers to grip its prize. Miraculously, the hilt found her palm and settled into her fist as it closed, to be held vertically for a few moments before plunging back into the mysterious depths to disappear."

"Fancy throwing it away," Addani groaned. "He should have used it, I would have."

"It was a desperate situation; the King was dying and only he was allowed to wield it as the true King of England. So, the weapon had to be sent back to the hand that gave it to Merlin in the first place."

"How could she breathe?" Lalena asked, puzzled.

"I don't know the answer to that, sweet Lalena, it was magical and Godly. That was only one part of the story, though."

"What's a knight and a joust?" Alyssa asked.

"Usually someone of great virtue, character, strength and bravery who upholds right against evil and wrongdoing, much as you, sweet one, and lived in a castle. They rode beautiful horses and met around a round table. A joust is when two knights rode a horse at each other holding a long lance to see who would prove themselves best."

"Why was it round?" Alyssa went on, her brow wrinkling in puzzlement.

"So, all those that sat at it were of equal status, no one knight could claim to be more important or powerful than any other, there was no head of the table, not even the King himself. And that is also much like us at the moment."

"Oh, are we acting out that story?" Lalena said, surprised.

"Is that what will happen to our swords?" Alyssa asked. "We have to return them to whence they came?"

"I don't know that, Alyssa. When we find them, we may get guidance from the Gods, they were the ones that empowered them."

"Was there a Queen?" Alyssa smiled softly as she asked.

"Yes, called Guinevere. She was very beautiful, as a Queen should be and again like you my love," I smiled back. "But she deserted her King to run away with a knight called Sir Galahad."

"Disloyalty!" Alyssa exclaimed. "How awful."

"King Arthur had her burned at a stake for her betrayal."

Alyssa nodded. "Although a sword thrust might have been more humane."

"What is a castle?" Bran put in.

"It was supposed to be a massive stone fortification. However, the ability to build such a thing never existed here so I expect it was actually one of our hill forts made into a stronghold with higher and stronger palisades. The period was immediately after the Romans leave this land."

"How do you know all this?" Sheelan asked, squeezing even nearer to almost sit in my lap.

I laughed. "I was taught it at college."

"Ah, that college place again," Alyssa said with a grin.

Sheelan tapped my leg. "What happened to King Arthur?"

"He was placed in a boat that drifted away on the lake with a fairy to guide it. It's said he was tended by three mystical women and may still be alive in a cavern or Fairymound somewhere. One day, when this country is in terrible trouble, he'll return and save us, although he may take the form of a different person."

"He should be here soon then," Lalena snorted.

"That is in the future Lalena. Maybe the reason we have had our swords empowered is to deal with this situation until Arthur is born? This land of ours will face much worse threats than the Romans, Lalena. When they leave us in about four hundred years' time, the Saxons and Vikings will come and after those, the Normans. Occupation will continue for many hundreds of years. King Arthur fought the Saxons."

"So, will our swords save our race?" Alyssa asked.

"Possibly, there must be a reason why that strange event occurred and made them powerful. That was on stone, just like Excalibur."

"Wow! It all happens here then," Sheelan stated brightly and giggled.

"Not right now, fortunately, sweetheart. We had better get to sleep, tomorrow we start our journey. It should be okay to travel along the track again and get to the first of the eastern villages. Maybe Chief Ragnar has news?"

"I do hope so," Alyssa replied. "Thank you for the story, we all enjoyed it, my love."

The morning was clear and dry so we could see the track was empty of any pursuers. The sun came out and warmed us, turning it into a pleasant day.

At last the village came into sight two hundred yards away and with us fourteen in all since Fran joined, a large group that could easily be seen. Yet there wasn't a soul anywhere and houses were closed up, making the place look deserted.

"That's odd," I said, turning on my horse to Sheelan. "I would have expected Chief Ragnar to be out by now. Let's get nearer."

At fifty yards there was still no sign of life.

"Maybe they think we are bandits," Alyssa suggested. "Give them a call, Sheelan, sweetheart, one of your special voices," she said, nodding in the direction of the houses.

Sheelan yelled out with all the power in her lungs, which was considerable. *"Hey there, is anybody home?"*

Nothing. Complete silence.

"Stay there for a moment, sweet one, with the rest," I said to Alyssa. "Come with me Sheelan, let's investigate."

We rode into the village surveying the scene.

"Is anybody home," I called again.

A door opened a fraction. A woman's voice asked, "Who is it?"

"It's friends from the fort," I called back.

The door opened a little more.

I waved, Sheelan gave a blistering smile.

The woman came out with extreme caution, slowly placing her feet outside her doorway as though the sky might fall on her the moment she was free of her house. Inch by inch she came on, hardly moving her feet and obviously ready to dash back in and bolt her door at the first sign of anything untoward.

I jumped down, Sheelan followed. "Don't you recognise me? Where is Chief Ragnar?"

"Oh, yes!" The woman came running forward then. "It's you, Queen Lauren. Thank the Gods, we were at a loss what to do and frightened."

I looked around. More doors were starting to open. "Why are you at a loss?"

"It's alright," she shouted back into the village. "It's our Queen. You can all come out." She smiled at me. "I'm sorry, Highness, we are very careful after what happened. You shouldn't be here either, it's far too dangerous for you. Chief Ragnar was killed by the Romans, Majesty. They came looking for you and Queen Alyssa but when our Chief said he hadn't seen you, they tied him up and beat him terribly, it was too awful to watch. He was old, so died of the fright and his wounds."

She really meant shock, but all these people understood was that he had died.

My anger burst through. "Those bastards, it's that bloody Quintus Veranius again. May the Gods bring a curse down upon his head and strike the swine with a dreadful pestilence that is excruciatingly painful but slowly fatal," I cried aloud, looking up to the Gods. "Why does he have to be so bloody spiteful. I think we have a score to settle with him in more than one way." I waved an arm to the rest of our band. "Come in, it's safe. Who are you, my dear woman?"

"Morgana, Highness."

"Who has been looking after you all since Chief Ragnar was killed, Morgana?"

"I have, Majesty."

"Then you seem to have held your people together, well done. I think you should become the Matriarch here and continue the good work, the village needs a leader. You mustn't call me by my title, Morgana, that is very dangerous for all of us. As you know, the Romans are looking for us so we have had to become outlaws until they settle down."

"Me! Be a Chief! Bu... bu... but I don't know wher... what to do."

"What you have been doing all along, looking out for strangers, keeping your people safe and the land and animal stocks tended."

"Goodness, do you think I can? Where is the other Queen?" Morgana asked, looking around our band.

Bran stepped between us. "Queen Alyssa was injured in a

fight a short while ago. Lauren is looking after us until Queen Alyssa is well enough. She's here, with us."

Sheelan helped Alyssa off her mount.

Morgana bowed. "My Queen, how are you?"

"Well, thank you, Morgana, thanks to Lauren. She saved my life."

"I'm so pleased to hear that, you must feel very weary. We know Queen Lauren is a Goddess so she would have cured you, Majesty. Come and take tea and food with us, please." She led us to what had been Ragnar's house, it was larger than the rest, accommodating of us all. "Please sit and rest, I'll get some women to bring food. I see the woman who came with the God Stan is with you again."

"She has come to stay this time," Alyssa explained.

"Send Freda and Juna out to check there are no riders or other formations of people on foot following us, please, Bran," I asked.

A veritable banquet came.

"Thank you, Morgana, this is wonderful. How have the crops been doing?"

"Well Highn..., oh, what shall I call you now?"

"Lauren, use our given names, please."

"Yes, well, Lauren..." she paused, looked at me guiltily as if she had transgressed a sacred oath and sighed. "The ground here is much more productive than our old home. Everybody was happy until those awful people came, thanks to Queen Alyssa allowing us to farm here. You're never going on farther, my Queen, sleep here if you wish. I'll get some women to bring bedding in and keep a lookout all night. You'll be safe."

"Thank you, it would be wonderful for us all to get a decent rest, it's hard being outlaws, Morgana."

"You should never be that, you have both helped us so much, it isn't right."

The clan looked after us well overnight, gave us breakfast and tea the next day and even packed food bundles for each of us.

"Thank you, Morgana, and your whole village. You have done very well. Look after your people, be sparing with food reserves during the cold time and have a good sowing in the spring. Farewell."

She hugged me. "You're the ones that need to take care, my Queens. Please do be careful and return to rule over us again one day."

"I hope that will be soon, Morgana," Alyssa replied. "We all wish that with our full hearts."

The morning was chilly, our horses snorted their breath out in diaphanous clouds and fidgeted on their feet, eager to move.

We left the village people, standing waving at our backs while we twisted on our mounts, waving to them. Then our band rounded a corner and we lost sight.

The weather soon warmed and seemed to be holding, what in modern times in Britain would be called an Indian Summer, in other words a late one. It made travelling easier and pleasanter. I had lost track of the time of year, other than it was autumn, perhaps October, so it would be Samhain soon, the end of the month and then the year would drift into November. We needed furs and a winter camp that would be secure, preferably not in a forest.

"Penny for them," Sheelan's voice cut into my thoughts.

She made me smile.

"I like to see you smile, darling. You've had a scowl on your face for ages and it doesn't suit you. I know why, I feel the same about Eva, but if we try to keep our minds focussed on our quest it might help. Remember what Alegia said?"

Alyssa reached over to place a hand on my arm. "Sheelan's right. Keep your mind on our quest, darling, be positive, that's what you tell me."

I nodded. "Thank you both. I got low, then I look at you two and my heart fills with love, summer sunshine and beautiful flowers with a wonderful fragrance."

"Ah, that's so lovely, thank you, my darling," Sheelan replied.

Bran rode back to us. "Is it the Belgae next, Lauren? It's been a while since I've been out here."

"Yes. Send a couple on ahead to let them know who we are, please."

She chose Nianda and Addani. They went at a steady trot while our horses just ambled along. They rapidly disappeared into the trees between us and the village but were soon galloping back hard. Their mounts skidded to a halt by Bran.

"Romans," Nianda rattled out urgently.

"How many?"

"I think about a patrol," Nianda replied, showing ten fingers.

I snorted angrily. "Let's dismount and go forwards in the trees, we'll get a better idea then. Verna, look after the horses and keep them quiet." It was snapped at her, but I knew what an idiot she could be so a sharp warning might get her to do the simple task allotted to her efficiently.

Her eyes goggled. "Yes, Lauren, I will, I promise."

"Okay, thank you, Verna." Perhaps I was being too hard on her?

Low scrubby foliage gave us good cover as we crept nearer the village. We soon saw the situation and I fumed even more at the injustice.

They had Mondar trussed up kneeling on the ground, his arms bound in front of him to a stake driven into the ground. His tunic had been removed and a brute of a man was about to set into flogging him with a multi-stranded whip. I knew what that felt like and determined to prevent the Chief suffering such pain.

The enemy group, for that's what they should be considered, comprised twelve, the unit commander and the one with the lash in the centre of a ring of steel formed around the punishment arena by the legionaries, their huge shields standing on end in front of each soldier, a gladius gripped to point outwards through gaps between.

Anger arose in my mind. How dare these barbarians flog a clan Chieftain. Whatever had occurred could not warrant this wicked act on unarmed civilians. Motioning with signals to half our group to work their way around the other side of the houses and so surround our enemy, leaving them open to attack from multiple directions. I plucked an arrow from my quiver, nocking it as a signal for our warriors to do likewise. They moved quickly, silently, gaining as close a position as possible to the circle of Romans, be it a bush, a wagon, or the side of a roundhouse's shade, anything that got them well within deadly striking range, close enough to do terrible damage.

The pig of a Commander was spouting something to the villagers, indicating the man with the whip and Chief Mondar with an arm, plainly warning all and sundry that if they failed to comply with his demands they would suffer the same fate.

Sheelan tapped my arm. "If we kill them all, won't Veranius come and destroy the village as a reprisal?" she whispered.

I put a finger to my lips, shook my head and stood, just as the brute brought his right arm back ready to bring the lash across Mondar's bare back. Drawing my longbow hard back to gain as much power as possible and the signal for all our group to stand in clear sight, the first two fingers on my right hand opened, the string whipped forwards sending my missile on its way with that fascinating fallowing sound. Half a heartbeat later it struck home.

A look of shock and horror gripped the brute's features as the arrow hit him in the centre of his evil back, lifting him off his feet to dump his lifeless body some distance away. The only sound was air escaping from his lungs.

The Centurion commanding had partly turned when he was killed, the arrow passing clean through his neck to stick out the other side. He gurgled for a few moments on the ground.

More arrows flashed through the air, all but one Roman dropped. Holding a huge shield in front of them didn't give any protection from an arrow in the back or straight in their ugly faces at such close range. I nocked another, took aim at the last remaining Roman fleeing as fast as his legs would carry him, and felled the swine as he reached the edge of the clearing. He nosedived into a bush. I grinned at Sheelan. "There must be no survivors this time, none to tell the tale."

I motioned us all forward. "Go inspect each of the enemy to ensure they're truly dead," I shouted as I whipped a dagger from my calf sheath to cut Mondar's bonds. "Come, my brave clan Chief, stand tall again."

The incident had only taken a few seconds so everybody was still standing agape at the speed of the event where they had been when we first saw them. But as Mondar stood, everybody erupted in joy.

The Chief had already been beaten, bruises littered his face and body yet he still looked bemused at the sudden change of fortune.

"Thank you, Highness, for your timely intervention." He tried to bow but was unsteady on his feet.

Grabbing an arm, I called to Sheelan. "Give me a hand here, my love. Let's get him to his home and tend the wounds."

Mondar was placed on his bed, his head dropped forwards.

"Bring my horse please, Freda, the medications are in the straddle bags. Why were they beating you, my Chief?"

"They are searching for you both, my Queens. I told them you hadn't been here, but they didn't believe me." He turned to Alyssa. "Thank you, my Queen."

Bran explained the event in the wood, our loss and Alyssa's injury. "We're looking for the Queen's swords. Have you seen or heard of them?"

"No, young woman. But nobody would harm them, surely? They are held in the highest esteem by all our tribes."

"That's my worry, what if another clan got hold of them. We fought a band of raiders when …" I paused... "when Queen Alyssa got injured."

"I expect they were found and taken to safety somewhere,"

Mondar said, nodding encouragingly.

I gave a half smile back. "Perhaps, Chief, but where? Addani, would you get a cart and have our people load the dead on it. Take them well away from here ensuring there can be no connection with this village. Leave the pigs there as if they've been waylaid, but remove our arrows, please. They live in fear of us when out in small units in forests like these."

"My people will do that, Highness. You have done enough in one day. They can take them north-east, away from us and Chief Mernae's village and dump their carcasses within the edge of the eastern forest. Now, sit and take food and drink with me."

"We have had to stop using our titles, Chief, the Romans will be alerted if they hear it."

Mondar looked at me aghast. "What am I to call such kind Goddesses as you?"

"Just a very plain Alyssa, Lauren and Sheelan. It will have to do for now. Have any strangers been this way?" I asked, "Anyone at all"

"No, none, my Queen, and it's late in the year so we don't expect any either. Folk tend to stay where they are as the cold time approaches."

"Yes, very true and sensible. Keep your eyes and ears open, please, any information could be vital."

We spent a pleasant evening chatting around the hearth. When time came for bed Chief Mondar wouldn't hear of us sleeping in our tents; each member was allocated a family to look after us and afford a bed for them. Apart from Alyssa, Sheelan and I, he managed to magic a spare house for us. We spent a peaceful night in each other's arms without fear of discovery again.

Chapter Seven

Omen

Come the morning we bade them our goodbyes. "Take special care Chief. If they ask again, tell them a cock and bull story that we went a different way. It might save you a flogging and keep them occupied and away from us."

"Dangerous times, Highnesses." Mondar replied. "Take good care of your small band of warriors. Give Chief Serobach my regards and best wishes."

I smiled at that. "It makes a change from fighting each other where you used to live. You can expand your land as far west as you like but keep in touch with neighbouring tribes as you do, you don't want wars between you."

He smiled. "I hope those days have gone, Highness. Farewell until you rule over us once more."

We rode back to the main track at a steady slow pace, to turn right onto it. It was another nice day for the time of year but even so, had a noticeable chill in it now. This early in the morning our breath still vaporised.

Sheelan shivered. "I need to hunt, Lauren. We must get some more furs together ready for the cold time."

"Yes, make a team up, Addani, Lalena and Merial perhaps. The rest of us will have a break and wait by this grove of trees."

Sheelan and her group vanished into the eastern forest on our left. The trees on our side comprised a small stand about two hundred yards long and looked fairly deep, cutting the wind off of us that had recently sprung up.

It looked peaceful, so I walked into it a little, remembering how much I liked forests and how one had brought me to this land in the first place. I stood barely within its confines, quiet and still, hardly a rustle from the branches on this leeward side. Then I heard the whimpering. A small animal was in trouble.

I ran back to the others and grabbed a cross bow.

"Alyssa, Freda, get a longbow each and Fran, give me cover. There's something in there and I'm not sure what."

Back at the perimeter we began inching in a tree at a time, making our progress slow. But better slow than go blundering into an unexpected situation. It was obviously a baby animal of some kind calling for its parents and I wondered if they had been killed and it was alone, or just hungry and awaiting their return at any moment. If they came back and saw us by their offspring it could turn into a volatile situation.

Alyssa indicated she was moving left, so Freda went to my right. They both had arrows nocked and ready to loose quickly.

I cocked my crossbow, indicating Fran to do the same, slipping a quarrel in to arm them. Flitting forward another tree, we stopped and listened again.

Whatever it was must have heard us and perhaps in desperation, gave a short bark. Now I knew not many animals bark like that, dogs, foxes and wolves, so it had to be one of those. But which?

Putting a finger to my lips I raised my eyebrows to Fran, she would take that as silence. Another tree on, flattening ourselves against it. Alyssa and Freda kept pace.

Alyssa signalled she thought it was just a couple more trees on by holding two fingers up and pointing in. She went out left and back in a sweep to get on that side and not spook it.

I saw Freda move, too. So now it was up to Fran and me. We lightly ran forward one tree on our toes and stopped again, peering around the trunk. Nothing.

Whimpering came again, I thought more desperately than before. The little mite was aware something was near but in its tiny mind, knew not whether enemy or a friend, so whether to cry out for aid or be quiet.

"Oh well, might as well get this over with," I muttered to Fran. On to the last tree, stopped, and using the tree's bole as a shield peered around it.

And there it lay, crumpled up in some twigs.

But I wasn't sure what it was. It looked like a wolf, but also like a hunting dog. There often wasn't a lot of difference between them, take Noda for instance, he is a cross breed.

I lowered my bow and walked to it. Oddly, it wagged its tail. I roared out laughing. "It's okay, we aren't going to get mauled to death."

The others came in. "What is it?" Alyssa asked. "And what's it doing in a forest with no parents? That's a point, we had better be careful they aren't around, they may have left it to go hunting. Noda, leave."

It was then I realised how Eva's wolf-dog Noda, had just taken to us and obeyed Alyssa. He had been sniffing the baby but, on her command, moved away and sat.

"It looks half-starved to me," Fran put in. "Look, its little ribs are sticking out. Ah, poor little thing."

I looked at Alyssa. "If we touch it and its parents come back and smell our scent, they'll kill it. But it does look bloody hungry," I finished, giving Fran a playful shove.

"I'll pop back to camp and get some meat," Alyssa volunteered.

"Is it old enough for solid foods?"

"Yes, I think so," Fran replied. "The parents feed it for a while to weaning, a few weeks I think. Maybe they had too many and this was the oddest looking one and just left it. Nature is very cruel, Lauren."

I nodded. "Yes, it is, and that isn't just the animal kingdom, either." But I also knew that parents would desert the runt of a litter, leave it to die of starvation or become a meal for some other predator.

She came and embraced me. "I know, Lauren, I know."

A shout went up outside the trees. For some inexplicable reason I grabbed the cub before dashing out, appearing in front of Sheelan holding it. "Is there a problem, sweetheart?"

She dropped the deer from her shoulders, looked at the cub, then at me and then back at the cub. "Only with that. Where did you find it?"

"I heard it crying in those trees."

"And you went in after it not knowing what was there?" She looked horrified.

"No, four of us went in. It seemed a bit mob handed when we found it. Isn't it sweet."

"It looks like Noda, a cross bred wolf-dog. What are you going to do with it, darling?"

Suddenly, I hadn't the faintest idea. "Well, I thought I would... um." My words faded out.

"You thought you would rescue it with your big, soft heart. But what of its parents?"

Alyssa grinned behind her. "She's always had a big, soft heart, I'm pleased to say."

"It's starving," Fran pointed out. "They must have abandoned it, Sheelan."

Sheelan grinned at me. "Softie. I wonder if it will take meat. I'll get some."

Alyssa laughed. "She's as soft as you are, Lauren."

Taal fondled its fur. "We have a pet wolf."

"Again," Lalena said, with a giggle. "I think Lauren collects them."

"Put it down and see what it does," Merial suggested. "It may run back to the forest."

I placed it on the ground facing the trees. It promptly turned around and sat looking pathetically up at me. "It can sit in front of me like Wolfy did. It's not going to eat much."

"It will grow up, and quicker than you think, Lauren, what then?" Sheelan pointed out, as she cut meat into small chunks and fed them to our new member. It gobbled them up.

"Well, Wolfy lived with us for ages and he was a fully grown wild wolf. This one will be tame and stay with us. Maybe it's a good omen, we should accept a gift from the gods, sweetheart."

Sheelan weakened. "Okay, you can keep it. Is it a boy or a girl?"

"I don't know, ask it," I replied with a laugh.

"I'll lift its tail up, we'll soon see," Addani offered.

"Oh, it's a girl, just like all of us," Alyssa said. "Couldn't be a better omen, could it?"

"That's what we should call her, then, Omen," I said. "What did you kill, Sheelan?"

"A deer and two wolves," she replied, then looked aghast. "You don't think... that I..."

"No, sweetheart, I don't. This Omen was very hungry, she hadn't eaten for a while. If they had been her parents they would have had the rest of the pack with them. Come on, let's go see your father."

Our approach to Serobach's village was as stealthy as the others. It was never possible to know what might be around the next corner nor what kind of situation we might abruptly run into, as had been proven at the last two villages, so care and caution was essential.

Alyssa brought her horse alongside. "It's very quiet, Lauren. Not a soul in sight."

"Sheelan, give them a call please. But first, we arm ourselves, longbows I think, so dismount. You too, Fran, best stay with me," I said.

"Hello!" Sheelan yelled as only she could, her words echoing around the trees and houses.

No response.

"If they didn't hear that they must all be deaf," Addani said. "Or..." she looked at me steadily, unblinking.

"Oh no, " I groaned, "not again. Right, approach mode everybody. Dismount!"

Motioning for half our group to go one side under Alyssa's control to work their way to the far side of the buildings giving us a multi-angled approach, I brought my force forward once they had scuttled over.

Closing at an angle of forty-five degrees each, we slowly got nearer the Chief's house, bows part-drawn and ready to loose, our nerves probably tighter than the strings.

My back was pressed up against the wall leading to the

doorway when I heard the groan. I nodded to the others. "Ready? In, now!"

Once through the door, people stepped sideways into the shade quickly and away from being silhouetted against the light. No attack came. A groan sounded once more.

"Who's there?" I snapped. "Answer, or we loose our arrows." It was a bluff, how we would be able to see a target in the gloom I had not the faintest idea.

"My Queen," a muffled voice said, through another groan. "Thank the Gods it's you."

"Open the door curtain, Addani," I ordered abruptly. "We must find out what has happened here."

Taal did that, Addani stood next to me protectively. Now light infiltrated the room it was possible to see people. Several lay in awkward positions, the way Death often leaves our mortal remains as He takes us to His lair.

A quick search found Chief Serobach beaten and barely alive. I knelt by him. "What happened here, Chief? Where are you injured?"

"R... Romans, Highness," he uttered through gasps of pain. "They tied me to a frame and beat me unmercifully. When my people took me down to treat me they came back and began killing them. Please Highness, go and check the other houses."

"Taal, Juna, Freda and Verna, go and do that please. Sheelan, tend your father. Fran, bring my horse with the medications in its bags here please."

Alyssa helped get Chief Serobach into the light. He was a mess, blood running from open wounds, the cuts on his back continued to bleed even now and bruising showed all over his body and face. But at least he was still alive.

Taal and her group returned and shook their heads. I knew that meant the worst possible news.

"Why didn't they kill the Chief, Lauren?" Alyssa asked.

"Because they expected him to die without help, slowly and in pain and as a warning to others not to disobey, my love. They had no idea we were this close." I returned my attention back to the Chief. "How long ago did this happen?"

"Half a day, Highness."

"Let's get after them," Sheelan said enthusiastically, "We'll kill them all, the bastards."

I stood and patted her arm. "And what of your father, who tends him?"

She looked sheepishly back. "Sorry Lauren, I was so wild. There are babies and children lying dead outside some huts, I thought we should punish them for this dreadful deed."

"You're angry and that clouds our visions, he's your father so your emotions are hurt. Take three with you and find out where they went and any other information you can muster. Don't engage, keep out of sight. I'll see to your father."

She bent and kissed his forehead, "Lauren will look after you, listen to her, father." Then chose Bran, Freda and Juna, they mounted up and slowly made their way off.

Taal brought medications, warm water and linen so I could wash his wounds. I applied a steeped garlic rinse, allowed that to dry, then put ointment on and bandaged his wounds. "We'll change them again later, I want your body to settle for a while first. Alyssa and I have patched you up. I'm afraid everybody has been killed," I said. "I'm so sorry."

He nodded. "I guessed so. My whole village wiped out. Now I'm here alone. I don't know what to do, Highness." There was desperation in his eyes as he asked for guidance from his Queens.

"We'll stay here a while. I want to know where that unit went and how many there are?"

"About a patrol I think. We didn't stand a chance, it was all so sudden."

"Some of my fighters will make a meal. You rest, Chief. Your daughter can help look after you, she's part of the Royal Family now."

He tried to smile, but his face was badly beaten about. "Part of the Royal Family, how amazing."

"Lauren will look after you, Chief," Addani said, encouragingly. "Try to rest and relax."

Alyssa brought some chamomile tea and helped him sip it. "Take it steady. Don't rush."

"Give him a couple of these painkillers, darling," I said, offering two tablets.

I took her, Addani and Fran to one side. "He can't stay here. Apart from it being open to Romans, he can't defend or feed himself."

"What can we do, Lauren. He can't possibly travel with us in his condition and we need to keep moving. It's far too dangerous staying in one place very long," Alyssa rightly pointed out.

"Yes, I know, darling. What about Morgana? She could use help and at the same time care for our Chief?"

They agreed with a nod. "Ask him, Lauren," Alyssa said.

Chief Serobach was no fool. He knew the seriousness of his situation.

"I would willingly put myself at her disposal, if she needed it, Highness," he replied. "How do I get there, I don't think I can ride?"

"We'll use one of your wagons. Don't worry, Chief, you have women organising your life now," I said, tongue in cheek.

He tried to smile. "Thank you, all of you."

Fran had a deep frown on her brow. "I see what you meant about coming here unannounced, everything has changed. I was lucky Haff found me."

"It changes by the day sometimes and why you and Stan wisely keep the portal location secret. You were lucky."

The rumpus outside must have been our scouts returning. I went to the door to nearly get knocked flying by Sheelan tearing in like a gale of wind.

"They've camped, Lauren, only a short distance away. Let's go pay back a debt for my kin, please?"

It was her father lying there all smashed up. I couldn't refuse. "Leave Verna and Fran here with the Chief. The rest of us weapon up. Let's ride."

A loud cheer went up.

Chapter Eight

The Baker

The campfire smoke gave their position away. We dismounted, tied our horses to trees a good distance away, got low and crept up to the edge of the small clearing they were in. As Chief Serobach had forecast, they numbered a small patrol, ten in all, they were lazy and hadn't kept it flaming so a haze drifted slowly through the trees where it lingered, the light breeze soon caught it and sucked it up into the sky. Now they were relaxed, having, so they thought, removed any opposition in the vicinity. Horses were tethered on the far side about thirty yards away, so they were a mounted unit and most likely mercenaries. The perpetrators sat around their fire cooking something in a pot, happily chatting and well within the range of our longbows some sixteen feet from us. At that distance, an arrow would go through two inches of solid oak, so their armour was useless against them.

There was something else; a strange silence here. No sounds from the forest, no birds or other noises that made a forest alive. Animals have an instinct of impending violence and become quiet so as not to attract attention upon themselves.

I put a finger to my lips indicating silence, then motioned Addani to take three with her around the far side and Freda a further three off to my right. No sounds, just signs.

Each unit moved through the bushes without disturbing them like avenging wraiths slipping unseen into position. Once at their allotted posts their owl hoots came over denoting they were ready.

One of the enemy looked up, said something to his

neighbour and pointed towards Addani's group.

I took a deep breath and held it. Had they been discovered? My fingers tensioned the bow string ready to draw and loose.

The second man stood to look around, saw nothing and burst out laughing, slapping the other on the back and said something in a foreign tongue while making flapping motions with his hands and cavorting around mimicking a bird, pointed to the seat and gave the other one a shove. He argued the point, but eventually sat They settled again.

My breath finally released.

Now we pay these vile horrors back for the despicable deed upon our friends, people we had grown fond of and they of us over the short years we had known each other. Standing, I shouted "**Now!**"

Our enemies immediately began to rise, hands going to their short swords ready to draw them from their scabbards.

But arrows were already in flight and in half a heartbeat hit them hard before they had even stood properly. The one nearest me flew backwards into the fire with the force of impact, a gasp emitting from him as he knocked the pot over scattering its contents. The others just collapsed and laid still. One had an arrow full in his face that had gone right through and stuck out the back of his helmet. Addani found one alive. She called to me.

"Which is his prominent hand?" I asked her.

"He held that short sword in his right, Highness," she answered.

My cold eyes looked at the wretch on the ground. There was no pity in my heart after witnessing what they had done. "Cut it off then, Addani."

She raised her long sword to bring it swooping down with all her might, slicing through his tunic and shoulder, leaving his arm dangling on a thread of skin, blood gushed, his heart pumping out in floods, he collapsed.

I walked away, leaving the soldier to die, as they had left Serobach to die. "Revenge is sweet. Leave the arrows," I shouted. "It will look more like they were waylaid. Search their bodies and horses, see if you can find anything of importance. We'll take the steeds, that will enforce the appearance of a raiding ambush."

Sheelan was staring at me. "You ordered his arm cut off, Lauren. Thank you, it was the one that struck my clans people down."

Nothing of note was found, at least nothing we could understand. "Let's get away from here, leave these swine for nature," Addani growled, casting a disdaining eye over the corpses.

"Take the reins of a horse each, they'll be great spares or as barter goods. Fran can have one. Now back to the Chief and let's get him to Morgana."

He tried to raise himself on an elbow as we entered, looking around our group to be sure we had all got back. "Are you all well?" he asked anxiously.

"Yes, thank you Chief. They are all dead, justice has been carried out," Alyssa replied.

"Addani, would you and Juna get a cart hitched, use two the village horses. See if you can find furs in the houses here and load those in it, we can lay the Chief on them."

"Yes, Lauren."

Serobach cried out a few times as he was lifted in, that was unavoidable. He apologised.

Sheelan fussed over him. "You'll get better now Lauren is looking after you, father. Won't he?" she finished hopefully, looking at me.

"I'll do my best, my love, I know he means a lot to you."

He took Sheelan's hand. "You've been a good daughter, I wasn't kind enough to you and treated you badly, I'm sorry for that, Sheelan. Now look at you, Vowed to a Queen, and a wonderful and great Queen at that. I'm so proud of you, as all our clan would be."

Sheelan kissed his forehead, turned and rushed back into the house sobbing.

The Serobach turned to me, puzzled. "What did I say wrong, my Queen?"

"Nothing, just everything that was right. She loves you as a daughter should her father and you showed her deep love back in those few words. She's just choked up. You made her whole year by just saying that."

The journey took two days, it needed to be taken slowly for the ease of Serobach's wounds, comfort and the state of the roads, requiring us to camp one night. When the houses came into view I hoped all was well there, it had been several days since we had left them and it was plain Roman patrols were in the vicinity.

Someone saw our group approaching which included a wagon, and that meant friendly people usually. A crowd had gathered by the time we halted.

After dismounting, Morgana and I embraced. "How are you managing?"

"Well enough, thank you, Highn... I mean Lauren. Why have you returned? Has there been a fight? Do you have injured? Is the other Queen hurt?" she was full of questions and looking at the wagon.

"Yes and no, Morgana. Do you know Chieftain Serobach of the Tradera tribe?"

"Yes, we fought each other often enough, fortunately, and because of Queen Alyssa and you, not anymore, Lauren."

"I have sad news. His whole village was wiped out by a Roman unit a short while ago. He is badly injured and needs help. We wondered if your clan would offer that aid and take him in, Morgana?"

She looked shocked. "Killed them all, High... I mean Lauren. That's terrible. It was probably the ones that came here," she pondered. "Of course we'll take him in, as one of us. We hold no grudge against him or his tribe, they were different circumstances and times. Let me see him, please."

She climbed into the wagon and sighed at his pitiful state. "Get him into the Chief's house, please, we can share it. That way I can keep a better eye on him. Where is that patrol now?"

"Have no fear, Morgana, we killed them, your village is safe."

Chief Serobach took her hand. "Thank you, kind woman. This gesture proves we live in peace and harmony. We must unify against the invaders."

"Her name is Chief Morgana, Chief Serobach, she's the Matriarch here," I explained.

"Where's Chief Ragnar?"

"That Roman patrol flogged him, he died of his wounds, Chief. I'm sorry."

"You did well ridding us of those brutes, Lauren. Thank you and your warriors."

"We must move on now. Help her if she needs it, but remember she's the boss here, so decides what is best for her clan. Try to work together, then I'm sure you'll get on well. We'll try to drop by again when the occasion arises. Goodbye to you all, until we meet again."

Morgana embraced me, Alyssa and Sheelan again. "Take care. You're still Royal Highnesses as far as I am concerned and always will be. We are all sorry to see you in this situation. And Sheelan, I promise to look after your father, he'll be in good hands here. Your little dog is cute."

I related the tale. "She's called Omen, because we felt it was one."

Morgana smiled. "A good name. I hope she lives up to it. Farewell, Highnesses."

We turned our horse's heads north again, into unknown lands, pausing at Chief Serobach's now empty village for refreshment. Then on, farther north into partially wooded areas.

"I have an uneasy feeling, Lauren," Sheelan said. "As if something is going to happen suddenly."

"Halt the patrol," I shouted. "Gather around Sheelan, she has something to tell us."

She repeated what she had told me.

"What sort of sudden thing?" Alyssa asked. "Can't you be more specific?"

"I don't know, Alyssa, but it will be sudden and very surprising," was all Sheelan would say.

"Mmm," Alyssa mused. "We'll change formation in that case. A scout out either side and one at the rear, they are the most likely places for any attack. Freda and Juna, take the left flank, Addani with Merial, the right, please. Call a halt if you see or hear anything out of the ordinary."

I looked at her, startled. "Well done, darling, you're getting the hang of military matters."

She blushed. "I'm sorry, Lauren, you should have done that. I don't know what got into me."

"It proves you're able to deploy our fighters now, which I am pleased about."

We rode at a walk for at least an hour through light woods, each with nerves taut as bow strings and not having the faintest idea what Sheelan's surprise might be. If a twig had snapped I'm sure we would all have jumped so high, we would have left our horses backs.

Suddenly, and just as she had predicted, it happened. The forest ended abruptly and what looked like a smooth track extended as far as we could see in either direction. It was wide, hard, flat with a slight camber and went in a dead straight line. I knew what it was.

"What is it?" Addani asked, stopping her horse from going on it.

"It's a Roman road," I replied. "They'll build them all over the place, but mainly between forts to move troops about faster."

They all sat and stared at me. Alyssa was the first to break the silence. "You know of these, Lauren?"

I nodded. "They'll begin clearing our lovely forests as well soon, That's terribly sad. Then it will be fields and crops. No hunting anymore. I wonder where it goes to? Shall we find out?"

"It's Roman," Alyssa almost snarled. "That means it can't

be much good, only major trouble."

I took my horse onto it. "Look, it's solid and flat, good to travel on. We'll stop when the houses start, there's no need to go blundering in."

Addani rode onto it, grinning all over her face as if she had just conquered Everest. "Come on, don't be afraid, it's safe and not rutted like the tracks."

Fran joined us. "They don't hurt, look."

With that the others came to join us.

It went on for some distance until we came across a different style of building than we were used to. A few at first, then gradually more until in the distance it became a small village. Mostly they were no longer round, now square or oblong, yet still of the wattle and daub type of construction than we were familiar with, some had windows and shutters the same as my hospital.

The group stopped in its tracks.

"We can't go in there as we are," I said. "We need to go back into the forest to leave our horses there with our weapons."

"Like we did in the southern forest, Lauren?" Sheelan added.

"Yes, exactly. We'll only wear daggers. Come on, let's go and see what this Romanised Celtic village is like."

As we approached people looked at us curiously, some pausing to stare as if we were out of context here. I wondered why? There was no abundance of weapons, we dressed the same as the locals so looked the same, yet still they gaped. I checked Sheelan to see if she had grown two heads, she hadn't.

Then I smelt the bread. We had been without it for some time and the aroma of it being baked and meat cooked was very tempting.

This particular house had a drop-down shade or large flap that could be used to close up the now open front at night.

The man looked me over, then Sheelan and following her, the others. He had suspicion in his eyes. "What do you want?"

We must have looked a rough lot having been living in the forest for some time, clothes weren't in the best repair and dirty.

"Good morning, friend," I said, as amicably as possible. "May we barter a loaf of two from you?"

"We don't barter here, only coinage is taken," came a gruff reply. He still looked from one to the other, mistrust written over his face. Perhaps he thought we were going to raid his shop?

"I meant barter coinage, friend," I added hastily.

"Oh, I see. Then yes, of course. What coinage have you?" By the look he gave me, he was plainly still wary of so many scruffy individuals having anything of value at all.

I pulled a silver coin from my tunic pocket. "Like this," I replied. "Is that well with you?"

"Mmm," he muttered, taking it to turn it over in his hand. "It's not a Roman one, is it?"

"My Queen had them made at the order of the Lord Vespasian. Is it any good?"

"It's silver, and good silver, too. Where do you live?"

It was a delicate question. We didn't live anywhere really but our home had been the fort, so I told him that. "The one over near the Standing Stones," I added.

"Oh yes, I know. It's almost deserted now I think. Most of the people are moving here to trade. These houses are brighter and with what the Romans call, windows in the walls, they let more light in."

"How many may we have?"

"For a good silver coin, one for each of you if you wish and a sausage and lettuce if you want, friend." He paused, looking down at my calf. "I see you wear daggers, that's why people look at you, the invaders forbid the wearing or carrying of any weapons. You're taking a chance showing them."

At least he had warmed to us. "I see, and thank you. We've been away for a while fighting, we were warriors at the fort and out of work now so get it where we can. Have you seen any bejewelled swords being bartered?"

"Jewelled swords? What would you want with those?"

"They belong to our Queen and she's asked us to return them to her. It's why we're travelling," I said, hoping it sounded logical.

"I see. But it would be more than a person's life were worth keeping a sword nowadays, especially an ornate one as you described, friend. I have heard it said that a soldier of this legion found some over that way."

I glanced at Sheelan. "Really, who told you this?"

"Another soldier of the legion, friend. He buys bread here and we got chatting one day about the old way of life. If he gets caught with them Legate will go mad, confiscate them and punish the soldier, he demands all jewels and gold found be handed in. So now we have no swords or bows, how are we supposed to hunt?"

"It's an all too familiar tale and one that is seriously resented, friend," I replied.

"Be careful, my friends. They are searching for a Queen and her consort they want to execute."

"Thank you, we will." I drew Alyssa and Sheelan aside by their arms as we walked away from the stall. "They might have our swords, my loves. It sounds very much like it."

"I wonder how many Queens they are looking for," Alyssa pondered, a glint of mischievousness in her eyes.

I stared at her. "Two I expect, my love. What made you say that?"

"But we are a family, it should be three."

"You mean Sheelan as well?"

"Yes, Lauren. We are all equal, aren't we? Sheelan takes the same risks as you and me."

I nodded. "Yes, she does, more sometimes, we must be hard people to look after and guard with our lifestyles," I said with a laugh.

Alyssa took Sheelan by her shoulders, looked her straight in her eyes and said. "I pronounce you our Consort, you will henceforth be known as Queen Sheelan."

"Me, a Queen! I am stunned. I never thought for one moment..." she trailed off to stand gaping at us.

I took her in my arms. "And now you're my consort as well, how lovely," I ended with a grin.

"And mine," Alyssa said. "Give me a cuddle please."

The others cheered.

"And rightly so, too," Addani said. "Sheelan has been a pillar of our clan and now our small group. Congratulations, Highness."

"Hi... Highness?" Sheelan muttered under her breath. "I'm a Highness now? What's a consort, Lauren?"

"What's a consort?" I replied with a chuckle. "Someone who rules the lands with a sovereign, like I do with Alyssa, I am her consort."

Sheelan giggled. "Coo, how wonderful, I'm almost a Queen."

"You are one, my love, that's what a consort is, and have the right to wear a crown."

"Yes," Alyssa replied. "With all the responsibilities that come with it. I know you'll take them seriously, Sheelan, as you have everything else."

"I will, Alyssa, I will. But how are we going to get our swords away from that soldier without getting caught?"

Alyssa shrugged her shoulders in dismay. "That will be very difficult and even more dangerous, my Queen Sheelan."

Sheelan blushed. "Me, a Queen..."

Addani and Freda came and took my hands. "We should all think this over, Lauren, try to get a plan together that stands a chance of working. Where is Legate now?"

I had to admit, I hadn't a clue. "Let's ask our friendly baker."

"Oh him," he said with a snort. "A brutal man, you should warn your Queens about him. He was quartered in a camp near that fort but since they've been building the town they call Sarum farther along this road, his headquarters have been moved there. It's really not a good idea to go there, my brave warriors, especially displaying any kind of weapon," he added, nodding in the directions of our daggers.

"Thank you, friend, we will take your good advice."

Chapter Nine

Justinus

"We need either a ruse or a very good reason to get anywhere near that town, it's just about the most dangerous thing you could ever dream of, Lauren," Addani viewed from her seated position on a fallen tree as she ate her bread and sausage. She snapped a part off and fed Omen, which, as all dogs do when food was in evidence, sat looking up at her pleadingly.

"Whichever way anybody looks at it, it's almost certain death," added Freda. "I mean, I'm pretty brave even though I say it myself, but that is taking risks to extremes, Lauren. Surely there's a better way?"

"I'm open to suggestions. At the moment I have no better idea than try to sneak in and grab them," I said.

Sheelan stood and paced about. "Shouldn't we go to see what the place is like before making plans? They may all live in tents for now until the houses are built, we know nothing of the town's structure."

"That's the best idea so far," I said. "But we can't go as one big group, we would stand out, it means splitting our numbers into two. A mob of fourteen would look very suspicious."

"Yes, I agree," Alyssa put in. "Let's say one group under Lauren, me and Sheelan, with Taal, Verna, Juna and Bran. That leaves, Addani, Freda, Leilan, Fran, Merial, Lalena, and lastly Nianda. How does that sound, Lauren?"

"Pretty good. You've paired couples and added individuals to each group. Your becoming a commander. Yes, that's what we'll do. Hide our weapons and horses well into a wood nearer the town. It means riding them among the trees out of sight and behind these houses, we can't go thundering through the village on them, although I would desperately love to," I said, a wicked grin on my face. "Can you imagine the look on their faces, they'll really have something to gape at, swords and bows, a lot more than a few daggers," I finished, laughing out loud.

"If anything goes wrong, we may have to do just that to get away," Sheelan pointed out. "We need a plan, Lauren."

"You're right. In that case, back to the horses and out along this road, it's the fastest way to travel. Let's get into the eastern forest where we came out on that track and disappear, maybe back to Serobach's old village and use that as a base. The Roman's won't fancy following us in there."

Heads nodded. We had a Plan B.

It took about an hour to cover the ground to the outskirts of Sarum, weaving our way around the village and finally to a wood, pausing to water the horses by a stream. We took Omen with our group. If we left her with the horses she may wander off and get killed, she was a wolf-sized snack.

What a surprise when we got there.

Sheelan grabbed my wrist. "Look at how well advanced the buildings are, Lauren. They certainly don't hang about when they get going, these Romans. Did you see that barracks on our left inside that stockade wall? Just one gate guarded by two legionaries, it would be difficult infiltrating that place and with that many huts in there, where would we start?"

"Yes, my lovely Consort, I did. Let's not worry about that for the moment. We need to find out what the town is like, where Legate is and keep out of his way. Now we split up. Meet you back here at dusk, Addani. Take care and no chances. Here, take a grenade and some firesticks, use it if you get in trouble, I can hear that go bang a long way off and it may slow up any pursuers. We'll all come here for our horses then execute that plan."

We hugged, and parted.

I watched them go, chatting away excitedly at the adventure they were on. Would I ever see them again? My only worry was Verna. She should have gone with the other group really, knowing how likely she was to shout out something she shouldn't at precisely the wrong moment. But Alyssa had kept her and Taal together because Taal was responsible for her now.

"Come on, Lauren," Sheelan said, breaking into my thoughts. "I can't wait to see what this place is like."

Buildings got larger and grander the farther we went in.

"Don't they remind you of those by the quay?" I asked Sheelan.

She nodded. "Yes, are these prisons, too?"

I shook my head. "More civic and residential. That looks like a temple being built over there to some odd God of theirs."

"What's a temple?" Alyssa looked puzzled.

"Oh, you don't have them, do you? It's a building where they go to worship their Gods because if they make them grand enough, they believe the God will go and live there. We don't have Gods like the Roman's, although we have some, like Andraste, our Goddess of war and victory."

"Do the Gods actually live in them?"

"I'm not sure."

"How odd. Which God will that be?" Alyssa asked.

"Phew, they have loads, maybe Jupiter, he's the King of their Gods, my love."

"Have they a God of war?"

"Yes, Mars, and a Goddess of love, called Venus, and to go with the king, a Queen, the Goddess Juno. Juna just missed being her by one letter," I joked.

We walked on. A large building stood at the back of a square.

"Is that a hospital?" Sheelan asked.

"I think that will be the forum where the Senators meet to discuss their laws and other things, much like Alyssa's palace."

"What's a Senators?" Sheelan queried.

"A Senator, he's a kind of elder, one that makes laws."

A young girl came to fuss Omen. She was a Celt. "Is it a wolf?" she asked.

"We're not sure, maybe a wolf-dog, a cross between the two."

"He's nice and fluffy."

I laughed. "He's a she and very young, like you. Are you fluffy?"

"No, of course not," she replied, giggling.

"Fluffy fur keeps them warm, the cold time is coming."

Her mother came over. "I know you from somewhere. Didn't you live at the fort?"

"Um, yes," Sheelan said. "There's not many there now. How do you find living here?"

"It's not bad but I preferred the way it used to be."

"Where did you live?" I ventured.

"We had a farm near the fort. Do you remember the festivals our Queens held? They were good days."

"If you farmed there, what do you do here? And what happened to the farm?"

"I work for a Roman Centurion. After our Queens were forced to leave and outlawed, many Celts were enslaved by Legate. I volunteered to serve, at least I kept our freedom, although I'm not much better than a slave." Her shoulders slumped. "My farm? I don't know what happened to it, we were taken from it by force."

"Do you know where Legate lives here?" Alyssa suddenly said. She had her hood up as I did, we had thought it best.

Fear came into the woman's eyes. "Why do you want him?" She backed away a few steps.

"We don't," I replied, trying to calm her. "We want to keep out of his way, that's all. It's the first time we've been here so don't know what each house does or who lives there."

"Oh, I see." She came closer again. "I'm sorry, my family had a bad time."

At that moment a wind blew, pushing Alyssa's hood backwards so it slipped off her face. "Ha," she took a gasp of breath and quickly put it up again.

112

"You're our Queen Alyssa," the woman cried out.

Before the woman could bow or shout out, Bran grabbed an arm and pulled her close. "Don't say a word, I shall have to kill you if you do, and I would rather not. But the Romans are seeking the Queens to imprison and execute them. Do I have your word?"

"I would never put my Queens in danger, we all wish they still ruled us instead of the pigs. I would still have my farm and family together."

I took her hand. "I am Queen Lauren, don't be afraid, but don't recognise or bow, please. What do you mean, family together?"

"My man was taken across the seas as a slave, Highness, it's only me and my daughter now."

"Shh," Addani said, "The Queens cannot use their titles, call them by the given names."

"I'm sorry, um, Lauren. That sounds so wrong though. I apologise."

"How are you and your daughter managing?"

"I would rather be on my farm, Lauren."

I embraced her. "I know how you feel. Our daughters cannot be with us, we miss them terribly. Your heart must pain for your loss."

"That's terrible, Lauren. Are they safely hidden away somewhere? My Centurion master told me Legate is going away very soon far to the west, so a new one will take over."

A glance shot between Alyssa and me. "Do you know who it is?"

"Gaius Suetunius Paulinus, Lauren. My Centurion, Justinus Agapus told me, he said he's a kinder man."

"We would like to meet your Centurion, if we may, we know him."

She looked blankly back. "You know Romans?"

"Yes, he helped us when the previous Commander was here, the General Scapula."

"Oh, him! He was a horrible man. Come with me, please, I will take you. Come Felice, be silent now, call them by their given names my child."

Felice came and took my hand. "You have a daughter?"

I went on my haunches. "Yes, Felice, two, and one day we will be together again."

She put her arms around my neck to kiss my cheek. "That would be wonderful, Lauren."

The woman took us along streets and into alleyways, eventually to a clean and spacious residence. "Let me go in first, please."

Sheelan grabbed my wrist. "Is it a trap, Lauren?"

"I don't know, but there are many of us. Give me that chunk of stone over there, please. If it is, I'll crown someone with it."

The flash of red material came as whoever it was approached through the house.

"By Jupiter, it's Queen Lauren and Queen Alyssa. Come in quickly, get off the street before neighbours see you."

I discarded the chunk of stone.

Justinus smiled. "In case, is that right? Tell me what's happened please. Here, sit down. Ruth," he said, turning to the woman. "Would you bring wine and food, please."

She bowed and went further into the house.

"How amazing," Justinus went on. "You all look in bad health and run down. What are you doing right over here, why aren't you at your hill fort?"

I explained the events since we had last seen him, Sheelan putting in her two pennyworth as well.

"That's terrible, and you're a Client-Queendom as well. I cannot apologise enough, Legate is very wrong. But he is going to fight in the far west, Highnesses, then you may be able to take your fort back. The new Legate is..."

I put a hand up. "Forgive me, we know, your servant told us."

"Ruth, yes, she is a great help. Unfortunately, I have to treat her much like a slave, it's expected of me but I try to give her and her lovely daughter a comfortable life. Her husband was sadly taken to Rome."

114

Ruth returned with food and wine.

She was about to leave when Justinus asked her to stay.

"Sit with your Queens and me Ruth, I like your company."

"Does Justinus treat you well?" Alyssa asked.

"I am virtually a slave, Highness. After we were taken from the farm and my husband vanished we needed a roof over our heads and food, but he does try to be kind."

"She's lovely and I think the world of her daughter, she's a sweet child. I would marry her, but this Legate won't allow it. If I lived at your fort, I could, couldn't I, Highness?"

It plainly came as a bombshell to Ruth. She sat staring at him, her mouth slightly open.

"Yes," Alyssa replied. "I would gladly give you the Vow blessing. Someone who cares so much for another deserves it." She leant forward and took one of Ruth's hands. "Would you take this man, that is just as important? You have a husband, but you may never see him again."

Ruth gulped. She looked distraught. "I don't know what to do, Highness. Justinus is very kind and looks after us but I love my husband, we spent many happy times together."

I saw the sad look spreading across Justinus' face. "You will have to be practical, Ruth. Life is hard, the chances of ever seeing your man again are next to nothing. You have a young daughter that needs a father figure and you need support in this cruel world. Your loyalty is worthy of a true Celt but we are also sensible. Care for your child, she must be your priority now."

"Thank you, my Queen," Justinus said. "But Ruth is free to make her own mind up, I shall not force her."

Ruth looked at Alyssa. There were unspoken words passing between them. The Queen smiled.

"I would," Ruth said softly.

"I am so pleased, we should celebrate and you should stay a while," Justinus cried. "By the way, General Scapula died while on campaign. That's why this one is going over there."

I looked at Alyssa and Sheelan and grinned. "My curse must have worked, then. It served him right, just deserts. But there are more of us in the town, I hate to burst your bubble, Justinus," I said.

"How many?"

"Another seven, too many for you to host in your small villa."

"It's bigger than you think, come, I'll show you."

It was huge. Several bedrooms, a garden and a pool.

"Wow," Bran gasped. "They look after you in the Roman army."

"I'm a Centurion and my father is a high official in Rome so I am privileged. Go and bring your friends here."

"Artorius and Aulus Maximus were asking after me at the fort, my people told me," I said. "Do you know where they are?"

"Yes, at the barracks along the road. Go with Ruth to get your friends, she'll be able to bring you back safely through the streets. I'll have a legionary find those two and bring them here. Go on, Ruth, you're free now, we live together, not as a servant and master anymore."

It was an excited bunch that made our way back to the horses. And that was a point, what can we do with those?

"Come with me Sheelan, let's see what's through the forest."

"Why are we going deeper in, Lauren?"

"To see if there's any grazing. We can't leave the animals tied to trees."

We found some open, rich grassland. Taking the horses through, each was tethered so it had a circle of grass to graze. Our swords we hid in bushes.

"A bit of a comeback memory isn't it, hiding swords?" Sheelan said, straight faced.

"It's called Deja vu, or already seen. Don't be sad, we'll find them."

Someone shouted for us to return. We shot a glance at each other, then ran back in case it was trouble.

Alyssa was pointing. "Look, here they come, Lauren."

It was a massive relief, they had survived intact.

Addani looked at Ruth suspiciously. "Who is this?"

"A Celtic friend," Alyssa replied with a smile.

Addani grunted acceptance. "We looked around but found nothing," she said, flopping down on a fallen tree. "It's a big place."

"We've done a little better. We have somewhere dry and comfortable for us all to sleep tonight."

"Really!" Addani shouted, jumping up. "Where?"

"In the house of a Roman Centurion," I replied, grinning, knowing it would perplex her.

Her face dropped. "How come? A Roman, isn't that dangerous?"

I patted her arm. "It's one of the Romans that helped us before. And he's bringing the other two you saw at the fort to meet us."

"Are you sure about this, it could be a trap?"

"They risked their lives for Alyssa so I don't think so, Addani. But we can take precautions."

"Like what?"

"You and three more stay outside. If nothing happens it will be safe."

Addani nodded. "That sounds sensible, Lauren."

"Okay, Ruth, lead on," Alyssa directed.

Chapter Ten

Reunion

Justinus welcomed us in. There was nobody else there yet. He frowned at our caution. "You didn't trust me, my Queen? I am a little hurt."

"Self-preservation, Justinus. I'm sorry, but one slip and we're dead," Alyssa pointed out.

He softened. "I can't blame you, any of you. Your problems have been many and dangerous, often downright painful and humiliating. Your warrior is interested in my home," he said, indicating Addani walking around in awe.

"It's amazing. So bright and clean, like your hospital, Lauren."

Justinus gave her a long hard look. "You call your Queen by her given name, not Highness or Majesty?"

"They have to, my friend," I put in quickly. "Even our daughters cannot use their titles, it's too dangerous under this Legate."

He nodded. "I hope that will change when Gaius Paulinus takes command. You should have the right to be addressed properly."

A call came from the door. Ruth went to go but Justinus took her hand and sat her down, smiling at her. "Stay with your people." He went himself.

"He cares for you, Ruth, and your little girl," Alyssa said. "He's a good Roman."

At that moment chaos reigned. Artorius shouted as he and his brother burst in excitedly. "My Queens, how wonderful to see you, especially the beautiful Queen Lauren." He bowed low.

"Keep the noise down," Justinus warned, crossly. "It's not safe for them at the moment with Quintus as Legate. They beat him in battle and captured his Legion's Eagle, so they aren't very popular."

"My apologies, Centurion." He saluted. "You took an aquila, that is some feat, my Queens, I admire you and your fighting prowess. We tried to make contact when we met this mighty warrior at your fort," Artorius said, pointing to Addani. "But she wouldn't say where you were. Now I know why." He burst out laughing. "She's a wise woman."

A smile flickered across Alyssa's lips. "Have you seen Marcus Danius?"

"No, Queen Alyssa. We think he may have gone back with the Legio Second Augusta under General Vespasian. Let me tell you a secret, Highness. The General liked you two Queens a lot, although he would never have admitted it openly. He thought you were marvellous and very wise, Queen Lauren. I bet that surprises you?"

It did, but I didn't let on. "Thank you, my friend. We're on a quest here, having lost our ceremonial swords. Have you heard anything of them?"

"A legionary in our barracks has some swords. If Legate finds out he'll in trouble because they are Celtic long swords."

"Have you seen them?" Alyssa asked, urgency in the question.

"No, my Queen. I just overheard him say to his friend he found some. Many Romans like your long sword, it has weight and reach, unlike our gladius."

"Did he say where he found them?" I asked.

"I'm afraid I have no idea, my lovely Queen. If I ask him, he'll deny it, because of getting discovered. I'll ask his friend for you though. He must keep them nearby, most likely in his mattress, it's where I would hide contraband. He's of the Legio Fourteen Gemina, not my Legion."

"What are you in now?"

"The Legio Ninth Hispana, the top legion in Britannia, Queen Lauren," he stated proudly.

That was bad news. "Be aware, your legion will be wiped

out in the near future, possibly in the north of Britain. I thought you had left and gone to live with Gweneth. What happened to that idea?"

He looked at me long and hard. "My Lord Vespasian always said you had a vision into the future. You can see this event, Highness?"

"If Lauren says it will happen, it will," Sheelan piped up. "She's been right about everything else."

"You don't pay proper respect to your Queen, young lady," Artorius scolded.

"You're speaking to Queen Sheelan, Artorius," Alyssa said. "As a Queen in her own right, she is an equal and entitled to call Lauren by her given name, as I am."

Artorius went down on one knee in front of her, bowing his head and saluting in the Roman way, much to her embarrassment.

"My wonderful Queen Sheelan, forgive me, I did not know and am unworthy. Your beauty shows your true Royalty. May I kiss your hand?"

Sheelan gingerly held it out and by the look on her face, half expecting he might bite it.

But he didn't, holding it softly to place the gentlest of kisses on the back, stood, and bowed fully again. "My exulted Queen Sheelan, I adore you."

Sheelan blushed full red. "Go on, don't be silly, I'm Vowed."

Artorius laughed. "I know you're Vowed to Queen Lauren, I wouldn't dare ask for your hand although I admit, I would like to more than anything, you are truly beautiful. You asked about Gweneth, Queen Lauren? I am afraid it didn't work out between us. She couldn't get used to me being a Roman and said it was Romans who expelled your Majesties from your fort. She held that against me."

"It was hardly your fault, you helped us. But people get an idea in their head and often it's impossible to shift. I'm sorry, I know you liked her a lot. Would you like me to speak to her?"

"She made her mind up and I respect that. I know many people hate the Romans for what happened at your fort but we're not all like Scapula or Veranius. You liked General Vespasian, Highness, and all of us. Leave her alone, perhaps she'll change her mind one day."

We sat around a long table and ate the fruit Ruth brought in, as Romans tended to do. In the evening, conversation returned to our weapons.

"I would like to go into the barracks to identify the swords myself," I said.

"Get in to look!" Aulus exclaimed. "Ber... ber.. but you're women, they aren't allowed in a barracks." Horror took his face.

"Then we'll have to become men for a while," I parried, with a grin.

At that, Aulus roared out laughing. "You can't do that, Queen Lauren, you're far too beautiful to pass as a man, you'll never get past the guards."

"Uh, oh," Sheelan said. "That's torn it."

"Torn it? torn what?" Aulus said, mystified.

"You made the mistake of telling Lauren she couldn't do something. Now she'll be all the more determined."

"The Queen's too short, that's the problem," Artorius put in.

I gave him a stern look. "There must be short men in your army, they're not all giants, are they?"

"Well, no," Artorius wavered. "That's true."

"Who would the shorter ones be?"

"There aren't many. I think there are two exceptions," Justinus said. "One's the aquilifer, the other the signifer. They claim those honours because of their bravery, not their height."

"Mmm," I mused. "The aquilifer is the bravest man in the legion, isn't he, and carries the aquila?"

"You couldn't possibly pretend to be him, it would attract too much attention, my Queen. And you have shoulder length hair," Justinus pointed out.

"A fair point. But you wear helmets, I can tuck my hair up inside that, Justinus."

"But he's well known, Highness. No, you'll get caught straight away. The signifer might work. He has a wolf's mane that covers his helmet that would help hide your hair and if pulled forward, part of your face. You'll need a uniform, I'll have to get one, I have a little more leverage than these brothers. Leave it with me, I'll try tomorrow."

"This is very risky, the most dangerous thing you've ever done, my love," Alyssa said, earnestly. "Are you sure?"

"It's for our swords, they are very important, darling."

"Who will go with you?" Alyssa asked.

I shook my head. "I have no idea."

"As we are both barracked there," Artorius said, indicating his brother, "It will have to be us."

"I would like one other of our people with me, is that possible. It will mean another uniform, Justinus."

He looked around our group. "Not Queen Alyssa or Addani, their hair is far too long. Lalena, Freda, Juna and Bran are too short, like you, Queen Lauren. Taal is too old, I'm sorry Taal, it's not meant to be derogatory. That leaves Merial, Leilan, Nianda, Sheelan or Verna. You choose, my Queen."

"Merial would rather stay with Lalena if she can't go, as would Verna stay with Taal, I think. I've never worked with Nianda, although I am sure she's brave, but I don't want to put it to the test on an extremely dangerous mission like this. In any case, Nianda is our fletcher, I cannot risk losing her expertise, we need arrows and quarrels. That narrows the field down a bit to Sheelan. She has very short hair so no problems with that, and I know she's very brave indeed, that's been proven beyond doubt many times."

She came and cuddled me. "Thank you for choosing me, darling. I'm your bodyguard in any case, I should be with you, Lauren."

"I would rather leave you here in safety, Sheelan, but I know you'll do your best and are quick thinking and sensible."

"Very well, my Queen," Justinus said. "You had all better stay here tonight. If you're seen wandering about in groups it will raise suspicions. Please treat my home as yours, I think you are all very brave, in fact Queen Lauren is so brave she would be my choice of aquilifer any time," he ended, laughing.

"After we have done this, Aulus and I would like to leave the Roman army and come to join you, Queen Lauren. Can we, please?"

"Don't you have to ask permission?"

"We have served our minimum time so Legate cannot refuse us. He might wonder why but we'll tell him we're going to be with Celtic women. It's not a lie, is it, Highness?"

I laughed. "No, it isn't, you're just stretching the truth a bit. And what of you, Justinus? Should you have a backup plan?"

He smiled, went to Ruth and put an arm around her. "I have one, Majesty. I can go into civil government, it's about time I began, my father has been urging me to for ages." He turned and looked at Ruth. "Isn't she lovely, such deep, dark hair, a beautiful face and wonderful gentle Celtic character, I couldn't ask the Gods for more."

She broke down and cried.

I understood why. A few steps took me too her. "Love him, Ruth, he plainly loves you and your child, what more could you ask for? You'll both be cared for here in comfort and safety and you'll have your freedom back."

"Nothing, my Queen. I am incredibly lucky."

Alyssa joined us. "You will have one of the best husbands you could wish for. Good luck in life, my dear. Now, we should get sleep, if we may, Justinus?"

We laid in next morning, what a luxury that was. There was no point in getting up because we couldn't go out and the uniforms hadn't arrived yet. Ruth brought us breakfast in bed, an unusual occurrence as we rarely had beds to have a breakfast in nowadays.

Alyssa got up after she had eaten and went out into the garden. She was back in seconds. "Darling, there's a pool out there, we could swim. Shall we?"

I could see her eyes glinting with the thought. "We all should, freshen us up, come on, you lazy lot, get your backsides out to the pool."

Some weren't keen but got dragged out of bed by one leg, an arm, or by having the mattress tipped over, much to the amusement of the others who nearly cried laughing.

The water was cool, to say the least, our nipples stood out like poles. We splashed and laughed for ages, it was great fun and freshened our bodies.

I had just walked up the steps the far end to get out and stood under the canopy of the passageway around the perimeter, when a trumpet sounded. I knew what that meant.

Legate!

What to do? Looking desperately around, I realised there was nowhere to go. We were trapped in this area in full view of Veranius. If he caught sight of us the game would be up. His guard would arrest our group and Justinus and Ruth for harbouring us all.

Justinus shot out the door. "Get back in the pool, stay down in the water." He vanished to welcome Veranius, who wouldn't want to be kept waiting.

I dived in again. Bobbing up, I quickly looked around. "Everyone, up the end as fast as you can. Keep splashing water about as though we're enjoying ourselves but stay low. Taal, keep Verna quiet at all costs."

Legate's voice sounded close by. Lifting my eyes until they were clear of the water, I caught sight of him standing in the door leading to this pool talking to Justinus urgently, it continued for some time.

It was cold in the pool, we had been in a long time, I started to shiver. That meant signs of early hypothermia. I began swimming lengths, turn, swim another, anything to try and keep warm. On the third turn at the house end I happened to glance up momentarily.

There, looking down into the pool was Legate, his eyes directed straight at me. I went under quickly, turning over to swim away.

Legate called something out in Latin.

I had not the faintest idea what it was, but hoped it wasn't *surrender now*, so waved back. As I turned the far end, I could see Veranius walking away. A sigh of relief left me. That had been close, too damned close.

Justinus came through and clapped his hands to attract our attention. "My Lord Veranius congratulated you on you superb swimming, Queen Lauren, and said how pleased he was to see Celtic people integrating so well with Roman citizens and our ways."

We all burst out laughing.

"Get out," I shouted. "Have you any towelling please, Justinus, we've all become very cold."

He sent Ruth through with a whole heap. After rubbing each other down, we got dressed.

"What luck we all went for a swim at that moment, Lauren," Alyssa said. "Had he arrived a few moments earlier we would have been caught."

"And it's as well he didn't recognise any of us in the pool," Sheelan added. "He looked straight at you, Lauren, right at your face. Why didn't he recognise you?"

"Because I was partly under water and it was the last place on earth he expected to see us, so it didn't register in his brain."

"What brain?" Addani snorted.

We all burst out laughing.

Chapter Eleven

The Signifer

The uniforms came about midday. Addani didn't fit into any, much to her chagrin and our amusement watching her struggle. We agreed the smaller the party the better, just Sheelan, me, Artorius and Aulus.

The brothers gave us a hand put the uniforms on correctly, we hadn't a clue how they went and they had to be right. Their eyes flitted up to our faces every now and again, a grin on them.

"You are very fit, Queen Lauren, as is Queen Sheelan," Artorius said.

I gave him a knowing smile. "You mean we have lovely figures, Artorius. It's normally only Queen Alyssa and us two who get this close, you're getting a privileged view."

He knew I was teasing him.

He bowed low. "I am honoured, Highnesses. You are all very beautiful. Here is the signum. It's the legion's standard, I had to smuggle it out. You're the signifer, not as important as the aquilifer but everybody knows him and you'd be exposed immediately. Are you ready? It's getting dark, Highness?"

"What's your signifer's name? For goodness sake don't call us Highness or Majesty in there."

"Of course. It's Aqualus Herculum, we usually call him Aqualus."

"And what of Sheelan?"

"She can be Dalium, his friend. Luckily he has red hair as well." He went to Justinus. "May we leave your home now, Centurion?" He gave the Roman salute.

He nodded, returning the salute. "Yes, be wary of all things, but not jumpy, a signifer wouldn't show fear. May the God Jupiter be with you. Go now, farewell."

"Who's Jupiter?" Sheelan asked of Aulus.

"He's the King of all our Gods, Highness, a very powerful God to have with you on this quest."

As Artorius had said, dusk was falling quickly and with our uniforms and helmets with the cheek pieces, nobody took much notice.

I pulled Aulus' arm. "How will we get past the sentry?"

"You're with us and in any case, you're the signifer, no one dare question you, my Queen," he replied softly.

I prayed he was right, we were only a few paces away now.

The rasp of metal was heard as two gladii were drawn. "Halt, who approaches?" It was in Latin, Artorius told me what the challenge meant afterwards.

I guessed it was so walked boldly up close.

"I apologise, signifer." Swords were returned to scabbards and salute given.

Artorius led the way in.

I couldn't believe it, and Aulus said I had an apology to go with it. We were actually inside a Roman military barracks. Huts abounded everywhere, laid out in neat rows and lines. I had expected tents, but legionaries must have demanded more for their homes. Someone was tugging my arm.

"This way, the fifth hut over," Aulus whispered.

He entered first, was out in a second or two. "It's empty, they must all be in town discovering the pleasures of Sarum," he grinned, white teeth flashed in the dark.

He meant they were probably all in brothels. "Which bed?"

"Along here, quickly, we may not have much time."

Artorius rummaged through the mattress for about a minute. "Ah, here's something," he cried pulling a sword out.

"Let me see, please." I took it but knew immediately it wasn't one of ours. It didn't glow for a start and there were no jewels on it, it was simply a plain Celtic long sword. I shook my head sadly. "I'm afraid not, put it back where you found it, please. Let him keep is plunder."

He had barely done that when the trumpet sounded.

"By Jupiter, it's Legate!" Aulus exclaimed. He ran to the

door to peer out. "He's on his horse and coming this way. I wonder if anybody has tipped him off?"

"Only Justinus knows we're here, he wouldn't, would he?" Artorius snapped.

"It doesn't matter this instant," Aulus said. "We must line up outside, if we don't he'll create a stink and we don't want that. Come, my Queens, put on your bravest faces. It's dark, he can't see you properly. Let me ruffle the wolf's mane."

We dashed out, standing beside each other in a line. Sheelan and me kept our heads down a little.

The black horse came slowly along the huts together with the General's guard, stopping in front of us.

I held my breath. The horse fidgeted, one leg to another. Legate sat still upon it, I assumed looking down. We all thumped our chests in salute.

Veranius said something in Latin. Goodness knows what it was.

I nodded, knowing it best not to speak, nobody did if they could help it.

Artorius did another salute and replied in their language.

Legate nodded, leant over and patted my shoulder. I nearly fell through the ground! What on earth had Artorius said?

One of his guards took a step closer, peering intently at me. He spoke to Legate for a few moments.

Veranius laughed and said something. The legionary to stand stiffly to attention and slap his chest with his fist extra hard.

They moved on and I gave a gasp of relief. "What did you tell him? And what did the other one say?"

"We had been drinking and that you had too many and what with the singing, you had lost your voice. I thought you had been recognised, actually I think you had, the legionary told Veranius he though he saw you at the fort and that you weren't a Roman then. But Legate dismissed it, he said you were the signifer, you weren't at the fort at all so how could he have seen you there out of uniform."

"Well done for quick thinking," I replied. "He didn't mean

that, though. He meant I was one of the Celts. Fortunately, he dared not challenge Veranius, so shut up about it."

"It wasn't quick thinking, it's what we would have been doing in Sarum if we hadn't been on secret missions, Highness." He laughed.

"Shsss, call me, Aqualus."

We were between two huts, he bowed low. "You're far too beautiful to be Aqualus, Majesty, he has a flat nose after it got broken."

We all laughed about that.

Back at the entrance gate the sentries hardly took any notice. One said something and gave Sheelan a slap on her shoulder that caused her to stagger forwards. Artorius returned a few words and burst out laughing, which we all did, I guessed it had been a joke.

"Walk slowly, Aqualus," Artorius whispered. "I told him we were going back for second helpings."

I think Justinus was genuinely delighted we were all back without incident but at the same time, disappointed we never found our swords.

"But it means Legate won't get his hands on them. I'll make a few discrete enquiries tomorrow in town with a few traders I know well. The main thing is you're both safe, Highnesses, even though you had a couple of narrow escapes. Better get back into your own clothes, I shall have to return those uniforms tomorrow."

Artorius had been chatting to Addani for some time. He sat beside me. "The tall warrior is amazing, Highness. So impressive and powerful and her hair is incredible, such a wonderful colour." He rested his elbows on his knees to stare at Addani.

I smiled. "You like her then?" and chuckled at him. "How tall are you, Artorius?"

A daft grin came across his face. "Not as tall as her. Why does she wear paint on her face?"

"To put fear into the hearts of her enemies, many Celts do it. Some shave their heads or dye their hair bright colours."

"You don't, my Queen?" His head tilted a little with the question.

"Sometimes I do. When I fight Romans," I answered, with a grin.

"I hope I will never have to do that, Queen Lauren, or Queens Alyssa and Sheelan. I didn't realise she was when we first met, I failed to show respect."

"She wasn't at the fort. Queen Alyssa made her one so we could support each other in these very hard times. Queen Alyssa wanted to thank Marcus Danius for helping her, that's why I asked after him. Now we should go to bed and you should go home," I teased.

"The Centurion said we could stay here tonight. Do you mind?"

"I suggest you go and talk to Addani. She has lots of stories to tell. But don't ask her after her man, he died recently, so she's upset."

"So that's her name. I didn't like to ask. I'm sorry to hear that. Was he a brave fighter, too?"

"His name was Falcon, so I expect he was. Ask her about being a slave and the risks we took getting them all out of that distant fort and of the forest fire on our return. She had a sister called Brevit, they were almost twins. Brevit was incredible and gave her life for me by attacking a bear that came out of trees and was standing an arm's length away behind me. She had no weapon, so ran at it to hurl herself feet first and knocked it down. But it took her up like a doll and threw poor Brevit at a tree that smashed her skull. She really was brave, just like Addani."

"She fought a bear with her bare hands! That's fantastic, Highness. And for you, she must have loved you a lot to do that, as my whole legion does."

"Go on with you, I'm Vowed. Addani isn't, she's just tall. See you in the morning."

Alyssa, Sheelan and me found a comfortable place to lay our weary heads. It had been a busy day, meeting Legate twice over the last two had been nerve racking. I had even

131

got a pat on my shoulder and congratulated on my swimming, so a couple of pluses, and from my mortal enemy, too, Veranius!

A sunny day welcomed us. Justinus was out taking the uniforms back, Ruth brought us breakfast. She seemed more cheerful now, having, I guessed, chewed matters over in her mind and decided to make the best of it. Felice came in to fuss Omen.

"Do you like dogs?" I asked her.

She nodded. "I would love one to keep, but mummy said no, because we are slaves."

"But you aren't now, Felice. Perhaps if I asked Justinus he might let you."

Her little face brightened into a broad smile. "Thank you, Lauren. I like you, you're very brave, yet kind as well and very beautiful."

I picked her up as I did Alegia. "I have a little girl like you but cannot see her because of Legate. Perhaps I will soon, in the meantime, you'll have to stand in for her. Do you mind?"

Felice giggled as I tickled her tummy. "No, I like you. Why are there three Queens, Lauren?"

"Because we support each other in different ways. Queen Alyssa looks after the fort, I look after Queen Alyssa, and Queen Sheelan looks after both of us. She's even braver and very lovely." I put her down.

She fussed Omen again, waved, and went skipping out of our room.

I laid down again and stretched. I had to admit, it had been pure luxury sleeping in comfort rather than in a forest. Even Alyssa had got to like this house.

"I wonder if we could put these window things in our

roundhouses, darling?"

"Possibly. I'll ask Bod about it when we get back again."

Her hand grabbed my wrist, an urgency in her voice. "Do you think we will one day, Lauren?"

"If this new legate is more reasonable, it's possible. What was his name?"

"Gaius Paulinus. I suppose he's a general as well?" Alyssa mused.

"Legates usually are, but they can't all be as bad as the last two, surely? Justinus mentioned he might be the Governor of all Britain so may not be posted around here. In that case we'll get a different one. He thought the Second Augusta might be drafted back under a General Gnaeus Julius Agricola."

"And what of him?" Alyssa half snorted. "Another brutal invader?"

I patted her hand. No blame could be attached to her mistrust of these high-ranking Romans, she had suffered enough under them so her wariness was understandable. "We can ask Artorius or Justinus when they get back, my love. At the moment there are campaigns going on far west and the north, so they may not be so interested in our fort. In any case, we're a Client-Queendom, darling."

"Yes, I had forgotten about that. Not that it seemed to make much difference before, they just ignored it."

The three men walked in. Justinus shook his head. "Nobody seems to have heard of them and if they are as special as you claim, Majesties, I'm sure they would have by now. What are you going to do?"

"Go back and see our daughters," Alyssa said. 'If we're allowed to."

"I paid Veranius a visit. He's going to the west in a couple of days but Paulinus is heading for Londinium. General Agricola will be coming here. I know him, hard, but fair and a stickler for detail. If your peaceful he'll probably leave you alone. I shall vouch for the fact you helped Vespasian and many of our legionaries, Highness. I hope that will help?"

"You are most kind, Justinus. We all owe a great debt to you," Alyssa said. "Shall we begin the journey back, Lauren. All we have to do is stay clear until Veranius has marched farther on, then we can go in. I can't wait to see our home again. I wonder if we'll be able to wear weapons, after all, we never attacked, only defended ourselves, didn't we?" Her eyes searched my face for answers frantically. It was all too much for her, Alyssa's life had changed so dramatically. She burst into tears.

I took her into a hug. "Soon, it will be soon. If this Agricola will listen to common sense we might be able to live back there as we did, wouldn't that be marvellous?" I chucked her under her chin. "If he knows anything of Veranius, he might appreciate what he did and why we fought. But we did, and Romans may feel they have a score to settle."

Alyssa sighed. "We were right to fight, darling, weren't we?"

"Yes, we were. But we can try to be peaceful as well, my love, can't we?"

It was time to leave. I was sorry in a way but happy in others. Sorry to leave our pleasant company, of a little security. But pleased we might be able to go home, we had been away for so long. I wondered how many people still lived there? Many tradesmen may have come here for a better living now that coinage was in use. Conversely, farmers would have to stay with their land to till and sow, raise new bloodstock and run a horse breeding program. They might welcome us, especially Alyssa, who had looked after them for so many years.

"Penny for them," Sheelan's voice penetrated my thoughts.

I smiled at her lovely innocent face. I told her. "I wonder what it will be like now, after all the upsets?"

She kissed my cheek. "Not the same, Lauren."

My fingers went to the spot her lips had touched. I realised she hadn't done that for quite a while. Like Madeil, she knew I had had problems on my mind and had not come close to distract me.

"With you there, it will be exactly like that heaven place I told you about."

She smiled back coyly. "Will it, I mean, will I? oh, err... I mean..."

I took her in my arms and kissed her properly. "Yes, it will. You're very sweet and patient with me, thank you."

Goodbyes were said, hugs given. Ruth was sad to see us go but she had a good man so she and her daughter should be fine. Felice said goodbye to Omen. She told me Justinus said she could have a dog and was delighted. So, my whisper in his ear had worked.

Artorius and Aulus promised to come to the fort as soon as they were free to leave, which should be in a few moons.

Inwardly, I was worried about them. Would they settle into a totally different lifestyle and environment? If not, I expect they could go and re-join the army.

"Until we meet again, my Queens," Artorius said, speaking for him and his brother. They thumped their chests in that odd salute of theirs and we walked away, back through the town to the wood and our horses and weapons, which were quickly donned. Someone in our band had gone back daily to check.

Then we were back on that Roman road moving towards the village where the baker had his stall. A wicked grin took my face, devilment filled my heart. "Let's not go through the trees, we'll gallop along this road for a way," I called out,

Addani grinned. "You're going through that little village, aren't you, let's go at full gallop."

I nodded. "Come on then, let's ride!"

Each dug their heels in the horse's sides and off we sped. The houses came in sight, people came out at the sound of horse's hooves thundering along the ground.

I drew my sword, waving it in the air, the others followed my example. We went through the central road screaming our heads off in a Celtic war cry, much to everybody's pure amazement.

Suddenly as the penny dropped, a rousing cheer went up. The baker waved. "Go, my Celtic Queens, and good luck."

We returned his wave and were out the other side before we knew it. Slowing our mounts to a canter and sheathing our swords, the group grinned inanely at each other, it had been an exhilarating experience after such a long time hiding ourselves. The ride continued until the forest path appeared on our left. It had been a rash thing to do but had given fellow Celts a boost they badly needed.

Chapter Twelve

Willon

We didn't rush, there was little point, so took a few days. Veranius needed to be well on his way west before we even thought of trying to find out if a return was possible and we certainly didn't want to bump into him with a five thousand strong legion along for the ride.

Alyssa had been quiet all along following our mad escapade on horseback through the village.

"What's the matter, darling?"

A soft smiled drifted across her features. "I was wondering if we can go home and if we can, what will it be like? We never know when he might return, and then..." She paused as a pained expression matched the emotions in her heart.

"And then what, Alyssa?"

"He would take his revenge, Lauren, and we might be killed. I couldn't bear losing you or Sheelan."

"It will take him ages to get to the far west. Then he'll have to organises his army, plan an attack and carry it out, several Moon's cycles I expect, Alyssa. Try not to worry. I'll get together with our leaders and set up a watch on the roads he has to come along, that way we'll get an early warning. I'll not see you treated like that again, my love." I blew her a kiss.

"You suffered as well, Lauren, that nearly broke my heart."

"As did poor Sheelan, my love. But we came through it all and are still a thorn in his side. Perhaps this Paulinus Legate will be better, Justinus seemed to think so. I want to see that beautiful smile again, Alyssa, not the frown you have had ever since we left Sarum."

"Lauren will get us back," Sheelan said, determinedly, as she pulled her mount close in beside Alyssa. "You know how clever she is?"

The Queen smiled then. "Yes, we all do. She has made a huge difference to our lives. Oh look, isn't that Chief Mernea's village ahead, our friendly Redgensi tribe?"

Bran came trotting back at the same moment from the lead. "Do you wish a stealthy approach, Highness?"

"Yes, Leader. Have everybody dismount and go in low and slow. You take the lead again. Taal, Verna, take our horses to the rear, please."

Bran bowed. "Very well, Highness."

"It seems very empty, Lauren," Alyssa whispered. "Where could they have gone? The people usually come out to meet us."

"I have no idea. They were fine the last time we visited. Freda, Juna, come with the Queens and me please, in close support. Longbows I think, Bran and Addani have a cross bow each. Here, Verna, look after Omen for me as well."

Bran and Addani skirted out wide to come in at right angles, a position which allowed for better overall vision. Our group began going close alongside the houses then, if anything or anyone came out to attack our two scouts, we would be better placed to take them down from the side.

The pair stopped by the shade of a house, using the shadows to best advantage. Bran signalled to Addani to move right.

I wondered why, splitting reduced the effectiveness of their bows, however, it gave them two different angles.

Our group's pace picked up, slipping quickly from one house to the next as quietly as possible. I beckoned Alyssa and Sheelan to follow. We got to within a house, everything was very silent, not even birds sang. I held my bow up and nocked an arrow, the signal for all to follow, but didn't draw.

The other two had no cover between them and the first house now. To go forward meant exposing themselves in full view and plainly Bran had suspicions about it. Something was very wrong.

I cupped a hand to my ear, indicating to Bran I needed to know if there was any noise.

She drew a finger across her throat, so nothing.

We waited. If anyone was in there they had either set an effective trap because we were at a stand-off, or they were too terrified to move.

Bran did the sensible thing, she yelled out. "Come out, if you don't we'll loose fire arrows at the thatch and you'll burn."

There was a long pause. Bran put her hands to her mouth ready to shout again...

Then an event occurred I had never seen before and would probably never again as long as I lived. A chair appeared with tiny hands holding it up one each side, probably in front of the child gripping it for protection from an arrow.

It was my turn to shout.

"Come out youngster, show yourself, none of my archers will loose if you're peaceful."

"Queen Lauren," a squeaky voice cried out in reply. The chair was flung out and a young lad followed it. He came tearing over as I squatted, to fling his arms around my neck.

"Willon! What on earth are you doing right out here alone?"

He sobbed. "I'm not, my mother is in there hurt. Will you save us, please?"

"It's okay, Bran, the natives are friendly, but injured. It's safe to go in. Tell me what's happened, young man?"

"That horrible man came to the fort looking for you, Queen Alyssa and Sheelan. He began beating people when they said they didn't know where you were. Mum and me had gone into the fort to ask Shaila for grain and he picked her out and flogged her on a frame. After he left, Shaila and some women cut mum down and tended her wounds. She said we should come to the eastern tribes because she had a friend here called Mayid. It took a few moons to walk this far, poor mum had to keep stopping so I could wash her wounds at streams. One afternoon we had to hide in an old roundhouse from a pack of wolves, it was terrible, I could hear them outside scratching and sniffing about. We huddled together at the back of the house. Next day, they had gone and we were able to keep walking. But when we arrived there was nobody here and I had to look after mum when she got worse. I found a bow and killed a wild pig. Mum helped me cook that and with the water I got from the stream, we managed. But she's got worse, Highness. Please come."

I took his hand and went in.

Bran had got her to the light and found cushions for her to sit on.

Deirdre had been badly beaten, as Veranius had done to us, I knew what she felt like. One last throw of the die to try and find us with threats and torture.

"My Queens, what are you doing here, the place is deserted?" Deirdre gasped through her pain.

"I'll get your horse, Lauren," Fran said, she knew what I needed. Soon, she was holding out medications and linen. "I'll get water boiling."

"I have some, over here," Willon called. "I was going to make mum a cup of tea."

I washed her wounds, gave them a garlic rinse that I allowed to dry on, put ointment on her open wounds and dressed her back, cut badly and deeply by the lash.

"That should ease the pain a little, Deirdre. Take these two tablets please, they will help."

"Thank you, my Queen," Deirdre replied, "It feels better already."

Then I teased the boy's mop of black hair. "You've grown up since I last saw you, Willon. Looking after your mum, killing for food, boiling water and goodness knows what else. And you managed to get your mother right over here for safety and protection, even though she is injured. I think that makes you a warrior and a good one at that. Now I want to look at your feet."

They were as I expected, bruised, blistered and bleeding from the long walk. Yet he hadn't mentioned his own pain, only his mothers.

"I'll mend your wounds now, my young warrior, bind them

up so you can walk without them hurting. I noticed you limping when we walked over."

He was as good as gold. Smiled at me, then gave me a cuddle. But coming into my arms released the strain he had suffered and then it all came out, he broke down and cried.

"It's okay, sweetheart, let it all go, I've got you. Only the Gods know what you've been through, you're a very brave lad." I sighed. "I cried once, just like you, there's a special name for it, so know how you feel."

His tear-filled eyes looked up. "You, Queen Lauren? You cried?" He seemed surprised I would ever show such an emotion.

"Yes, she did," Bran said. "Lauren had been through a lot as well back in the southern forest. She saved us from death several times but doing it took all her reserve strength. Lauren was very brave, just like you, Willon."

"We'll stop a day or two here, Bran. Deirdre can't move at the moment, she needs to recuperate. We left horses here in a field by the stream, would you go and get some please?"

Bran's wicked grin came through. "From those Roman swine we killed, I remember. Come on Taal, Verna, we have a job to do."

"You were a Princess last time I saw you, Lauren," Willon said. "Mum and me came to the ceremony when Queen Alyssa made you her co-ruler. You deserved it, now you're Queen Lauren."

"You can call me Lauren, Willon. Most do for now, we cannot use our titles until the Romans stop hunting us."

"Can I have a cuddle tonight, please Lauren?"

"Yes, I think you've earned it. I'll get Fran and Juna to stay with your mum, they'll keep her company and an eye on her. If she gets any worse or needs anything they'll call me. But now she's been tended and had medication, she should be fine," I added that to boost his spirits.

By the end of the second day, Deirdre was improved and sitting up. She had even been for a few short walks with Addani, who had really taken to Willon as we all had and showed him how to use a sword. I gave him lessons in the cross bow but had to cocked it for him otherwise he wouldn't be able to. He picked it up as soon as he held it so knew would be a natural and excellent shot. He had sneaked in with me and Alyssa one night to sleep between us, but the next night he had to go to cuddle his mother. It made a change from her cuddling him and it proved that his father refusing to allow him a cuddle didn't make him any weaker, he'd been strong and loved his mother deeply, a young boy who had a little of his childhood back with a parental fuss.

Deirdre wasn't properly fit, but we needed to move soon. I agreed we could spend another day and go the next. Addani volunteered to sleep in Deirdre's house so I had another night with Willon tucked up close. He's a sweet boy and appealed to my motherly instincts so it wasn't all one-sided. What worried me and nagged at the back of my mind, was why the Redgensi had left their land and homes? What had occurred here to force them away? They were war-like, we knew that from our first meeting at the ravine so the whole thing was a complete mystery.

When I asked her, Deirdre confirmed the place was deserted when they had stumbled upon the collection of huts.

Another fine autumn day greeted us, which would make travelling easier. I got out of our tent and ran through a few exercises to loosen my body up.

"Shall I start breaking camp, Highness?" Bran asked.

"Yes please, Leader. We must start for the fort today. Get Verna to collect water in small pitchers that we can tie across each horse. Send Taal with her."

Willon came out of our tent, yawning his head off and stretching his arms as high as they would go. "Are you going away today, Queen Lauren?" He sounded downcast.

"We are all going today, young Willon. You and Deirdre

are coming with us. Would you like that?"

He rushed over and gave me a cuddle. "I love you, my Queen. You helped me once before, now you have again. Thank you."

"Can you ride a horse?"

"Am I big enough"

I looked him up and down. "You were big enough to save your mum's life, so I guess big enough for a horse."

At that moment Verna came tearing along the track waving her arms frantically. "Highness, Highness, oh, I mean... Lauren, there are Romans coming."

"How many? Are they in uniform? Make a proper report, Verna."

She ground to a halt and hung her head. "I'm sorry. Two, walking, and yes, they are in uniform."

Two? That seemed odd. Roman's would think twice about coming into woods at even cohort strength, certainly not in twos. "Where is Taal?"

"Taal stayed behind to watch, Lauren. I'm sorry, the other word popped out."

She looked terrified, eyes wide open, frightened I might take the action she had threatened her with. But we were miles from anywhere so no damage was done.

She shouldn't have been sent out, just the two of them, so it was partly my own fault.

"It's alright Verna. Stay here and look after Omen. I think you might be made the official Omen carer. Would you like that?"

Relief showed in her eyes. "Thank you, I think I would like that job, Lauren, I love dogs."

I smiled at her. "Here then, take her. Nianda, Bran, Sheelan, Merial, Lalena, to me with longbows. Would you stay here, Alyssa, and look after the reserve, please. Not that I think we'll need it, but one never knows." I kissed her cheeks. "Thank you."

We split, three to a group, running along each side of the track until we found Taal.

"Where are they, Taal?"

"Coming down the track any moment now, Lauren. Have your other unit in the bushes over there, then we'll have clear shots from both sides."

The sound of voices wafted on the light breeze. Whoever it was spoke in Latin, so definitely Romans and they were scuffing their shoes on the gritty track surface so weren't being very quiet, either.

Holding my bow up, I nocked an arrow, everybody followed my example.

Voices came loudly now, they could only be a few yards away. Then there they were, as bold as brass, Artorius and Aulus Maximus,

I stood. "Release your draws," I shouted.

Everybody popped up from the undergrowth.

The men stood stock still, I would say, stupefied at our sudden appearance.

"What are you doing here, Highnesses?" Artorius asked.

"We were starting the walk to your fort."

"Where, might I ask, are your supplies?"

"We have none, Queen Lauren. Aulus said we could live off the land like you do."

"It's just as well we had to delay here, in that case. You have no bows and you can't get near enough to an animal to kill it with a gladius, not now the leaves are falling. Come back to the village, we have spare horses you can have."

"Is the tall warrior with you?" Artorius asked, looking about for Addani.

I laughed. "Yes, Addani is back at the village. Just be careful, she bites."

"She doesn't, does she?" He said it with an air of uncertainty.

I can't say I blamed him, she was an imposing woman, tall, a mass of lovely chestnut hair flowing about her shoulders, a painted face and was a formidable fighter. I recalled how in awe of Brevit I was when we first met on the practice ground. "Addani's fine when you get to know her, she's in

144

that house over there, go and have a chat. Do you like her?"

He grinned back. "She wonderful."

"I guess you do then. You'll have to treat her the right way, no youthful behaviour with pranks, she's rather serious and likes a fight. She also lived alone for many years so is very independent. Have you ever herded cattle?"

He looked blankly back. "No Highness, why?"

"Because she used to have a farm."

"Oh, I see. I'll need other clothes in that case."

"You'll need to win her over first. Go on, talk to her, you did the other day. If you're stuck for a subject talk about fighting, you'll get her full attention."

"Thank you, Highness, I will." He ambled off, no doubt mulling over the things I had told him.

"You're match making," Sheelan said. "It's forbidden."

"No it isn't, Alyssa did it for you."

She grinned back. "Yes, I suppose she did. Anyway, you did it before when Lalena was alone and you matched her with Merial, Bran told me, and me with Squirrel. But what if it doesn't work out?"

"'Then no harm is done. It's simply a gentle push, those involved have to decide themselves. You tried with Squirrel, like Madeil did with Teal but if it doesn't come together they split and find another. I think Addani is very capable of fending for herself. If she likes him they'll make it, if she doesn't, they won't. He's obviously besotted so will take my advice. If she's hesitant he may have to do some brave deed, she would admire that."

"What kind of brave deed?"

"I don't know, one on the spur of the moment, save someone from dreadful danger, fight an animal of some kind, there are loads of things a person can do that's brave."

"Like all the things you've done, Lauren," Sheelan said, closing the gap between us and kissing my cheek.

"I don't consider them as brave, they were necessary, so had to be done."

Artorius wasn't with Addani long, he came out looking

very glum. I guessed Addani wasn't very impressed with Romans in the first place after what they had done to our people and indeed to their three Queens, so had given him short shrift.

Chapter Thirteen

Brave Deeds

Our expanded group moved out the next morning. It was raining, so miserable and a chill wind picked up which made it worse.

I rode to Willon, who had his own horse but was plainly not liking the conditions. He hadn't ridden much before so wasn't enjoying the experience. Had it been warm and sunny I wouldn't have been concerned and although he had done amazing feats getting Deirdre away from the fort, even though she was hurt and across to the east and safety, a remarkable achievement for so young a lad, the weather had been fine. He had been incredibly brave but was still only a kid.

"Hello Willon," I said, as my mount came alongside his.

He looked totally unhappy. "Hello Lauren."

"My goodness, have we a cold and wet Willon today?"

He nodded, dejectedly.

"How about if we tied your horse to Sheelan's and you sat in front of me?"

That cheered him up and after a quick reshuffle he was cuddled up to my tummy, Sheelan one side, Alyssa the other, his mother behind us. Verna happily took Omen.

"Not many young men have three Queens as an escort, you're very lucky, Willon."

Merial came galloping back from her position as lead scout. "Highness, there are wolves on the track ahead."

"How many?"

She looked puzzled. "Not many Highness."

Merial had never sat in on a teaching session so didn't know how to count. "Do they look aggressive? It may be our friendly pack. And please stop calling me Highness out loud, not until we all know it's safe."

"They are sitting down. Does that mean they are friendly?"

"Bring the other scout in close, who is it?"

"Lalena, Lauren."

I nodded, that made sense, they were partnered. "Get her back in case we have to take action."

Merial went galloping off, soon to return with her Lalena.

We approached slowly, stopping about fifty yards away to sit and study the pack's actions. I couldn't see Wolfy among them, nor did I recognise any from the friendly lot but wondered if some were the parents of Omen. She had been with us for a while now so probably wouldn't return to the wild and I didn't want her killed by a strange wolf. Although, having a cub with us may swing the balance between a friendly or an aggressive pack. They would have got the scent of Omen by now.

"Here, take Willon please," I said to Alyssa. "I'll go forward a little to test the water." I had an odd feeling about the situation so stayed on my horse this time, gently urging it towards the gathering of wolves. They hadn't howled as our friends usually did, simply sat looking with all eyes directed at me. I noticed some had their ears flattened back, that wasn't a good sign.

"Arm with cross bows," I shouted back, at the same time slipping my own from the left side of my horse and cocking it.

The click seemed to galvanise the wolves into action. They stood almost as one, heckles rose, the big black leader began snarling, displaying his ferocious fangs and red gums and took a few paces towards me.

I grabbed a quarrel from my back quiver, aimed and was about to squeeze the trigger when the animal made a lunge forwards, snapping ferociously at my horse's forelegs.

My mount reared defensively, flailing the air with its front hooves which saved it from the Wolf's teeth but flinging me off its back and onto the ground with a thud, where I lay a little stunned and unarmed, having dropped my bow as I fell.

My horse fled backwards.

I found myself staring into the predator's cold eyes a few feet away.

The wolf made a dive at my throat.

I rolled, foiling its attempt but felt its hot breath on my left cheek as I lay on my side. The animal was still within striking distance and I expected it at any moment.

Something red moved quickly beside me, a flash of steel glinted as a sword buried itself deep into my attacker. An arm grabbed one of mine whisking me to my feet.

"Collect your strange bow," Artorius said as he returned his gladius to its sheath. "Come, Highness, Aulus has your horse, let us retreat."

I turned to my right, to find Aulus not only holding my horse but supporting me as well.

He smiled. "Teamwork, Highness. Artorius killed the wolf, I rescued you."

It had been close, nearly the closest I had ever come to being wolf meat. My rearing horse had saved it from being bitten and in the process had caused the wolf to pause before it tried to strike at me, so we both ended up in one piece. My only injury was to my pride.

"Thank you, my friends, I think I owe you my life, or at least for saving me from serious injury."

They beamed back. "Our very great pleasure, Highness," Artorius said. "We'll not allow the beautiful Queen Lauren to be hurt."

"Let's go and teach those wolves a lesson," I shouted as I mounted again and drew my long sword. "Charge!"

The thunder of hooves got them off their backsides ready to receive us, then quarrels flashed and the whole pack lay dead within a minute.

"Make a camp, Bran, we can't waste good fur skins with the cold time not far off."

Tents would be a problem. We had one each plus and extra and our larger one, so with two men, Willon and his mother as extras, we had to reorganise.

I called Bran over, "If Deirdre went into Lalena and Merial's tent, Willon can come with us. Maybe a couple of our women could find someone willing to share a tent each, Fran perhaps, just until we get back to the fort, that would free a tent for our brave Romans?"

Addani touched my arm. "Artorius can share my tent, Lauren." She smiled at him and took a hand to lead him away.

"Aulus can share with me," Bran said.

"Wer... wer... with you?" I stammered, staring at her in amazement.

A smile flickered over her face. "That's the first time I have ever seen you lost for words, Lauren. Addani isn't the only one that can recognise bravery and commitment. They could both have held back and waited for some of us to save you but they didn't. They went in on foot to a pack of angry wolves, that was courageous."

I gathered my senses from the shock. "Okay, if that's what you both want, it solves the problem." I admitted to myself I was surprised at Bran, but then she had never shown the slightest interest in anyone before so I had no idea of her sexuality. Obviously, not all the female warriors were lesbians but that notwithstanding, we all got on remarkably well.

Once skinned and dried the furs were slung over the horse's backs and we rode on. The weather improved so Willon wanted to ride his horse again. He looked so tiny on it but had good control so I was sure he would become an expert horseman.

The days stayed dry and without further incidence until the Tradera village came into sight. We had left it deserted after finding Chief Serobach so badly beaten and his whole clan killed by a patrol of Romans. But now we could hear voices.

Bran came back from the lead. "There's somebody there,

Lauren. What are your orders?"

"Send a recce party in, please, through the trees to maintain secrecy. You choose, but only two, I don't want to risk any more than that."

She selected Freda and Juna. They quickly filtered into the undergrowth and vanished.

"Keep our horses quiet," I called softly back, hoping Verna had at last mastered the art.

Our scouts soon came back. "Celts, Lauren, many women and children."

"Very well and thank you, Juna. Mount up. We'll go in slowly. Willon, bring your horse next to mine, we are going in together."

"We, Lauren?" He seemed surprised.

I smiled. "Yes, we, Willon. You're a warrior now so entitled to lead a war party." I was sure that no danger existed and leading in with the first wave would be a great adventure for him. "Keep weapons sheathed," I called back.

As we came into sight every soul stopped what they were doing and clustered together. Children were made to go into houses, others held in parent's arms.

"We come in peace," I called. "I have a child as well, next to me on his horse."

Chief Mernea strode out of what had been Serobach's home. He bowed. "My Queens, thank goodness it's you. Welcome."

I jumped off my mount, went and helped Willon down and taking him by a hand, walked into the centre of the village. "Why are you here and not in your own village?"

"The Romans came, we had to flee. But as night fell I realised wolves were about so came here to ask for help but found the place empty, Highness. We stayed on, hoping to return in a while and take up where we left off. We need to, our seeds are sown."

At that moment Artorius and Aulus came in. Mernea put his arms out in front of his people protectively. "You are in league with Romans, Highness?" he asked, horrified.

"No, Chief, we are not. Our heads still have a price on them and while that lasts we remain outlaws. These two brave legionaries saved Queen Alyssa from imprisonment and me from wolves only a short while ago. The wolf pack you heard is killed, every one. They asked to join us, not us them. Be calm, my good Chief, I understand your wariness."

He visibly relaxed. "Have you seen the town, Highness? It's amazing."

I nodded. "We went there in search of our ceremonial swords, Chief, but never found them. Have you heard anything yet?"

Mernea shook his head. "I am afraid not, Majesty. But you're all welcome to stay and take food with us."

"Thank you, we will."

The evening was spent pleasantly around the hearth of the Chief's house. It was packed with people, everybody wanted the latest news and to hear of our adventures. I let Sheelan do the talking, she seemed in her element.

All the villagers were surprised to hear she had become a Queen, so they had three now to look after them. Eventually, one by one, they left for their beds and so did we, sleeping accommodation being supplied by the people here. How wonderful to lie on a mattress again, sheer luxury.

Sadly, the morning came all too quickly. Alyssa looked disappointed, I knew she had liked the cuddles at night now they were getting cooler, although and to be truthful, she liked them at any time, as did Sheelan. It meant us changing over each night so each got a fair hug from every member of our *family*. But we knew Veranius had gone past the fort now and was well on his way to what would become Wales, that rugged, mountainous and wet country where he would meet stiff opposition.

I noticed Addani kept Artorius near her now and chatted a lot so they appeared to be getting on well. Bran, who was our Leader, took Aulus out in front with her. From my point of view, it kept our Romans occupied and busy, so I was happy. They learnt our ways, our customs, how to hunt and a host of other things as well with two excellent tutors. They also understood military matters, the need for scouts and small patrols and were very willing to take part.

Today, Willon wanted to ride with me so poor Omen got Verna, although she had looked after her well and was mindful of her welfare, so at least Verna was good at something.

Alyssa kept laughing at me as I answered the multitude of questions Willon threw at me. It reminded me of Alegia, how she would ask a million things as we moved along and that made me sad. It must have shown in my demeanour.

"Shall I take Willon now?" Alyssa asked. "I think you have been very patient and answered all his questions so far. Go and chat to Sheelan, darling."

I smiled at her as I handed him across. "You have called me that for ages, thank you, sweet one."

"I know you were missing Alegia and it hurt, I can read your thoughts. Perhaps we can see them again soon, that would be wonderful, wouldn't it?"

"Alegia may have a little friend," I replied. "That would be good, too."

Sheelan beamed at me as I pulled my horse in beside her. "Had enough of questions?" she teased.

"I don't mind, but it brought back memories so Alyssa took him for a while."

"I have a funny feeling, Lauren," she blurted out.

Oh dear. I knew only too well what that could mean. "What sort of feeling, sweetheart?"

"It's not like the others, it's different, lighter somehow, it feels bubbly instead of sick. Maybe it's a good feeling, something nice will happen?"

I gave her a long, hard look. "They never have been before, not even when Madeil had them. It always turned out to be a horrible experience. Have you any ideas what it might be?"

"No, Lauren, my love. They rarely tell me, just come in my tummy."

"Mmm," I mused. Tummy feelings had never come out well so far. But where else would she get them? "Let me know if anything comes to mind, sweetheart, won't you?"

Chapter Fourteen

Serobach

We checked Chief Mondar of the Belgae out but all was well there, apart from a woman having cut herself, I treated her. It was a relief nothing worse had occurred with the wolf pack so close. We stayed overnight, departing early the next morning.

"It's the Ickera next and Matriarch Morgana. I wonder how her and Chief Serobach are getting on?" Alyssa mused.

"I hope, well, darling. She had to nurse him back to health and he was badly knocked about so it would take a while, and that should create a bond."

Freda came trotting back from the lead. "The village is in sight, Lauren. Shall we dismount?"

"Let's get a little closer first, to about short arrow range. We'll stop and check then."

She nodded and went back to retrieve Juna.

As we rounded a bend the houses came into view. I held a hand up, halting our column.

Alyssa came close alongside. "Is anything wrong?"

"I don't know, I'm being a little cautious, that's all, sweet one."

She lowered her head a little. "Sweet one, how lovely."

Someone came out of a hut, took one look at our group with Romans in it and dashed to the Chief's hut.

"Dismount," I yelled, then walked forward with my horse.

Morgana and a wobbly Serobach appeared, coming to the front of their people.

"I come in peace, Chief Morgana, as we all do. Please don't be alarmed at our two Roman guests, they elected to join us. Are we welcome?"

Morgana ran forward to hug me. "Of course you are, Highness. How wonderful to see you all again and seemingly in good health. Please, my Queens, come into our humble homes and join us in celebration."

I was a little bemused, there were no festivals at this time. "You are celebrating something special?"

"Your safe return, we are so pleased, Highnesses."

I drew Morgana to one side. "How are you getting on with Chief Serobach? And how is his health?"

"We get along fine, Highness. His health needs attention though, he's not a well man after what happened."

I nodded. "I understand. I'll look at him shortly to give him a check over."

"What have *you* been doing, Highnesses?"

"Now there's a tale Queen Sheelan will be only too pleased to relate, after she's said hello to her father."

"A Queen now, I can't get over it," Serobach muttered, shaking his head slowly. "From that untidy, scruffy and hopeless youngster I had, to this elegant and brave young woman. I am very proud of you, daughter, you do our family and clan, great honour." He stood to address all the village. "Hear this, Ickera people, this is my daughter, a Queen at the hill fort. My heart bursts with pride at her achievements."

They embraced, it was wonderful to see. The whole village cheered and clapped.

Sheelan went bright red.

"We have another very courageous warrior here that we should all toast and congratulate, Morgana," I called out.

She looked around, puzzled. "Who, Highness?"

"This young man here beside me. I have never known a child as brave, as bold and resourceful in my life before. His mother should be exceptionally proud of his feats and achievements, but mostly, of him. Allow me to introduce, Willon."

The congregation stared at me as if I had gone completely mad. How could this diminutive child have become a great warrior?

"Highness?" Morgana queried. "This little boy?"

"Tell the story Queen Sheelan, if you please."

And she did, as only Sheelan could, captivating all that stood around her and the young lad she kept by her side. "Then we found him and his mum in a house."

"That is truly amazing. All the way from the fort? It's hard to believe."

"It's all true," Deirdre stated. "He is a loving and wonderful child. Thank you, my son."

"Now, Chief Serobach, I need to look you over to see how your recovering. How do you feel? Are you eating well?"

"Morgana has been great, Highness. She's cared for me better than a wife," he finished with a laugh.

My return smile amused him. "Perhaps that's not a bad idea, Chief?"

"Ha ha, she's far too independent. No wonder she became a Chief. I don't mind living under her command. She's a good Matriarch, I'm impressed."

"Your wounds are healing well, Chief. You'll be back to normal very soon. What will you do then?"

"Stay here and help out wherever I can. I have no tribe now, no point in going back to the village, is there, Highness?"

"I'm afraid not, my dear Chief Serobach, and I am so sorry. If you're happy here then make this your home, that's my advice. You may find a new wife in time." I patted his shoulder.

"And what of you and the other Queens? Where will you go? Are you still outlaws?"

"A lot of questions for an injured Chief," I laughed. "As far as I know we are still outlawed by Rome, until the situation changes we live in the wilds. However, we intend to try and see our daughters in the fort, it should be possible now Veranius has gone west. That's our basic plan but it's a loose one that can be altered as necessary. We need to get Deirdre and Willon home as well, possibly with Shaila to look after his mother until she's fully fit and to tend poor

Willon's feet."

"You're good Queens, you still care for your people before yourselves and take risks for them. I hope they appreciate it? Highness."

"Our first priority is to our subjects, whether they appreciate it or not," I replied with a chuckle.

Morgana entered. "How is he, Highness?"

"Much better for you looking after him, my dear woman. You have done remarkable things."

"I have done my duty, Highness. Now, will you all join our celebration, please? You too, Chief Serobach."

"I am sure our group would be only too pleased, Morgana, thank you for going to the trouble."

Alyssa settled on my left, Sheelan to my right. They seemed happy which was wonderful, especially for Alyssa. I had been worried about her for some time as the events changed her whole world. The poor darling didn't understand much of it but had shown great resilience and courage. Somehow, she had also retained most of her youth, although small lines were showing around the corners of her eyes and mouth. I had hopes that once back in the fort she would lose those as well. But all this depended on who came as Legate here and what they were like, as well as their attitude to us?

"Here, Highnesses, some food for you all."

"Oh, Verna, you made me jump, I had been so fully in thought."

"I'm so sorry, Highness," Verna gurgled. "I didn't mean to startle you, I didn't, really." Fear enveloped her face.

'I smiled back. "Don't worry, it was my fault for thinking so deeply and actually rude of me during a celebration. Thank you, Verna."

A huge smile of relief lit her face. "It was my pleasure, my Queen." She backed away.

Sheelan dug me in the ribs. "You were kind to Verna. Perhaps that's a better way than shouting at her, she might try harder."

"She's a disaster area and you know it, but that's her way,

some people are. She's chatting to Taal now more so seems happier and more respectful of her feelings."

The night was a long one. Nobody seemed to want to stop. Perhaps it was because of the chance to relax without fear for the first time in ages and folk were making the most of it. Goodness knows what time we went to bed, early in the morning I thought, so we didn't get up until nearly lunchtime.

Sheelan woke first. "I'll see if there's any porridge, Lauren," she whispered, nodding with her head at Alyssa still sleeping.

She was half out the tent, then returned backwards.

"Porridge?" Bran called grinning. "Thought I would save Her Majesty Sheelan from making the trip. Our unit is packed and ready to move, whenever your Majesties wish."

Alyssa stirred. "Thank you, Leader. We'll need a few more moments I am afraid."

"Yes, your Majesty," Bran replied, and departed.

Within a short while it was goodbye time again. We seemed to be doing them a lot lately, too many times maybe?

Serobach gave Sheelan a long hug. "Take care my wonderful daughter but do your Queenly duty as well, your people will expect it of you, as my people demanded it of me."

"I will, father. I will try to be as you were. You looked after our people, it wasn't your fault a greater power came upon us. You take care, let Morgana look after you."

We hugged, mounted, and took the road to the west and our fort... and what awaited us there...

We camped in a wood the first night, halting late afternoon to give our hunters a chance to kill something to eat. It needed to be substantial now we were eighteen strong, so Sheelan went with them. Although a Queen, she was better than anyone else at the hunt and wonderful at tracking so if anybody could fell a deer, she would.

"Shall I erect your tent for you, Majesty?" Artorius asked. "We use them in the Roman army so know how they work."

"Thank you, young man, my Queens and I would be grateful. How are you getting on with Addani?"

"Very well, Highness. She's incredible, but I think you are even braver. She has told me of your adventures when you rescued them and Bran related the whole story of the Babrani, how they captured them all, the struggles you had in the forest and mountains, how you saved them in the lake. You should be a Centurion, Highness, or even better, a Legate," he added, with a chuckle.

"I'm pleased you're both finding your feet with our Celtic people. There are many feasts and festivals you don't know about yet and some traditions that might appear abhorrent to you, like cutting the heads of the vanquished off. The Celts believe that a warrior can come back and fight at their side if they remain intact so to prevent an enemy doing that, they separate the head from the body."

"I have seen that on a battlefield in Germania and wondered why, Majesty."

"I try to dissuade them because I feel if a warrior fights bravely, they should be left in peace to travel to Otherworld."

A shout went up. Sheelan and her hunters had walked out of the trees; she had a deer across her shoulders.

I smiled to myself, betting she had been the one to shoot it and pleased the hunt had gone without incident. When Brevit took one out they invariably ended in a disaster. That was never intentional of course, it always seemed to work out that way

Juna sat beside me. "Sheelan is a good hunter, Highness. She showed us how to be much quieter and use cover better, she killed the deer."

I won my own bet. "Sheelan," I called. "Leave the offal well away, please, there's a love. Our friendly pack live around here somewhere, I'm sure they would appreciate the meal. And if any other pack came around looking they wouldn't bother us if it's clear of the camp."

She waved cheerily back, chose Nianda, Taal and Verna to accompany her for safety.

After the meal, we went to our tents and sleep. Bran organised a watch rota so a guard was there to warn us of trouble.

Alyssa sat under the furs looking at me. It was an expression I had never seen before, one of puzzled worry.

I folded my legs up under me to sit beside her. "What is it, my love?"

She sighed. "Tomorrow we will see the fort once again. While that will be wonderful, what do you think we should do, darling?"

"I'll send a couple in to scout around first while the rest go onto the small wood where we camped last time. Let's get an idea what's happened and if any Romans are still there. We can't go walking straight in, although I would love to, we must exercise a measure of caution, darling." I leant and kissed her cheek. "Try to get sleep tonight, we are going to have a busy day tomorrow. Sheelan's funny tummy hasn't resolved itself yet either, there might be a surprise in store and it's usually a nasty one. But we can deal with that once we know what it is."

We cuddled, brought all our furs in as well, the nights had a definite chill to them.

Chapter Fifteen

Joy

At last! There it stood atop the hill, our home, our fort, our Queendom. It looked quiet, something was missing.

"There are no guards!" Sheelan exclaimed, excitedly. "Let's go in."

"None we can see, sweetheart. We don't go rushing in, as much as I'm sure you're tempted to. Taal, Nianda and Leilan, go in on foot please, carry no weapons of any kind. We'll go farther on into the wood and set up camp. Meet us there once you have finished looking around. Pay particular attention to the palace, the hospital and any empty houses in case Romans are hiding in them. Check the north gates as well, please. If you can, talk to Shaila and get any latest news. Be ordinary people, no fighting, no weapons on show, that could cost you your lives. Good luck."

They jumped off their horses, handed them to Juna and Verna, their swords, bows and daggers being distributed among us all. And away they went. I called upon Madeil and Brevit to watch over them during their sortie.

"I was waiting for a shout from the fort," Alyssa said. "They did last time we stood here."

"It may be a ploy to get us nearer or even within the fort before they spring a trap, my love. Let us go and make our camp and await our scouts."

The wood was more open now leaves had fallen. Some still clung to the branches desperately, but would be swept away when the first gales came roaring in from the north-east. Then it would be bleak in here, there were very few evergreen trees to use as windbreaks.

Bran got some people making a fire, others getting tents up before the night fell upon us.

"May I unpack some meat, Highness?" Verna said, quietly. "I could get a meal cooking."

"Thank you, Verna, that's a good idea. I'm sure everybody is hungry."

"What do you think has happened at the fort? Will Taal be alright?"

"She has Nianda and Leilan with her so yes, I am sure Taal will be fine and they'll all be back with us soon. Try not to worry, Verna."

Sheelan sat beside me. "She's worried about her, Lauren. That's a change in attitude. I hope it lasts."

We huddled around the fire Freda and Juna had got going. The snag was, with it so large and no leaves on trees, I suspected it could be seen at the fort. I called Bran.

"Yes, Highness?"

"A couple of things, Bran. Why have people started calling us Highness and Majesty again? Secondly, as we have a large fire that's visible for a considerable distance, we should keep our gear packed as much as possible in case Romans come out to see who it is."

"They called you your titles while away from here, it didn't seem to matter so much in the middle of nowhere, Highness, and as long as spoken quietly, no harm was done. I had also wondered about the fire and why nobody had come down to see who we were. Even if they couldn't see actual flames, the glow would show for sure at the fort and they'd be aware there is a party in here."

"Post a guard at the edge of the trees, please, Addani perhaps, she'll take Artorius, that will keep him busy," I ended with a laugh.

Addani took two furs, I guess they would need them out there.

It was almost dark when Artorius came running in. "Highness, our scouts are returning, they have a woman with them."

164

"I wonder who that is? Very well Artorius, thank you. You may return to your post now."

It was an impatient wait that dogged my nerves. Then, out of the murk strode Addani and her man, together with Haff.

"Highness," she cried out. "How lovely to see you all again," she went on, looking around our group. "You have more than when you went," she said, a smile on her face.

"We seem to collect people," Alyssa replied. "They needed Lauren's help. This young man had been incredibly brave, we all admire him. Ask Sheelan about his adventures, I think he's a little shy."

"What news, Taal?" I asked, the question had been burning my heart out.

"There are no Romans there, Highness, not one. I asked Shaila what had happened and it seems Veranius took every able-bodied legionary with him to the west. Please come back, your daughters want to see you."

I stared at Alyssa, who seemed equally dumbstruck at the news. "No Romans?"

"No Highnesses, not one. Oh, do return to your palace, I'll lead the way if I can have an ember from your fire?"

Alyssa stood. "We go home, right now. Come, my warriors, you have all been very brave and loyal, true Celts to us Queens."

Addani went down on one knee. "It was our very great pleasure and duty, my Queens. I can't wait to see you back in your palace."

"But it was open to the weather when I went in," I said. "I hate to burst the bubble, it will need cleaning."

"It's done, Highnesses," Haff said. "We got Agneta back in to tidy it up once the pigs went." She saw our two Romans and backed away. "Romans, Highness?"

"The ones that tried to help us so are also faithful, my dear Haff," I reassured her.

Bran got everything ready to move, gave Haff an ember, then dowsed the fire with soil.

Our group left the wood. It seemed like a dream, going

home. "How is your tummy now?" I asked Sheelan.

"That feeling has suddenly gone, Lauren."

"This must have been the event. You're allowed to have more of those feelings, Sheelan, as many as you like."

Everybody burst out laughing.

Agneta waited at the palace doors, giving us a wonderful curtsy. "Welcome home, my Queens," she said. "I hope you can stay here again now. You have a new dog, Highness," Agneta said, fondling Omen.

"It's a wild wolf cub, Agneta. We found it alone and starving so rescued her. Call her Omen. It feels amazing to be back, too." I could see the flickering of a large fire within, made up to warm us.

People thronged about, cheering, clapping and singing.

Alyssa was beside herself with excitement. "We must get the girls back in the annex as it used to be, darling. Selene and Fallow, our daughters and Squirrel, we can sing and dance again, how wonderful. Do you know where they are, Agneta?"

"Shaila will bring your daughters, Highness, and I will go to find the girls, if I may. They were staying with families."

"Yes, my child, please do. Go now, take my fur and keep warm."

Shaila came in like a hurricane, rapidly followed by Alegia and Betany, who was walking now. Hugs and tears went everywhere.

"Mummy Alyssa and mummy Lauren," Alegia shouted through her tears of joy. "You've both come back."

I picked her up, not so easy now she was older but this was a special occasion. "Don't you remember what I told you a while ago, that if ever we were separated I would come and find you again and we both have, as has Sheelan." I turned and smiled at her. "Here Sheelan, you must join in the happiness as well. Take Alegia and give her a big cuddle and kiss." I bent and collected Betany. "Hello my daughter, are you pleased we are back home again/"

She nodded. Neither of us had spoken to Betany much, she was too young to talk but she knew of our proximity and must have thought of us as mothers.

I kissed her cheeks. "You have grown up, Betany, and you have a sister and now we are a family. Perhaps Queen Alyssa would have a crown made for you now you're old enough?"

Shaila was hugging us all then. "How wonderful to see you all back in your fort, my Queens. Everybody missed you so much. Some have moved to the town, mainly tradespeople but Toler's still here in his forge and Bod still works his wood. I don't think either will ever want to leave you."

"And what of the Romans. We found Deirdre and Willon, he told us what happened. The poor little lad, he did remarkably well. I wonder what they'll do here now? I wouldn't want them to come to any harm and Deirdre still isn't well."

"I'll get them put up in the fort somehow, Highness," Shaila replied. "Please don't worry. The Romans got ordered to the far west. Veranius came and took every man he could, that left us alone. He said another man was coming, a General Paulinus, so we're wondering what he's like?"

"Our friend Justinus, said he wasn't too bad but might go to Londinium so another General may come to this area and live in Sarum, General Julius Agricola, he's the one we are likely to meet. Justinus said he was strict, but fair. It all depends on how he views us against the uprisings in the west and north. They are pushed for legions at the moment so might allow us, as a Client-Queendom, the freedom to look after our own interests. He won't be long in making his presence felt, I am sure. But for now, let us rejoice in being at the fort and a family again."

A swirl erupted by the door and in stepped Selene and Fallow. They both bowed, then Selene did a twirl around to end in a flourish of a curtsy.

"Come here, Alegia, let's show their Majesties how well

you have learned to dance since they last saw us. And I have a surprise, Highness, may I bring it in?"

Alyssa laughed. "A surprise, Selene, how lovely. Yes, please do."

She went to the door and beckoned, there was another flurry and in came the drummer and pipes Selene motioned to them and beautiful music filled the palace accompanied by three graceful dancers, Fallow had come on wonderfully, too. But Alegia was brilliant, matching Selene perfectly.

I turned to Alyssa, who had tears streaming down her face, clapping her hands and dancing small steps herself. "Dance with them, my love. It will do you good and make you happier."

Her look of hesitation was momentary, then she was dancing so beautifully with them and her singing voice echoed around the palace walls as it had done before, in the joy of life and living.

How long they danced, I didn't know. None seemed to tire in the least, cries of laughter rang out to mingle with sobs of joy at being a reunited family again, it had happened so suddenly.

Shaila and Agneta got a fire going in the annex so it would warm up, beds were already there but were taken out and dusted. Water was brought and anything else they needed. Shaila turned into a genie, producing things we never dreamed of.

"And now Highnesses," she said loudly. "Another surprise." She clapped her hands as the signal for women to bring in food and drink. Our tables were soon full to overflowing.

"Look at all this, darling," Alyssa cried. "How can we ever thank you for being so thoughtful and caring. Aren't they kind, Sheelan? So much food we could never eat it, so please have any village people come in and join us. Addani, please go and call them."

The night turned into a glorious exultation of our return, a homecoming well overdue. However, whether or not it was permanent we had no idea, that was for the future. Now, we were joyful and very happy to be with our people once more.

Chapter Sixteen

Gnaeus Julius Agricola

A kiss came upon my shoulder as I lay cuddled up to someone. Who it was, was another matter. We had all got very merry yesterday evening and people got mixed up, tired, and laid down wherever they found a place, so it may be Sheelan or Alyssa. I smiled to myself. How wonderful to have two women that loved me so much and welcomed me into their lives. An exuberant, excited feeling welled up within me and I spun to take whichever one it was into my arms and kiss her, only to find a very startled looking Squirrel there as I embraced her.

"Oh, Highness," she uttered.

I let go quickly. "Squirrel, what are you doing kissing me in my bed?" It sounded like a terrible accusation, it wasn't meant to be, I was fond of the woman.

"I... I'm so sorry Highness, but you were so peacefully asleep I didn't like to shake you and I know Sheelan did that sometimes. Please forgive me." She hung her head.

"I'm sorry, Squirrel, you just made me jump, I expected someone else. But thank you for thinking of such a lovely way to wake me. What do you want, my dear woman?"

"Selene is out in the fields dancing with Alegia, they took Agneta with them so I wondered if you would like breakfast?"

I sat up and kissed her cheek. "I'm sure we would all love it. Where is Queen Sheelan?"

"In the practice area with Freda and Juna working out, Majesty."

"Then the Queen and I would love you to bring breakfast. Tell me, what made you come into the palace?"

"I apologise for the intrusion, Highness, but I heard

Sheelan mention they were allowing you to stay in bed because of last night so I thought you might be hungry now the morning is getting late."

"Then you were right, my dear Squirrel."

She went to leave, but I caught her wrist. "Do you remember the mountains when we only had meat for breakfast? Now we have porridge again, how lovely."

"I do, Highness. I remember how you worked out how we should survive, to attack the fort and rescue our people and to get us safely through the forest and fire. You saved all our lives. Thank you. I think you're amazing, a Goddess."

A smile flickered across my lips. "Remember this, I saved my own life as well so I had to do whatever I did to survive."

"But you didn't have to do it for everyone, Highness." She kissed my shoulder again. "I'll get your porridge," Then dashed out the door,

"What was that about?" Alyssa asked, an amused smile on her face.

"To be honest, I'm not sure. Why do I attract red-heads?" I muttered. "Squirrel may be lonely. I'm not certain she's sure about her sexuality yet having failed with Sheelan and then seeing Addani and Bran pair off may have made her feel isolated. There's not much I can do about that, though. If she isn't inclined towards women she has a problem, because there aren't many men in our group and those that are, are usually in a relationship already."

Alyssa nodded. "Perhaps now she's in the fort again that may resolve itself, an attraction to another person is not only a physical thing like facial features that please the eye or a good bottom or legs, it must be chemical and biological too. It's a mix of things that makes one person drawn to another. Get them wrong and it won't work. Yet, and it's happened to me, a person can fall in love at first sight. I think all those things come together in one big swoosh and your heart is captivated."

I had just opened my mouth to reply, when Alegia came in like a whirlwind, dragging Selene by one hand and Fallow by the other. "We've been dancing," she announced, as if it was the most unusual thing in the world to do.

"Oh, I see," I replied. "Like you did every day and all last night. You'll wear your two friends out, my little Princess."

She grinned, then came and sat beside me. "It's wonderful having you both back again, mummy Lauren and Alyssa, I didn't like it when you had to stay away." She pouted, a tear trickled down her cheeks.

I took the child in my arms and cuddled her. "We didn't like having to live in the forest much either, sweetheart. We both missed you terribly, our hearts were breaking."

Alyssa leant and gave Alegia a kiss. "It was horrible not having you with us. But we found a friend for you, a very brave one who will live in the fort with Shaila's women from now on."

"Where? Can I meet her please mummy?" Alegia squealed excitedly, her tears suddenly forgotten.

I slid out of the furs and got dressed. "It's a little boy called Willon. When his mum was beaten and hurt by Veranius he took her all the way to the eastern clan's villages on his own, fought his way there, killed animals for food and cared for his mother. That's being brave, isn't it, just like you would be."

Alegia slowly nodded her head. She knew the score, what it was like out in the wilds and how dangerous it could be, and she had been with a band of warriors, not alone. "I think he's the bravest boy in the fort then," she stated, firming her mouth and giving a couple of sharp nods. "I saw what those Romans did to Deirdre, it was spiteful. Willon must love his mummy a lot to do that."

"I guess he must, sweetheart. Come on, let's go see Shaila." I took her hand as we left the palace, making our way to Shaila's abode near the north gate. I thought to myself that it must be getting rather full now after I had taken several people there for support and protection. There had been Hahn and his mother, Lateal, and now Willon and Deirdre. But somehow Shaila had not let me or them down

173

and they had happier lives than the miserable existence they lived out before. We looked inside the hospital, I was pleased to note it was empty.

Shaila came out to welcome us. "Good morning Highness. How lovely it is to be able to call you all by your rightful titles again. It never seemed right or respectful just saying your given name."

I embraced the woman warmly. "It was necessary, my good Shaila, we accepted that. Is Willon around?"

"Yes, your Majesty, he's learning how to make paper. I'll get him."

I heard Shaila say I was outside and before I knew it an excited youngster came flying out ready for a cuddle. He quickly ground to a halt when her saw Alegia standing beside me.

"Good day, Willon, aren't you pleased to see me?"

He grinned. "Yes, of course I am, Lauren. Who is this?" he asked indicating Alegia.

"May I introduce the Princess Alegia, Willon. Alegia, this is Willon, the brave young man I told you about."

Alegia curtsied. "I am very pleased to meet you, Willon."

Plainly Willon wasn't without manners, so responded by putting his right arm across his waist, bowing low, taking one of Alegia's hands to his lips and saying. "My lovely Princess, the pleasure is mine."

It was charming, and more suited to a much later age than the roughness of this one. Where he had got any of it from was a mystery, he had probably seen adults do it once, but it won the day.

"I need to look at your feet, Willon. Perhaps Shaila would bring a stool, please." The bandages came off, the wounds were healing well. "You can wear shoes now, my lad, they are fine."

"Why were his feet cut?" Alegia asked.

"Because he walked all the way to the eastern villages to save his mummy. I tended them there and he rode a horse back, young Princess."

174

Alegia put her arms around his neck and planted a kiss on each cheek. "For being so brave, Willon."

The lad grinned. "Thank you, Princess."

"Would you show me what you're doing, please Willon?" Alegia asked.

He held a hand out and they drifted away into Shaila's big roundhouse.

Shaila was as stunned as I was. "Well I never did," she said softly. "What a charming young lad. They seem to have hit it off."

I laughed. "He is quite an amazing boy, look after him well, please Shaila. If he wants to come to the palace with Alegia, that's fine, he's rather special to me. May I ask how Hahn is now. Did he and his mother stay during our troubles?"

"Troubles, Highness? Absolute brutality more like it. Yes, they are both still here. He's a polite young man as well, we all like him."

A blur came out of the house and flung its arms around one of my legs. "Hello, Highness, I've missed you," Hahn cried loudly.

Going on my haunches brought me to his height. "And I have missed you," I replied, ruffling his hair. "Do you like it here?"

"Yes, your Majesty, thank you for letting us stay."

"You should thank Shaila, she found you a place in her group. You have put weight on as well," I pointed out as I tickled his tummy. "Has your mummy, as well?"

He giggled. "No, she's the same. May I call you Lauren, like Willon does, please?"

"Of course, why on earth shouldn't you? You and your mummy are special, as is Willon and his mummy, and those that are special to me call me by my given name. Not many do but you and Willon can. And if you want to see me come to the palace and ask, it's as simple as that."

He gave me a cuddle for that. "I had better go back, Lauren, we're making paper."

Life slowly began to return to normal. People came to Alyssa to solve their problems, Toler worked his forge, Bod took over where Crenn had left off and everybody else took up where gaps had been left through death, violence or moving into Sarum and other local villages.

Alyssa sidled up beside me. "I think it must be Samhain soon, maybe in a few days, darling."

"It's important. You should hold it and let the people celebrate one of our Celtic festivals fully and well, they've missed several, my love."

She cheered up. "Yes, we should, what a wonderful way to pass a couple of days, cold or not. Do you remember the last one, it was freezing? Oh, I'm sorry darling, you were still hurting badly then, but bore it so bravely."

"A lot has happened since then, Alyssa. Several festivals have been missed, last Samhain, for one. I wonder what this cold time will bring? We've heard nothing of the new Legate for well over a moon's cycle, Lauren. Perhaps they'll leave us alone?"

I screwed my lips up. "Rome will never do that. The new man will come, soon probably, to impress his flavour of governance upon us. I wonder what it will be?"

People arrived asking for an audience with the Queen.

"I'll take a walk to the hospital while you see to your people, darling. I want to check stocks of herbs for the cold time. That reminds me, I need to ask Stan for more medications. I'll make a list and send it while there. Shan't be long."

Sheelan jumped off the bed. "Can I come, Lauren?"

"Of course, if you wish, I'd love your company."

Outside the air was cold. A fresh north-easterly wind blew down the centre of the houses, making us cling more to the west side for protection.

"Boo!" The voice made us both jump. "Hello you two,"

Madeil said. "It's wonderful to see you back in the fort doing the things you used to, darling." As always, Madeil giggled at using the word "*darling*".

"Made better by such a wonderful surprise, my love."

She trailed a foot, hands behind her back, her head at a coy angle. "I'm sorry, I should have been with you more recently. Am I forgiven?"

"There's nothing to forgive my love. You do amazing things, I can't ask for more than that."

"Sheelan has been by your side," Madeil went on, turning and smiling at her. "I am pleased about that. Now a Queen, how lovely for you, Sheelan. You will look after Lauren for me, won't you?"

"Yer... yer... yes, Madeil, I promise I will," Sheelan stammered in some kind of confusion, eyes wide open staring at the vision.

Madeil stepped close and kissed me. "I must go now, but will see you soon, perhaps at Samhain. The new Legate is on his way, be careful, darling." Her giggle faded as she vanished into thin air.

"Phew," huffed Sheelan. "She always puts me in awe of her. Madeil was really nice."

Shaila came out to meet us. "Good day, my Queens. Do you need something?"

"We popped along to check the herb situation and to send a message to the God Stanley. Have you some paper?"

"Yes, Highness. I made a few small containers for you to put them in so they don't get wet if it rains. I looked through herbs stocks and had a few of the women go refresh them. Deirdre and Willon went to help, as well. He's a nice lad."

"His father was strict, tried to treat him like a man before he had a chance of a boyhood so he never had the parental love he should have had. We should make up for that if we can, Shaila."

"I understand, Majesty. When Madeil first came here she had nobody at all, we all gave her that and brought her up as our own."

I smiled. "You did a good job, she was wonderful. Now, I must write this letter. Our stocks have got low, especially field dressings, ointment and antibiotics, there has been so many injuries. I hope Stan is still at the hospital and able to supply them. It's been ages since he left, over a year now," I mused, looking vacantly at Shaila. "Now Fran has returned she could add something. I'll call her."

"They are wonderful ointments and those pills are really amazing," Shaila nodded.

Fran's cheery face appeared around the doorpost. "Hello, did you call Highness?"

I explained what I was about to do. Would you like to add a line or two?"

She grinned. "Love to, let him know how to lose weight, dash all over the place here," she laughed. "Can I come with you?"

"Let's venture into the forest now, come on."

It was light enough for just two of us but Fran wanted to help so Sheelan and me let her. We went to the spot and waited. Sheelan looked around nervously.

I wondered if it still worked? Maybe it would stop one day and never appear again. As I thought that, the strange translucent curtain formed just in front of us.

Sheelan went close to peer at the mist's odd appearance, paused, but didn't go into it. We put Shaila's small container on the end of the pole and pushed it through. Once out, the letter had been delivered, the pole's end was empty.

"It's gone," Fran said, stating the obvious.

Alyssa was brimming with excitement when we got back. "I've worked it out, darling. Samhain is in two days. Has Shaila got the fare ready?"

"She didn't say when we spoke to her. I'll call her," I finished.

She must have run all the way, panting and red in the face when she got permission to enter.

"Please take you time, Shaila," Alyssa said. "There is no need for you to run like this, you're an elder. We all know

178

how faithful you are and trust you to come as soon as you are free. Now, what about the Samhain fare?"

"I thought you would like to celebrate it, Highness so organised the grain for bread and beer, vegetables and meat. Much like we do for the Spring festivals."

"Excellent, Shaila. You are a treasure. Let us offer a sacrifice to the Gods for good weather, a dried sheaf of wheat I think. Corann can do that during the late afternoon."

A trumpet sounded.

We looked at each other in shocked surprise.

"That Legate has arrived." Shaila muttered. "Be careful my Queens, the Romans are very unpredictable."

The tramp of many feet sounded through the houses as part of a cohort entered the fort to form the aisle of honour that Legate would travel down. It brought back memories of poor Squirrel and the terror she went through when Veranius had her crucified for trespassing upon it.

"Have you the parchment?" I asked Alyssa. I gave her a hug; her face was strained and white with worry.

"Yes, my love, ready to hand over, if I get the chance."

I knew what she meant. The last beast had not been interested in the slightest, its presence interfered with his plans of control and plunder.

"Take it one move at a time, we'll be polite," I said, taking her into my arms for a few moments again, I never knew if I would be able once Legate arrived, it all depended on this new Roman. It was plain how she felt, I must have looked the same. A dreadful fear inside of us that brutality would rear its head once more, a fear neither of us dare show, yet we both felt within our hearts.

His appearance surprised me as he entered the north gate seated on a short, brown horse. He was young, pleasant looking with chubby cheeks each side of a round face and a kind of half, but firm permanent smile. I knew of him and many of the campaigns he had been on from my history studies so had expected a grumpy looking, older General.

He stopped before us and looked around. We both bowed.

"My Lord, we welcome you to our hill fort."

He nodded, then jumped off his horse to stand looking us over. "You are the Queens of this domain?" It was a softly put question, not a demand.

"Yes, my Lord," Alyssa replied.

He nodded slowly again. "I am informed you're a Client-Queendom, which is a little unusual, but there is another in the north. I was also appraised of the help you offered General Vespasian while he was camped nearby and of the services you afforded him. Would you do likewise for my men?"

"Certainly, my Lord. The great General Vespasian was very kind to us and we wished to show our appreciation."

His head nodded slightly yet again. "He said you were very helpful and cooperative. For that, he allowed you to govern yourselves. I shall do the same. All the Roman army needs from you is help with our wounded and sick in your hospital, that I am told by Centurion Justinus Agapus, is located here. May I see it, please?"

Alyssa shot me a glance and smiled. He had obviously done his homework and got all the facts together. And more importantly was a reasonable person. "Queens Lauren and Sheelan will take you there, my Lord."

"And you are?" He asked with a smile.

"Queen Alyssa, my General." She bowed.

His face kind of erupted into a grin. "Three Queens, again most unusual. Perhaps that makes you three times politer. Thank you."

"This way, my Lord."

Agricola looked all over our hospital. He seemed happy, came to us and did the Roman salute. "It is modern and impressive for a hill fort, my Queens. There are unusual implements here so you're plainly an educated woman. I note you are armed. It is generally forbidden to carry weapons due to the uprisings in the west and north but because I have received such glowing reports about you and how helpful you have been, you and your people may carry them for hunting and ceremonial uses."

"Thank you, my Lord, you afford us a great privilege. We still hunt, especially during the cold time for both meat and furs," I replied. "How is the General Vespasian, my Lord?"

A broad smile flicked across his face. "That is the first time a native of this land has ever asked after the health of a Roman General. He is well, has had a successful campaign and is in Rome at the moment resting. I shall pass on your enquiry, I am sure he will be pleased. He liked you all very much. But I understand you fought part of General Veranius' army and defeated him. Is that so?"

"Yes, my Lord, that is correct." It was pointless denying it, Justinus probably told him.

"Two legionaries of the Ninth Hispana told me what happened here so I am not in the least surprised or angry about it. You had the right to retaliate under the circumstances as you are a client-Queendom and had helped Rome, it was incorrect to be treated in such a manner. That was appalling and I am disgusted and apologise profusely. I hope our association will be a pleasant one. Shall we walk back to Queen Alyssa? As you're an allied domain, Rome should pay you a tribute, did you know that?"

"If that is your wish, my Lord," I answered, diplomatically.

"I shall see to it immediately, and that you're paid right back to when you became a Client-Queendom, a season's award at least. Your red-headed Queen says very little," Agricola said, looking at Sheelan.

"That is very kind of you, General. Queen Sheelan is in awe of your greatness, my Lord. I know of your campaigns and am equally in admiration."

His head nodded very slightly. "Thank you, I appreciate that. You will find me reasonable, Queen Lauren, if you are with me," he ended, as we stopped beside Alyssa.

"May I offer you the same invitation we did to the General Vespasian," Alyssa said, with a bow of her head.

"He attended a festival. He told me, and thoroughly

enjoyed it. I would certainly accept even though it might be cold. May I bring some of my Centurions with me?"

"Naturally, General, we would love to meet them," Alyssa replied. "It is in two days' time. I shall arrange for a special chair in honour of you."

"I am based in Sarum, not in the camp General Vespasian used. We use the road my army laid, it is much faster than coming through the forest. But to save you sending a messenger, I shall arrive mid-morning in two days. Thank you. I like your little dog. It is young, is there a history?"

Sheelan told the story of Omen and of how I had befriended a wild wolf previously and had it stay by my side of its own free will.

"I think you have many stories to tell, Queen Sheelan, and you tell them so well." He gave his Roman salute, mounted his horse and vanished, along with the legionaries.

We let out a collective holding of breathes.

"He seems a reasonable man, much like General Vespasian, asks for things and says thank you, politely," Alyssa almost sighed. "What did he say at the hospital?"

"For us to tend any wounded or sick and for that he would leave us to govern as Vespasian had done. He also gave permission for everybody to wear and carry weapons and will have a tribute sent to you as payment for becoming allied to Rome."

"Did he know we ambushed Veranius?" Alyssa asked, nervously.

"He asked about that and I told him, yes. But he also knew what Veranius and Scapula had done here and he wasn't pleased about their treatment of us. He said it had been our right to retaliate. He apologised."

"He apologised! Wow, that's something for a Roman General. So, we are free, my darling," Alyssa cried loudly. "He had a nice face, I had a feeling he would see reason." She spun around the palace on her dainty toes, dancing gaily, a soft song came from her.

It warmed my heart to see her happy again. A load had

been lifted that she had borne in her heart for such a long time. Now that load was gone, dissipated like dry dust in the wind on a hot summer day.

Chapter Seventeen

Samhain

"Gather our people, please my loves. We must make a proclamation, they should all know how they stand with the invaders now the Legate has changed and been here," Alyssa breathed. She was delighted with the outcome, her face showed it in no uncertain terms, she looked stunning. The fort was hers to govern and that plainly brought joy to her heart.

"I shall call all Unit Leaders, my love. You should tell them, it is your right."

"We are equal, my Lauren, we all go out and tell them together, including Sheelan. I am so relieved, it had worried me for some time," Alyssa admitted.

"Send a patrol out for the maidens today, so we can put on a good show for Legate and his officers, darling, straight after your speech. Use Freda's Guard and Ecole's units with wagons."

Alyssa nodded. "A good impression, yes, a wonderful idea. I'll have Selene and Fallow take charge of them when they arrive, they know what to do."

People gradually began gathering. None from the far farms, word of mouth would travel fast enough. All the closer families would come, keen to know what the state of affairs was now. By mid-afternoon we made our way onto the palace frontage.

I looked at Alyssa, at her lovely face now full of health and vitality at being these people's sovereign once more, her eyes bright, hair a richer red.

A hush descended over the crowd.

"My good people. We all wish to thank you for staying near the fort, even under such a barbaric rule, that took great courage. The new Governor is like the General Vespasian and is allowing us to rule ourselves as we always have done. He is aware we fought and beat Romans but considers our cause just because of the way we were treated under a Client-Queendom treaty. He has decreed we can all carry and use our weapons to supply meat and skins for the cold time. More importantly, he and his officers are coming to see our Samhain celebration even though it may be cold. These Romans salute us, are trying to understand our ways and are reasonable about them. All we have to do is help with their wounded and sick legionaries as we did under the General Vespasian and as far as they are concerned, that is it, nothing is demanded of us." Alyssa turned to me, her eyes asking if I had anything further to add.

"Thank you, Queen Alyssa. Furthermore, Rome is to pay us tribute, something that will help us barter money for goods in Sarum and hopefully create better lives for you. That is where the Legate will stay, not near this fort, so they won't be breathing down our necks anymore. Has Queen Sheelan anything to say?"

"Me? Oh, well, yes. He seemed a good and a fair General so please go about your lives without fear and live happily. Thank you all for coming." She giggled. It had been the first public speech she had ever made in her life.

There was a loud rippling of voices as the news sank in. People turned and hugged each other, shook hands, some danced, swinging their partners out on crossed hands. The sight was pleasing.

We returned to the palace, the people eventually went to their homes. Bran organised the wagons and escorts, they left soon after. It meant a night out so they provisioned and took tents. I went out to see them depart. Freda and Ecole waved goodbye, I returned it. They were a strong unit so should be fine. One thing was sure, no Romans would attack them.

Alegia and two young lads came tearing in. "Mummy

Lauren, can they stay overnight with the maidens, please?"

"What on earth for? Are they going to learn to dance?" I teased the boys.

"They wanted to see us dancing, mummy. Can they, please?"

"If mummy Alyssa agrees, I don't see why not."

Actually, it wouldn't be a bad idea to have boys around Alegia, all she had ever known were women up until now. She was a mature child well in advance of her mental years so knew the difference between boys and girls. I felt it would round her life's knowledge off a little.

"Yes, bring your two boyfriends in if you wish," Alyssa said, grinning at Alegia.

She didn't deny they were, just smiled a thank you. "There, I said my mummies wouldn't mind," Alegia said to the pair. "They are very understanding."

"Hello Willon and Hahn," I called. "Go and look after the girls when they come."

They both laughed. "Yes, Lauren, we will."

My shoulder was being shaken. I leaped up, moving to grab my sword then remembered I was in the palace and not in a tent in a forest. I rolled away from Alyssa to see who it was.

"Old habits," Freda said, earnestly. "They take a while to fade. The maidens are here, they are about to enter the annex so I thought I had better warn you, Highness."

"Yes, sensible, Freda, thank you. I'll come and see them. Are Selene and Fallow in there?"

Freda nodded a reply. "Also, Alegia and the two boys, they seem excited. I'll pop along to the kitchen and organise breakfast for them."

I got dressed, slipped a crown and sword on and went into the annex to investigate.

They all rose and bowed.

"Selene?"

"Here, Highness."

"Queen Alyssa, Sheelan and I are putting you in charge of the dancers, I don't think there is anyone better. Keep noise down, please. I see there are some new faces."

"Yes, Highness, they all wish to serve you."

"Thank you for coming, girls. Food is provided, if you want anything at all ask Selene, Fallow or even the Princess Alegia, they will try to help. Please don't be afraid to ask about something you're not sure about."

"May we practice a little, Majesty?" Selene asked.

"Yes, of course, you need to get routines together."

A hubbub spread around the room, keen faces looked at me.

"Remember, the other Queens and I will be through that door in the next room so not too much noise if possible."

"Are they all here?" Alyssa asked dreamily, when I returned. "I can't wait to see them dancing again."

Pipes sounded, followed by a light tapping of a drum.

"Oh, hark, it's magical," Alyssa said, jumped out of bed and went skimming around the palace on her toes.

It brought joy to my heart. How wonderful to see her so full of life and energy again. "I need to call Verna, so you should put something on."

"Call Verna? What for, darling? You said she was a disaster waiting to happen. Has it?"

I smiled ruefully. "Fortunately, not recently. I need her to look after Omen while the festivities are going on. She isn't used to this much activity or the noise."

A guard called Verna and Taal were outside. Alyssa gave permission for them to enter.

"You called me, Highness," Verna almost whimpered, head hung.

Had I terrified her that much? But she had deserved it on several occasions, especially the sneeze, it had to be done. Admittedly she had improved since.

"Yes, Verna. Would you take Omen and care for her

during the festivities, please? She may be fine after she gets used to the strange noises, you can join in then."

"Oh, is that all. Certainly Highness. I said once I might like that job, and I do."

"You have Taal to help, you're excused Guard Commander duties for the two days the festival is on, Taal. You can be together more then."

They both bowed. "Thank you, Highness, you are very thoughtful."

"Here, take Omen then," I said, holding her out.

The noise from next door drowned out their replies as they left.

The maidens were plainly enjoying themselves and I didn't want to burst their bubble but was curious why it had become so loud. As I entered it soon became perfectly clear. Selene, Alegia and Fallow were running through routines so gracefully, everybody was applauding them, including the two boys.

Selene waved as she saw me standing in the doorway but kept dancing, which was good, I didn't want to disturb their flow.

Alyssa appeared beside me. Everybody bowed. "Please don't stop," she called. "I want to join you." And she did, wonderfully, amazing each of the maidens with her deftness, lightness of foot and grace of movement.

"Majesty," they cried at the end. "You dance so beautifully, far better than any of us. We can only try to humbly meet your elegance and skills."

"Thank you, girls. It's meal time, will you all come in the palace and join us?" Alyssa had a way of winning people over. The dancers sat in a semi-circle and listened avidly to the tales she unfolded, of her youth, the caverns and how she loved dancing and singing. "Fallow and Selene might sing with me, if I ask them nicely."

A chorus of cries and clapping erupted.

The two women sat either side of the Queen, Alegia nestling in front, then they mesmerised the whole room with their wonderful voices. Alyssa didn't seem to tire and went on until late.

I had to remind her the girls were up early in the morning so needed sleep. "We should let them rest, Alyssa."

"Of course, how rude of me," Alyssa said. "But thank you all for joining us. Go now, sleep in the annex."

"You look fantastic, darling," I encouraged. "As does Sheelan. Being here and free has rejuvenated you both. You sang and danced superbly."

A coy smile too her face. "Did I? It was so joyful, I couldn't stop."

It was the first day of Samhain. Selene had got the maidens up and dressed, had their breakfast and were ready to go but I asked them not to dance until General Agricola arrived mid-morning. They could practice though.

Bran had sent a lookout well past the north gate to give us warning of his approach.

I had worried the new moon might fall on this day but it was still two days away, so the Romans weren't likely to march into the mist and appear somewhere else instead of at our festivities.

Alyssa wanted us in full ceremonial dress. "We should show this General we aren't the barbarians they believe us to be and know how to respect a special day. Sheelan too, she has a beautifully jewelled sword as well now we have recovered the older ones and everything else from the Stones, she is the same as us, I wish we could find our best ones though, darlings."

I sighed. "They must be somewhere and someone must know, it's all a matter of time. We'll use our other ones for today as you say, and our best crowns, my love. Do you want a hand?"

She smiled. "Yes, I would love that. Having you near is very special. I remember the first time I met you and I came close, I so wanted to take you in my arms and kiss you. But that really would have put the wolf among the hens, it was too soon. The pain I felt sending you to another hurt so much but Madeil was a good choice, I am happy with that."

As I lifted the scabbard strap over her shoulder the scent of lemon balm enveloped me. It was wonderful, I kissed her neck.

"Thank you, Lauren, that was lovely. Now we should dress Sheelan. Take off your tunic and trousers, please, there's a gown for you on the bed."

Sheelan didn't hesitate, unlike the first time Alyssa had told her to undress. Goodness knows what she thought was going to happen, poor Sheelan was very hesitant and shy.

"Turn around, please," Alyssa motioned with a twirl of a hand. She nodded. "We all look regal now, as three Queens should."

Bran called if she could come in. "They are approaching, Highnesses," she said, looking at the three of us standing fully dressed. "My, you all look so amazing."

Music sounded, the maidens had begun dancing which meant Legate was coming along between the houses.

We went and stood on the palace forecourt as his legionaries took up position either side.

I had asked permission for our dancers to use the hallowed centre, perhaps to escort him enchantingly along with their greeting. He had agreed readily.

The maidens came into view first. It was plain the soldiers were captivated by them, as was Legate, who wanted to be in their midst. They played up to him, bowing low, offering laurel wreaths which I knew he would like, it was the sign of a victor in Rome. He smiled and laughed with the girls.

They arrived before us. General Agricola beamed happily, he seemed delighted.

We bowed. "My Lord, may we welcome you and your Centurions most humbly to our Samhain celebration?" Alyssa said, bowing again.

Agricola thumped his chest in their odd salute. "Thank

you, my wonderful Queens. I have never had a more charming escort, they are wonderful dancers and very pretty young women. Is there a magic about the Celtic appearance that makes it so beautiful?"

"Would you honour us by accepting wine in our palace, my General?" I suggested.

"Wine would be most welcome. Vespasian said you were very civilised. He told me there is a Queen Cartimandua who governs a Queendom in the north of Britannia. You helped to sway her to a Client-Queendom, I understand. The Queen fought, but I also know why. She did as you, tried to protect her people. General Gaius Paulinius informs me she is having problems with a rebel called Caractacus. Have you ever met him?"

As he walked and sat, so did half a dozen Centurions.

"Yes, my Lord," I replied. "He is a conceited man who wants to do battle in the old ways in the open field, charging at the head of a mass of warriors. As I understand it, he was defeated by General Scapula and fled farther west."

Agricola nodded. "That is so. But another battle occurred in a mountainous area and the remnants went farther north and are now threatening Queen Cartimandua."

"He threatened us, my Lord," Alyssa put in. "Claimed that after he had beaten your forces and driven you back into the sea, he would return and take our fort from us."

The General sighed. "Don't these rebel leaders understand the might of Rome? They will be destroyed and it doesn't have to be that way as you can see, my Queens. Britannia will be governed by Rome, there is no doubt about that, we can bring in overwhelming legions that are well trained and steady in battle. Yet you beat Veranius, how did you manage that, or am I asking for military secrets," he said, smiling.

I laughed. "No, my Lord. We used ambush tactics. It's the only way Celts will ever win, certainly not in formal battle. But you know this already."

"We are well aware of that, especially in forested areas. That is one reason forests will be cleared and new roads laid.

Broader fields produce more crops and cattle to slaughter. An agricultural society will mean you won't have to take on the dangers of a hunt and I am sure you know all about the risks involved, my Queens. Breeding more cattle will fill the gap left by the lack of deer. Grain will be more abundant so your people will gain all round. Good highways allow for greater speed of travel. There are roads going north and west now, especially north-east where rebels still defy us. We shall be sending a top legion there soon."

"The Ninth Hispana, my Lord," I replied. "Be aware of ambush. You may lose your legion."

"How can you know that?"

Sheelan spoke up. "Lauren knows lots of things of the future, General. She told of your coming, showed us how to make your war machines before you got here and the special bows we use."

"I am intrigued. Show me the bows?"

Sheelan gave him the cross bow. "It's used on its side, my Lord, with a short arrow called a quarrel or bolt. Like this," she cocked it and slipped a bolt in.

"This is amazing. But I shall not loose an arrow on a festival day. What of the longer bow?" He passed the crossbow to circulate around the Centurions.

I handed him mine. "It has a hard draw, General. That is what gives it the power."

He stood and tried the draw. "Mmm, it is very strong. Why did you need it?"

Alyssa explained about the wild tribes, their shield walls and how our arrows would pierce them and kill the person behind. "It was Lauren who showed us the secret, my Lord."

He stared at me for a while, head slightly angled, not quite sure how I would know of such things. "I honour you as a warrior, Queen Lauren. I won't ask where you or your knowledge comes from but I will say this, you have defended your subjects as well as possible. You tried to cooperate with the previous Legates, it wasn't your fault that failed. I am not surprised you beat them." He paused a second, then laughed.

"Would you like to visit our festival field now, my Lord?"

"Yes, Queen Alyssa, I would. Can you explain what it is about, please? Come, Centurions."

"Samhain is a very old festival, my Lord, it denoted when cattle are herded in from the fields to overwinter in the byers and when some are slaughtered to last over the cold time. There is a feeling that as the seasons change, the boundaries between this and Otherworld are more easily passed. Then the Aos Si, the spirit of the fairies can come into our world. So, we celebrate with a feast and leave them food to sate their desires and ask them to look over our livestock until the spring. The souls of our dead may also come to revisit their homes seeking hospitality. You will see empty spaces left for the spirits to use. The Celtic people believe our dead can return, especially in times of crisis and battle and can fight by our sides. Sometimes people will wear costumes and act out a play or have games like apple bobbing. Although it can be a cold time, we try to make it warm in our hearts, my Lord."

"How unusual, but then Romans have such beliefs of our Gods and Goddesses."

Large fires had been prepared on the lower field, Toler had placed the chair used for Vespasian in the centre of our benches so Agricola would have a good view of the fun.

"Here, my Lord, sit and watch our celebrations."

He seemed to enjoy it, as did his officers. Wine was freely supplied and drunk by all. As with Vespasian, Agricola's foot tapped in time with the music our maidens danced to.

When darkness began to fall, Corann came to light the fires and give the offering. He held the sheaf high above his head. "Duward y bryniau ac Otherworld, yn derbyn y sied non fel arwydd o ddiolch I nt am gynhaeaf da, a gobeithio y bydd yr Amser Oer yn."

A hush fell over the field, a special and magical moment had fallen. Holding the sheaf with one hand he somehow used a match, I wished he hadn't, but I had forgotten to warn him.

General Agricola started a little as it flared but said

nothing.

The sheaf burst into flames as Corann released it to drift downwards, on fire and settle on the ground as ashes.

"Felly, yoddir yr aborth, efallai y bydd Duwiau'n ei dderbyn dyda calonnau agored a llawerrydd," Corann shouted.

"Who is that man?" Agricola asked Alyssa.

"Our priest, General."

"A Druid?"

"Our priest," Alyssa repeated, knowing that if she admitted the fact, Corann would probably be killed.

"I see, a priest," the General said. "Why did he light a sheaf and allow it to burn like that?"

Alyssa explained the sacrifice.

"And what did your priest say?" Agricola asked.

"When he held the sheaf up he said, *Gods of the hills and Otherworld, accept this sheaf as a token of our thanks for a good harvest and we hope, a safe passing of the cold time.* The second, shorter proclamation was, *So the sacrifice is given, may the Gods accept it with open hearts and joy.*"

To save her further explanation, the men began their ritual dances, closer and closer to the fires, each trying to outdo the last until they leaped right through the flames, some catching alight and had to be put out from the water butt placed nearby.

It had got chilly. Alyssa had furs brought for the Romans to slip over their shoulders.

After a long day, Agricola rose to leave with the Centurions. Immediately legionaries were surrounding him. He waved them away. "I don't believe I am in any danger with our hosts," he stated. "Thank you for a wonderful day and evening. If you need anything send a messenger to the Senate buildings and ask for me." He saluted, mounted the horse a legionary had brought down, and they all left.

Chapter Eighteen

Vanished

As General Agricola promised, we were left in peace. All we had now were our own problems. First the swords, that still had not been resolved. Nor had we discovered what their power was to be used for. And after a period without Alyssa at the helm the fort needed building up again, it had become run down, the people despondent and weary. But now she injected new enthusiasm, as she did after our dreadful battle here when the place was a wreck.

"I need to visit Shaila to see what food and fur stocks are like, whether the previous Romans raided our grain stores. Do you wish to come?"

"I shall stay here, darling, people need me to give judgements and advice, there have been many since we returned. Sheelan might go with you. Isn't it a new moon today?"

I had forgotten about the letter I sent in the excitement of the new Legate and his kindnesses. "Yes, you're right, so I shall need help if Stan did his magic. Come Sheelan, let's go to the forest and find out."

She grinned. "Sending messages into the future, it's madness. I hope it works though."

Shaila came out as we passed her house. "You're never going to the mist again, are you, Highness?" she asked tentatively.

"We left a message, remember? Now it's a new moon so the time for a reply."

"It's dangerous, my Queens, please be careful."

"Going anywhere is dangerous, Shaila, even just into the forest. We never know what lurks there waiting for a meal. We have bows and swords but may need a hand. Are there any volunteers?"

"I'll ask." Shaila went into the darkness of the women's

house and called out.

Seconds after her vice faded, Willon and Hahn came tearing out. "We'll help, Lauren," Hahn cried excitedly. "What must we do?"

"Where is Alegia? I thought she had come here to play?"

"She did, but said she was going into the forest a little while ago to see if anything had arrived. What did she mean by that, Lauren?" Willon asked. "What might arrive, and from where?"

A feeling of horror took my heart. "Come, all of you, we must find her quickly, she's in terrible danger."

The little sun that had been warming us was taken away by the trees, it became cold and damp. It reminded me of a deep, dark Fairytale forest depicted in films and cartoons in the future, mysterious and brooding, danger lurking all around. A light mist lay along the ground as the sun tried to penetrate the canopy, making walking a bit difficult.

"Look," Sheelan shouted. "The mist is there. But no sign of Alegia. There's a box farther over, I wonder if she's hiding behind it?"

We ran as fast as our legs would carry us, calling her name.

"Alegia, where are you sweetheart?"

There was no sign of our daughter.

"Search around, all of you, but don't go near that mist, whatever you do," I warned.

Sheelan went westerly with Hahn, I walked easterly with Willon in tow. We went for some time but there was no sight of Alegia.

"We had better go and see if Sheelan has any news, come on Willon, be sure and hold my hand. At least we have a lot of time left before it gets dark."

Sheelan appeared in the distance. I could see she only had Hahn with her.

"No sign of her along there, Lauren, I'm sorry. Where could she have gone?"

I looked at the mist. "Through there, although I hope not.

She has no idea what's on the other side."

"What *is* on the other side?" Willon asked curiously. "Isn't it the same as this? I've been through mists before and they don't hurt you, Lauren."

"This one is very different, Willon. If Alegia went there she'll be lost, alone and in serious trouble. She doesn't understand how it works."

Willon gaped at me. "Is she lost and in danger, Lauren? That's terrible. She should be rescued."

Before I could move a muscle, he slipped my hand and went diving through the strange curtain to disappeared from sight.

"Oh, by the Gods," I shouted in anguish. "I'll have to go after him, Sheelan. Stay here with Hahn, please."

"No way, my love. If it's that dangerous and you go through there, we go with you."

"Please stay here, sweetheart, you're not equipped for what lies on the other side," I implored.

There was little time, the longer we stood and discussed this the more danger our children were exposed to in the twenty-first century.

"We have swords and bows," Sheelan argued. "We can fight."

"It's not like this through there. We can't fight people like we do here. Please stay."

"NO!" Sheelan stated.

She said it so firmly I took a hasty step back.

"I have never disobeyed you before but I love you too much to let you go wandering off into goodness knows where. I'm coming, and if I do, he'll have to come with me."

I stared at her for a few moments, we were wasting time. "Let's go then. Hold one of my hands and one of Sheelan's, Hahn and whatever happens don't let go. Promise?"

Hahn didn't look at all perturbed about what might happen, he just grinned. I expected he viewed it as a great adventure. "Okay, Lauren."

I shook my head in disbelief, both these lads were fearless.

"Hold on very tight. Now!" The nauseating feeling came, I felt very sick. "Are you alright, Hahn?"

"I feel ill, Lauren."

"It will pass."

Suddenly, as quickly as it began we were through. There was nobody in sight.

"It's different," Hahn said. "It isn't a big forest anymore, Lauren."

"No, it's a wood. Come on, this way."

I led on along paths hoping they were the right ones when abruptly, we were out in the open and in time to see a plane flying way overhead, its contrails showing against a clear blue sky.

"Look Hahn, that's an aeroplane flying in the air, a jet plane in other words, there are people inside it going many, many miles away. We must go on farther, across this field more."

He was rooted to the spot gaping into the sky. "People, right up there! Wow, wish I could. What are those white clouds coming from it?"

"They're called contrails, condensation vapour caused as the plane flies, it's very cold up there. It looks slow but its going very fast indeed."

In the distance houses stood and cars went along the road in front of them. One had been my own home and memories of poor Lalena came back when she was here with me after the big battle.

"What are they?" Hahn asked, pointing at the traffic.

I sighed. "Cars, Hahn, a chariot that people sit inside without a horse." I was beginning to panic. There was no sign of anybody ahead.

"Mummy," a voice came from behind us. We turned to find Alegia, Willon and Stan holding hands and a group of very puzzled people with them walking towards us.

Alegia broke free and ran at full speed, as I ran to her. We met in an almighty collision halfway, I scooped her up in my arms as big as she was and swung her around and around.

The relief was enormous, a great weight lifted off my shoulders.

Her arms came around my neck to hug me. "I'm sorry mummy. I went to see if the parcel you asked for had come and it had. I ran to see what was in it but as I got there I tripped on something under the ground mist and went flying forwards through the big one. I saw Stan a little way ahead and called out. He came back to see if I was alright."

We both had tears of joy running down our cheeks.

"What are you doing right over here?" I asked. "You should have come straight back through the mist again, not go wandering around."

"Stan said I should see what it was like here first, a quick look, so we all came to see the horseless chariots and that flying thing. Aren't the houses funny, they're square with holes in the walls."

"Who are all these people?" I asked Stan.

"They happened to be walking along. When they saw Princess Alegia and how she was dressed, they came to say hello."

A man came forward. "You carry a sword and longbow, and there are daggers on your leg. Why?"

I looked at Stan for help. "Should I tell them?"

"She's acting out a game in the forest, that's all," he said, quick as a flash. "They all need to go back to it now."

A strange drumming noise came across the field attracting attention. Travelling along the road were three tanks and a few military lorries.

"Ah, I see," the man said. "It's an army festival through the ages."

"Yes, that's right," Stan jumped in. "They are forming up farther along the wood. Why don't you go see?"

I grinned at him, that had been quick thinking. And looking at the kids it was plain they weren't the least worried about their environment, they simply took to it without question, apart from about a million of them Stan had had to answer.

"You did a very brave thing, Highness," Stan said. "Coming here after Princess Alegia. She could have been anywhere."

"Highness?" the man queried. "And a Princess? Exactly who are you?"

"She's a Queen in that game and this is her daughter, the Princess Alegia," Stan went on.

"Oh, I see. Come on, June, let's leave them to their odd hobby."

"But it's fascinating, Harry," June replied, curiosity in her eyes. "Could we come and watch?"

"It's far too dangerous for bystanders now the tanks have arrived," Stan parried. "You might get hurt. Are you insured against such things?"

"No, and I'm not risking the kids in an odd environment," the man retorted. They wandered off.

"Where are we?" Willon asked. "Why did you say we're in a game? What were those big things going along over there?"

I looked at Stan, who was grinning all over his face. "You tell him, that might wipe the smile off your face."

"Me! Crikey, err, let me see... How does one explain it?"

"They can't count to two thousand for a start so that's going to be difficult," I grinned back.

He thought for a few moments. "You see all of this forest, and how many trees there are?"

Willon and Hahn nodded.

"And you know how long the four season's cycles last for, one cold time to the next?"

They nodded again, plainly having no idea where this conversation was going.

"That's how many years farther on in time you are here, from the fort you live in, a four-season cycle for every tree here, very, very many indeed. A lot has changed since your time, young Willon, even our clothes. The fort isn't there anymore either. I said you were in a game because those people would never understand you came here from the past and we can't risk having anybody going to your time, they'd

202

never survive. Those big vehicles are modern armed chariots, but very different from your kind, young man."

"Bravo, Stan," I said, and clapped his inventiveness. "That's not a bad explanation. Now we had better go and find the mist before it vanishes and we're stuck here permanently. Come on, all of you, quickly."

"How are things back there," Stan asked as we walked.

"Not bad now we have a decent Roman General in charge. The previous two were brutal. We lost our ceremonial swords, too, if you find them, would you please let me know where?"

"Yes, of course, Highnesses. How do you like the future, Queen Sheelan?" Stan asked.

"I prefer it where I came from, thank you."

He laughed. "Look, there it is. You had better go quickly. I have to admit, I never thought I would see any of you again, let alone look after a Princess, it's been wonderful. Goodbye my Queens, Willon and Hahn, you are very brave young men, goodbye Princess Alegia. Say Hi to Fran for me too."

We hugged. "Quickly," I called out. "It's starting to vanish."

Holding hands, we ran through as fast as possible, to land in a heap the other side. I knew we were back, because the cardboard box Stan had sent, was just beside us.

I took hold of Alegia. "That was very naughty coming into this forest alone, sweetheart. Please don't ever do that again. We'll always come in together, promise me?"

"Yes, mummy."

I huffed out. "Are you okay, Sheelan?"

"Yes, I think so, Lauren. It's a strange place, isn't it?"

"It certainly is, and not anywhere you should be, my love. Now, shall we see what Stan has sent us?"

All heads nodded. The kids were the most excited, peering in and lifting things out.

So many questions followed I didn't know whether I was coming or going. "Now, we put everything back in and take it to the hospital. We'll use the pole across-ways, then you two boys can get underneath and help."

It was a stop-go journey until Shaila heard us and got women to help.

"You've been ages, Highness, what happened?"

"We went to the future, Shaila," Willon shouted with great enthusiasm while jumping up and down, as if they did it every day of the week.

"The future! You didn't, did you?" Shaila asked, unbelievingly.

I nodded. "Only briefly, Shaila," I replied, and explained what had happened. "So fortunately, no harm done, although it gave me an enormous fright, it simply turned into an interesting experience for them all."

She stared at us. "The future, all of you. By the Gods, I'm glad I never came with you," Shaila muttered.

"It was fun," Hahn stated unashamedly. "We saw a flying machine and chariots that didn't need a horse to make them go and they growled at us. Can we do it again, Lauren?"

"No, we most certainly cannot," I replied, chuckling. "You two lads are far too brave for your own good. Let's put the box into the hospital and let mummy Alyssa know we're back," I said, jerking Sheelan from her daydream of people in strange clothes and odd transport systems.

Alyssa was horrified when she found out. "They all went?" she uttered. "And survived?"

"We were only there long enough to find Alegia and chat to Stan. He had just put the parcel through so was the other side. Then we came back before the mist went away. Stan sent the things I asked for so our hospital is a real one again. Don't worry, darling, we are all unscathed."

"It was exciting," the boys shouted.

Chapter Nineteen

Wounds

Gnaeus Julius Agricola kept his word, we hardly ever saw him. I knew from history that the Romans had plenty of problems about now. There was Caractacus playing up in the west having incorporated Chief Damarion's Silures tribe into his army. I wondered where Chief Damarion was now, nobody had heard anything about him. The last we had made contact was with his wife and son when she gave us away at the south gate and we fled for our lives. It wasn't only our domain that had serious problems either. King Venutius was stirring up trouble near Deva Victrix, what we now know as Chester, gradually working his way over to the east coast and further into Brigantian territory, the land of the Brigantes tribe and Queen Cartimandua. The Roman legions had gone to suppressed the insurrection caused by Venutius but now they were pushed for forces so were thin on the ground.

"What are you dreaming about?" Alyssa's voice shattered my thoughts.

"I was wondering about Queen Cartimandua. Her ex-husband is trying to wrest her Queendom away from her. The Romans should send support."

"Isn't that the Roman's problem, my love, not ours?"

"It's Queen Cartimandua's problem so a Celtic one. Perhaps we should offer her refuge?" I mused.

"That means she would give up her Queendom. I can't see her doing that, can you? We hung on here rather than retreat too far, she'll do the same," Alyssa answered.

A sigh left me. "You're right. And having to worry about her domain isn't helping us find our swords. That should be our next aim, restarting the Quest. It seems to have got pushed to one side as we came back to the fort and met

Agricola, as nice as he is. Thinking of Cartimandua's fort, or whatever she has, isn't getting us anywhere nearer retrieving those."

Sheelan sat on the bed, still in a dream.

I sat next to her. "What's the matter?"

"I still can't believe I went to the future and came back again. How far is it, Lauren?"

"It's not how far in distance, we were still here, it's distance in time. Two thousand years into the future, sweetheart. You looked just as beautiful."

She went coy. "Do I... I mean did I?"

I pushed her backwards to the far side of the bed nearest the wall. "Of course, you were and are, exactly the same person."

"This mattress is lumpy at the far edge, I'm glad it's wide and we all sleep near the middle cuddled up."

"We can't have it lumpy, not for Queen Sheelan," I teased. "Shall be give it a shake?"

"There's something very hard inside, Lauren," Sheelan muttered. "What can it be?"

"Let me feel." My hand went under so I could grope upwards and perhaps find the clod of earth or whatever it was Sheelan was complaining about. I found a long thin object. When I took hold of it, a glow came right through the mattress.

"It's one of our swords," Sheelan yelled excitedly. "How did it get in here?"

"There's more. Get a dagger sweetheart, we have to slit this open."

And out they tumbled, to crash onto the floor in a jumbled heap, sheathed in their individual decorated scabbards, three beautiful swords encrusted in brilliant jewels.

Alyssa dashed over, to stand looking stunned. "Does this mean they were here all the time, even when we were travelling all over our domain searching for them, Lauren?"

I nodded slowly. "Most likely. But who could have put them here? Not Shaila or Haff, they would have told us. Our

Guards and units were with us in the forest as were Toler and Crenn and his assistants. Anyway, the mattress had been sewn up neatly, I can't see Toler doing that, it's more likely a woman's handiwork. The palace was deserted, so whoever it was had plenty of time as long as a Roman didn't come along."

"The main thing is we have them," Alyssa cried, joyfully. She reached out and picked hers up. It glowed brightly for a while, fading to a soft luminescence. "It seems alive, Lauren, a buzzing feeling. Is yours the same?"

Sheelan was too curious to wait, so grabbed hers. The result was identical. "It kind of hums in my hand, I wonder why?"

I admired mine, they were all incredibly beautiful, holding it up and twisting it so the jewels sparkled in the firelight. I drew it from the scabbard, that odd sensation of power tingled my hand and arm. I felt invigorated, as if I needed to do something, a desperate urge to put this sword to use, so I swished it through the air as if striking an enemy. The balance was perfect, light, and easily wielded and controlled, it was the swoosh it made that startled me, louder than an arrow in flight. My mouth dropped open as I stared at the weapon in my fist, glowing lightly. "There's raw power in these, we must find out the purpose of it. I wonder if the Stones will tell us. We were shocked at the event when we held them there last time as the power came to us and Sheelan was changed. Perhaps we should return and place the tips on a Sarsen or the Altar Stone?"

"Was there some purpose behind their disappearance," Alyssa muttered.

"You may be right. Look at all the events that occurred during our search. Finding the Chiefs and making Morgana a Matriarch. The events in Sarum and then finding Willon. Now, after all that, we're back home. Like a round table, only over land instead."

A guard called a Roman wished an audience.

"Who is it?" Alyssa asked.

A pause... "Justinus Agapus, Highness."

Alyssa confirmed. "Good day, Justinus, to what do we owe this honour?"

He gave her an odd look. "I have come at Legate's request, Highness. We have three injured legionaries that aren't healing, he asks if you would help, please."

"Where are they?"

"Forgive me, but I took the liberty of leaving them in your hospital, Queen Lauren. I hope that is alright?"

"Perfectly, Justinus. Come on Sheelan, we are needed. I feel we should put our best swords on, go on Sheelan, wear it."

"You have the swords, Highness," Justinus asked, amazed. "Where did you find them, out in the forest somewhere, in a village nearby, where?"

"Right here, Justinus, sewn into that mattress. Do you know anything of it?"

"No Highness, but I am very pleased they are safe."

"Follow us, please Justinus."

Shaila came out as we got to the hospital entrance. I began to wonder if she either stood waiting all the time or had eyes in the back of her head. She was always helpful and caring, I could ask no more. "There are injured, Highness?"

"Yes, Shaila, please come with us."

Justinus had allocated a bed each, so two sat on an edge while the third lay.

At a glance it was plain they had been hurt for some time. "When were the wounds inflicted, Justinus?"

"Fourteen moons ago, Highness. Our surgeon tried to heal them but his efforts didn't work. They were sent back to Sarum from the north but our hospital isn't ready yet and in any case, Legate said you were far better than our people, so told me to come here. We brought them on a wagon, Queen Lauren."

The eyes of the legionary we stood in front of went from Justinus to me like a yo-yo. "Are you really a Queen?" he asked.

208

"Yes, she is a very great Queen," Justinus replied tartly. "All of you pay her due respect, otherwise the General will hear of it."

I thought it a little harsh, they hadn't put a foot wrong so far. "I'm sure our patients will be polite and well mannered. This is Queen Sheelan, and there is another Queen called Alyssa. This is a Client-Queendom, so allied to Rome. Now young man, what is the problem?"

"Oh... err. My problem Highness... Yes, I have a sword cut in my left side."

"Take off your tunic, please, while I see to this man." Going to the next, it was plain where his would was, a gash across his left cheek.

"Shaila, would you bring warm water and a garlic rinse as well, please."

"Can I leave you then, Highness?" Justinus asked.

"Yes, thank you Centurion."

"You are polite to your slaves, Highness."

"We have no slaves here, everybody is free. Shaila does things because she wants to, not because she has to. She is an elder and I respect her as she respects me. What is your name?"

"No slaves... Erm, name... it's Barrius, my Queen."

"You will have a scar, Barrius, and it's infected. We need to reduce that. I need to see what your body temperature is, so hold this little tube gently below your tongue, please don't crush it, it's glass."

"I will, for you, beautiful Highness. His name is Laenius," he said, indicating the soldier lying down. "He's very sick." He motioned me nearer. "The General doesn't think he'll live."

"Let me be the judge of that when I examine him. Mmm, you have a temperature, so get into bed and don't move, understand? Queen Sheelan will come and dress your cut."

He grinned. "Yes, Highness. She has beautiful hair."

Sheelan had gone to see the next man. "He's till bleeding, Lauren," she called.

I dashed over. He had a sword wound across the left shoulder, it was deep, nasty, a little infected and as Sheelan had said, bleeding. "Sheelan, get some linen from the women's house, a bowl of water and then my needle and small bottles from the dispensary. Look for a packet with sutures written on it and the needle we use with it, please." I was pleased she had learned to read a little, and luckily, we had practised on the boxes and bottles in here, so she was familiar with all of them.

She soon returned. "Here, Lauren. Shall I swab the wound?"

"Pop back to the palace and bring Fallow, she knows about these things, thanks. When you come back, would you dress his facial wound please, my love."

Sheelan stared. "Fallow? does she?" She saw my look of urgency. "Yes, I will."

Shaila saw to the first legionary, cleaning his wound and letting the rinse dry.

"Come here Shaila, and hold this pad onto this wound tightly, please. Pressure should help stop the bleeding. I'm going to give them a jab each."

Loading the syringe, I went to the first legionary. "Bare your upper arm, either one. I'm going to stick this in you for a few moments, it won't hurt."

That done, change the needle and onto the next then finally, our worse casualty. "This is to combat infection. I'll give you a couple of pills to swallow as well, after treatment." Now the wound was cleaner, I could see the extent of the damage. Deep, but not fatally hitting arteries. Threading the needle, I looked at him. "This will hurt, but that wound has to be closed up. I'm sorry. Grip your teeth on this thick leather, that will stop you biting your tongue."

He didn't look very keen about it. But nodded.

"If it hurts, grip the side of the bed hard. Ready?"

He sighed. "Yes, Highness."

He fainted after a few stitches, that saved him being conscious right through the process.

Sheelan appeared with Fallow.

"Get a big field dressing, please, then bind his wound for me, Fallow." Back to the sword thrust. "And what are you called?"

"Sestius, Highness. Are you going to sew me up as well?"

I smiled back. "No, Sestius, simply put a dressing on it. Here, take two of these. I want you lying down as well. In fact, you all can, have a rest here, that's a Royal Command. How is his wound Fallow?"

"The bleeding has eased, Highness. Will it knit after that amount of time?"

I shrugged my shoulders. "Let's hope. The bleeding kept it alive and fresh, so it should. We need to ask one of his Gods for help. Which is best?" I asked of Sestius.

"We have no God for healing, Highness, perhaps Ceres the Earth Goddess and Maia, the Goddess of Growth."

"Yes, I think they are a good combination. Will you both pray to them for him? He needs all the help he can get. Now settle down. I'll come back later to close the shutters and keep the night chill out. Shaila will come in now and then, if you need anything, ask her. I'll ask her to light a fire in the hearth for you."

"You have Romans in the hospital?" Willon asked when I went into the women's house. "They hurt my mother, Lauren. Shouldn't they be punished?"

"It wasn't these that hurt her, Willon. Not all Romans are horrible, some are very fair and understanding, like the new General. We cannot paint everybody with the same brush."

"But they got hurt fighting Celts," Willon insisted.

"Only because Caractacus fought them. If you hit a person, they will retaliate, won't they. It was Scapula and Veranius that were bad and why we went into the forest and fought them. I'll tell you a couple of secrets, Scapula has died fighting in the west of Britain, and Veranius will as well, so the curse I put upon them worked. Does that make up for the hurt they inflicted on Deirdre?"

He had a wicked grin. "Yes, I suppose it does, Lauren. Can

you put a curse on a person then? You are a Goddess, so I suppose you can."

"Why don't you and Hahn go and say hello. They have nothing to do and nobody to talk to, much like you before you came here. But be polite and don't talk about how your mum was hurt, it was Veranius that did that."

Alyssa asked how they were.

"Bad wounds, all of them, my love. We've done all we can, they must rest and recuperate now."

Chapter Twenty

The Cure

After a short rest, my next port of call was the hospital to check on our three patients. Sestius looked a bit feverish, so he got a thermometer under his tongue with strict instructions not to bite it. Barrius, with the cut face, seemed to be doing well and it was healing nicely. Bed three held poor Laenius with the cut shoulder. He was red in the face, so was next for the thermometer. It read high.

"You feel hot and possibly sick?" I asked.

He looked too weak to answer. It was serious. I called Fallow.

"What do you need, Highness?"

"Remove his dressing, please, while I see to Sestius." I gave him a couple more painkillers and told him to stay still. "Have you been out of bed?"

"No Highness."

Something said he wasn't convincing. "Look into my eyes, Sestius."

"I would happily look into your beautiful eyes all day, Highness."

I ignored his chat-up line. A spinning sensation took me as my gaze went deeper and deeper, until I saw his actions, running around and messing about. I released him.

"Ha," he gasped, as he fell back on the bed. "What happened?"

"I looked into your soul to find the truth. You lied to me, Sestius. When I say stay in bed, I mean it, not for you to run around here messing about, do you understand?"

He sat with his mouth open staring at me. Then bowed. "You must be a Goddess to be able to do that, you read my innermost feelings and secrets, Highness?"

"Yes, and that goes for all of you. Do what I tell you, otherwise I shall send you back to Legate with a messenger to tell him why. Do I make myself perfectly clear?"

"Yes, Highness, you do. I won't disobey again." He saluted.

"Good. Instead of playing pranks you would have been better occupied dabbing Laenius' forehead with cool water. In future, look after him, otherwise he may die." They looked duly berated.

I went back to Laenius. His wound was red and angry. I prepared another shot and dispensed that, got Fallow to help lift him up to take more painkillers and had her cool his brow with water. "Stay with him, please Fallow, I shall return soon."

Alyssa was grinning as I entered the palace. "You told a Roman off, Lauren, how funny."

"He wasn't doing what I told him so he got a dressing down, the same as he would have at his barracks."

"You should have seen what she did to Veranius," Sheelan said, laughing. "After tipping him off his horse she warned him not to underestimate her as she was a Goddess. He deserved it, the pig. He went skulking off back to the camp."

"I would have loved to have seen that, darling. How are they?"

"One I am worried about, the other two will be okay. I may move there tonight, he is critical. Would you mind?"

"If you believe that is what's needed, then no, of course not. Sheelan will keep me company. Ask Squirrel to join you."

"Yes, that's a good idea, I will. Thank you." I called her.

"What do you want, Highness?" Squirrel asked, a worried look on her face.

"Why are you worried?"

"I've done something wrong, Highness."

"Just because I call you it doesn't mean trouble, Squirrel. I want you to keep me company tonight in the hospital. There is a very sick Roman there I am concerned about. Fallow has looked after him all day, but she needs a break."

Squirrel smiled. "Oh, lovely, I will Highness, thank you. I used to mix herbal cures for you before our troubles began. I don't mind looking after sick people."

Laenius was in a fitful sleep when we arrived. The other two looked guiltily at me like a pair of naughty boys. "Have you stayed in bed?"

"Yes, Highness. The young woman looked after Laenius all day."

"Squirrel and I will stay tonight. We'll sleep on the other side." I realised the fire had gone low, it was chilly in here. I called Shaila.

"I'll get it made up immediately, my Queen. I have been very busy and it slipped my mind, I am sorry."

It was soon flaming and shedding light and a little warmth around the room, flames reflecting off the white walls. I closed all shutters and almost both doors, leaving one a little open for fresh air.

Laenius was still hot when I felt his brow. But I didn't want to wake him to take pills, he might during the night, he could take them then.

Squirrel got fresh water and some furs. "It's cold tonight, Highness," she said in explanation. She shivered.

"Come in with me then, I'll cuddle you if you're cold, we'll warm each other up."

She didn't need any second telling and squeezed her body close to mine. We dozed off quickly, it had been a strange day and I had felt weak after our experience but had only time for a short nap.

A kiss on my cheek woke me. It was fairly dark but I could see Squirrel's face inches from mine. "What is it, Squirrel?"

"That man has been moaning a lot very loudly, Lauren, I mean Highness."

I slipped out of bed and across to his side. His brow was still hot, hotter than it had been earlier. "Get some of the pain tablets, Squirrel, and my syringe."

We struggled getting him up, so I asked Barrius to help.

"He's in a bad way, isn't he, Highness," Barrius said. "He's so hot, and that isn't good, is it?"

My head shook in the negative. "He's far too hot, must be over a hundred, so critical." I sighed. I had only lost one to a wound before and I didn't want to lose Laenius, my need to save him was almost overwhelming, but it was touch and go. As I bent over him my sword hilt touched his head, I know it did because I felt the bump. I looked, but there was no mark. I thought myself a clumsy cow, as if the poor lad didn't have enough to contend with without me whacking him with a sword hilt.

"I'll get a couple more furs and put over him," Squirrel said, and went wafting out the door. She must only have gone to Shaila's house, she was back in moments to lay them over him. "I know you did that once before when people got hot, like Brevit, to make them even hotter."

"I also plunge people in snow, that happened to Brevit. But we have no snow. Why did you kiss me instead of shaking my shoulder, Squirrel?" I was sure I felt the heat of her blush.

"I thought it might make you jump, Highness."

I laughed. "You wanted to, didn't you? I don't mind on my cheek, Squirrel, but I don't want another redhead saying *I can, can't I*, I have two lovely redheads back at the palace that I think the world of." I gave her a hug. "Come on, in bed, I'll cuddle you again. Are you lonely, Squirrel?"

"Yes, I am a bit, my Queen, thank you for asking."

"You're a lovely person, Squirrel, why not talk to Leilan sometimes?"

She sighed. "I'd rather talk to you..." Her words faded without finishing the sentence.

I felt for her, it's hard being lonely, even harder when the person you admire and want to be with, won't, or cannot be yours.

The sun shone next day, although it was cold. I got up, stretched, and went to Laenius. He was sleeping peacefully and apparently had no temperature, which was a surprise. I couldn't believe it. He was cooking up only a couple of hours ago and possibly near death. "Squirrel," I called.

She was by my side in an instant, all wide eyed and ready to help.

"Take his dressing off please. I'll check the other two."

Sestius was much better. His temperature was normal now he had stopped moving about. I checked his wound, it was healing well, but needed another couple of days to settle.

Barrius' face would have a scar, we knew that from the start, but not a bad one. His wound was almost healed too. "How is Lanni, I mean Laenius?" he asked.

"Come and see." We went over.

Squirrel was staring at me. "He's cured, Highness, look at his wound."

It was a miracle. His shoulder had cooled to normal, the redness gone, the wound was knitted together and well on the mend. Yet only last night I didn't give much for his chances.

"What had happened here?" It was a self-question. We had administered the usual drugs. They might have worked but never this quickly. Then I remembered my sword hilt had touched him and what that Voice had said at the Stones, that they could be used to cure. Had that transformed him from near death to cured in a couple of hours?

Shaila came in, opening the doors and shutters as she did. "How is the bad one?" She asked. "Oh, by the Gods, he's nearly well, Highness. There, that proves it, you must be a Goddess, I've said it all along when I have seen you bring people back from the dead, now this." She went on one knee and kissed my ruby ring.

"Stand up, Shaila, you're embarrassing me."

"Her Highness brought people back from the dead?" Barrius cried in amazement. "Truly you are a Goddess then, a Highness Goddess." He went on one knee.

"Barrius, I want you to touch my sword, please. Lovely, isn't it, and it is very special."

It glowed.

He looked puzzled but did what I asked.

"Look," Squirrel exclaimed. "Laenius is sitting up."

"Is there any food?" he asked, sitting scratching his head as if nothing at all had happened over the last twenty-four hours.

"Shaila will bring some," I replied. "I hope breakfast for you all. How do you feel, Laenius?"

"Where am I? and who are you?" He sat looking around at unfamiliar surroundings.

"Hello Lanni," Barrius said. "You're at a hill fort's hospital. This is Queen Goddess Lauren, she cured you."

"A hospital at a hill fort? But we were fighting them on that mountain."

"You got injured, same as us. Our people couldn't cure the wounds and you were getting worse so we were sent back near to Sarum. These are nice Britons, Lanni, they'll look after you."

His handsome features broke into a lovely smile. "Thank you, my beautiful Queen and your lovely helper, I'm sure she made me much better just by being by my side." He took Squirrel's hand and kissed it. "You have lovely hair, you must be Diana, Goddess of the Moon, the Queen must be Juno, our Queen of Gods."

Squirrel blushed like mad and giggled.

"Is that the sound of wonderful raindrops falling from the Gods?" Laenius whispered in her ear.

"I'm going home, can't stand this much charm," I laughed. "Fallow is on her way. Remember what I said, Squirrel, to have a friend you have to talk to them."

She smiled. "I will, Highness. He was nice, wasn't he?" She came and hugged me, planting another kiss on my cheek. "You don't mind, do you?"

"No, but not all the time. Go chat to Leilan. Laenius was piling on the charm, as men do when they want to win your

218

affections, then you suddenly find yourself pregnant. Be sure what you want in life, it's very easy to get hurt emotionally."

"You had a disturbed night?" Alyssa put the question as I entered the palace, although it was more of a statement. "Your patients are cured as well, even the bad one you thought might die. How did you manage that?"

"My sword hilt touched him by accident last night, this morning he was well. Our weapons have amazing powers, as the Voice said."

"Go on, go to bed with Sheelan, she fidgeted all night so won't mind a lie-in."

"I didn't, did I?" she said, horror struck.

'No, you didn't sweetheart, but it's a good way of getting you to look after Lauren. Especially as Squirrel has taken to kissing her," she finished, laughing.

"I'll tell you about it later. Come on Sheelan, I need to have a fuss made of me." I was asleep quickly.

Chapter Twenty One

A Call for Help

The three legionaries had been returned to the barracks. I was pleased with their progress, especially Laenius, who had been knocking at Death's door for a while. Now he was back to full fitness and enjoying the delights of Sarum's prostitutes on a period of leave, so how long he would remain fit was anybody's guess.

Barrius' cheek healed in a day without the hint of a scar. He was delighted, knelt and kissed my ruby ring. "My Goddess Queen," he said, his big brown eyes looking up at me.

Little Squirrel had tried to make friends with Leilan, but that hadn't worked out, so she moped about the fort looking very glum.

I bumped into her as I walked to the hospital one morning. "Good morning, Squirrel, how are you today?" It was blatantly obvious she wasn't in the least happy.

"Good morning, Queen Lauren, although it never is for me."

"Walk with me, sweetheart. You used to work in the hospital for me, why did you stop?"

"I didn't think you wanted me anymore once you and Sheelan..." her words trailed off.

"Of course I want you, but you went off with Fidgeon and Jeela and as you're a free woman, I didn't come to demand your return. You can go there anytime you wish, especially if we have casualties. Fallow, while paired with Selene, would chat to you. She's very knowledgeable about biology, you should learn it, then you could begin treating people yourself."

She brightened. "I would like that, Highness, thank you."

"You'll meet people, all sorts of people. We're here, let's have a look inside."

Shaila came in. "I have a wounded soldier," she said.

"Have you? Who is it and where is he?" I asked.

"Hahn, Highness, he's cut a finger."

He stood, very embarrassed at doing such a thing. "A knife slipped, Lauren."

"Go and see Squirrel, she's a very good nurse." I watched her; she seemed good with children, much like Madeil was and teased him a little, enough to make him laugh, but not feel stupid.

"There Hahn, all better now," she finally said as she applied the sticking plaster.

Hahn looked at it oddly, then beckoned her low as if the whisper, but gave her a peck on her cheek instead. "Thank you, Squirrel." He ran out, ready to continue whatever he had been doing.

Alegia was round the side of the house playing throwing sticks with Willon. They spent a lot of time together now, which I was pleased about. Willon and Hahn gave her a childhood she may have missed otherwise.

Willon ran across. "Alegia's really good at throwing sticks, Lauren, she beats me every time."

"Alegia has had a lot of practice, Willon. That's what you must do. But she should let you win a few times, otherwise you'll get fed up playing it and won't want to anymore." I said it loud enough for Alegia to hear. I saw a smile hover on her face.

"I think Squirrel will come back to the hospital now, Shaila. Having a little job will help her loneliness."

"Is she? I didn't realise. She can always come in the women's house for a chat, Kwail, Lark and Mona often do, she could talk to them, they're her age. Or is it something else?"

I smiled. "I don't think she's sure, Shaila, but only she can decide."

"Sameon comes in at times, he's a nice young man. I'll see what I can do, Highness."

"No matchmaking, Shaila," I laughed.

Alyssa smiled as I walked into the palace. "Problems of the heart?" she asked.

I shook my head. "I'm not sure, Alyssa. Shaila's going to try and help."

A trumpet sounded.

Legate was here.

Alyssa stood and brushed the front of her robe down. How wonderful to see her do that again after so long in a tunic and trousers, although admittedly, they had shown her figure off to perfection.

The lines of legionaries came to stand either side, forming the hallowed ground.

He jumped off his horse and smiled, giving the Roman salute. "A fair day for the time of year, my Queens."

"Would you take tea or wine with us, my Lord?" Alyssa asked.

"Thank you, wine I think. How are your supplies of it?"

The question surprised me. "I am unsure, General. I'll call Shaila."

Agricola gave me a funny look. "You call without sending a messenger? You have amazing powers, my Queen. I shall have a few amphorae sent to your fort for the service you did for my three legionaries. How you saved Laenius, I cannot imagine, we had given up on him. So, a small reward is due, thank you. But that wasn't the main reason for this visit. You met and befriended, Queen Cartimandua once when General Vespasian was here?"

Alyssa and I nodded. "Yes, General. She was a sensible Queen."

"She's allied to Rome, as you know, but is in extreme danger from an insurrection caused by her ex-husband Venutius. It goes back a way to when they separated. He's trying to remove her from the throne by attacking with other tribes from the west. A previous Legate sent a legion up to quell an insurrection there a couple of years ago to secure her position. I wondered, if she was forced out and needed sanctuary, if you would kindly offer it?"

I looked at Alyssa, it wasn't my decision, she was by far the senior Queen here and giving protection to Cartimandua might place our fort in danger of attack.

She smiled back. "Yes, the Queen would be most welcome here, my Lord. We all have choices to make, whether to help those in trouble or ignore them. She is a Celtic Queen, like us, so we cannot turn our backs upon her if she wished refuge our fort is open to her."

Agricola smiled broadly, slapping a knee. "I knew I could count on your support. Queen Cartimandua has always shown her loyalty to Rome. By the way, the tribute I asked for is on its way by ship. You will receive it soon. Is there anything else I can do for you?"

"No, my Lord, thank you for your generous offer. We have the Winter Solstice soon but I am sure you would rather not attend that, it's at the turn of the year, a time when the weather is very cold. It is held at the Standing Stones over beyond the small forest."

"What are those stones for? I saw them on an inspection of the area. They are impressive. Did your tribe put them there?"

Alyssa shook her head. "No General, they have been there for many years. Queen Lauren can tell you more about them."

He looked at me expectantly.

"Nobody knows who erected that monument, my Lord. It has been there for at least two thousand years, the same time the pyramids were erected in Egypt. It used to be intact until a few years ago when a very important woman warrior from this fort was killed in a battle and was interred in the lower field barrow. There were three losses and each time one was interred, Nodens came down and wrecked the circle a little more, the display He put on was amazing. Because of that, it lies as you see it now. Mystical powers abound there and a strange aura permeates the area."

"I shall stay clear of it then and leave your religious temples sacred for you. If your God Nodens is that great, I do not wish to transgress His path." He stood and saluted in his Roman way, but paused. "I am surprised you know of Egypt, my Queen, you seem to have vast knowledge. Neither could I help notice the swords and daggers you wear now. They are truly beautiful and plainly show your status as Queens of this lovely land. Care for them." With that gem, he departed.

"What a change from the other two," Alyssa breathed. "I hope he stays for a long time."

"About another three and a half years, my love. Then he'll be relieved of his post and return to Rome."

She laughed. "If you say so, darling. Who am I to disagree with a Queen Goddess from the future."

Peace reigned for the several months. We had the occasional Legionary in for treatment, which meant Agricola still had faith in us.

One day Freda came in. "A strange Roman is outside and urgently requests an audience with Queen Lauren, Highnesses."

I nodded to Alyssa. "Better let him in, let's see what he wants."

He was tall and wore the uniform of a Centurion. He politely held his helmet under an arm. Striding across the room. He saluted us, then did a very surprising thing. He went down on one knee in front of me.

"My venerable Queen, we ask you most urgently to attend General Agricola at his residence in Sarum. He is very ill and needs help immediately. I implore you to come with me."

"Stand, Centurion. What is your name, please?"

"Ligarius Manimus, Highness."

"What exactly is wrong with the General?"

"He is very unwell, too ill to move from his bed. Please

come. Our physicians can do nothing."

His explanation wasn't much help. "Did you travel by horse?"

He nodded. "For greater speed, the matter is most urgent my Queen. You have cured all sent to you, even Laenius, who we all thought would die, so we're sure you can help. The General particularly asked for you. Please come."

I huffed. Goodness knows what the problem was and they are putting all their faith in me. What if I fail? There are no guarantees and I haven't the skills Stan has and I can't go dragging him back here from the future. But neither can I simply leave him to his fate, Agricola has been good to us.

"I shall have to go, my love," I said to Alyssa, "I would like Sheelan with me, would you mind?"

She looked glum. "I shall be alone, Lauren."

That was true, and I didn't like leaving her without support. "Who else? I haven't a clue."

"What about Squirrel? She says she's lonely and it will give her a chance to see what the rest of the world is like."

"It's tempting fate. You know she has the hots for me," I replied, laughing. "But she's good with medications and has been studying with Fallow, so is more knowledgeable now about the human form. I'll call her."

"Go on, I trust you," Alyssa grinned back.

Squirrel came flying in. "You called, Highness?"

Ligarius looked at Squirrel, then at me. "You never sent a messenger, Highness? You must be a Goddess as is claimed, I bow before you, oh mighty one." His fist hit his chest so hard I had concerns he might have broken something.

"Squirrel, get all medical equipment packed onto two horses in straddle bags, we're going on a mission of mercy."

"Me and you, Highness? Wow, right away." She shot out the palace bubbling over with excitement.

I embraced Alyssa and Sheelan. "I would rather one of you were coming but I know you have duties here, darling," I said to Alyssa. "I'll think of you a lot, both of you."

"Only a lot?" Sheelan retorted, grinning.

"All the time then, but remember, I must think about the General, too. Come, Ligarius, we must go to the hospital and get what I need." With a final wave, I left the palace.

"Thank you, Highness. We're at a loss, the General hasn't responded."

"Why didn't you bring him?"

"We dare not move him, my Queen."

That didn't sound very good, I kept that opinion to myself though. We entered the hospital where Squirrel was busy getting supplies into straddle bags.

Shaila appeared as usual. "Is there anything I can do, Highness?"

"No, Shaila, thank you. This is going to be hard, I would have preferred to effect a cure here. But there are no options. You can care for any illnesses while I'm away, some medications will be left. Take care."

"You too, Highness. You're going into the Roman's homes, I hope they treat you as a Queen should be, with great respect?"

"I can assure you the Goddess Queen Lauren will be. May I lead, Highness?" Ligarius asked. "There is a new road through the forest, it is faster."

Out the north gate, soon leaving the rock behind where the portal formed to come upon a good road. I realised it would be where the road was near my home in the future, the very one Lalena and I had run across when we had been time-shifted and the same road we had all galloped through the village on only a short time ago.

Sarum loomed in the distance. Ligarius took us to a large villa on the outskirts with many guards around its doors.

Legionaries thumped their chests in salute. I smiled back, entering an atrium.

"In here, Highness," Ligarius indicated.

The room was light and spacious, patterned flooring in black and white gave it a solid base, it was warm to my feet, so he had central heating.

Agricola held a hand up weakly. "Thank you for coming,

my Queen. Now, please try to cure me."

Even through his smile he looked dreadful, a grey pallor dulled his normally bright skin and rosy cheeks.

"Hello General, how do you feel?"

"Not my best, Queen Lauren, I don't seem to have any energy, not even enough to get out of bed without assistance."

"Have you been sick?"

"Yes, many times, it saps what strength I have left."

"I must ask you a delicate question, but I do need to know. Have you been to the toilet and if so, may I see it?"

He looked surprised. "It isn't the place for a great Queen, Highness," he said, doubtfully. "I can't tell what it was like, it's washed away."

"It will help me diagnose what is wrong with you, General, so it's important."

He hesitated.

"I do need to see, I'm afraid."

He gave in. "Very well. Ligarius will escort you."

It wasn't the cleanest of places. "This needs thoroughly washing down, Centurion. Please get that organised immediately." I knew a slave would do it and it was a distasteful task but had to be done. We returned to the General.

His forehead was hot to my touch. "Squirrel, bring the thermometer please."

He took my hand, squeezing it slightly.

"I'm putting this under your tongue, hold it gently." It proved what I suspected, he had a raging temperature. He must have felt terrible and was suffering a high fever with remarkable calmness.

I don't think Squirrel had got over the villa yet, it was in complete contrast to our homes. She walked around with her mouth open.

"Squirrel, find my needle and antibiotics please, you know where they are, you loaded them, sweetheart."

"Yes, Highness." And away she went, to return quickly.

"Here Lauren, I... I mean Highness," she corrected. It was plain that out of my sight and earshot she called me by name. Her cheeks went red.

"You're my medical assistant here, Squirrel, we must work on names, it's easier and more practical."

A light came into her eyes. "Thank you, Lauren, it's an honour."

I gave Agricola a shot of anti-tetanus as well and a couple of painkillers. "When was the last time you were sick, General?"

"This morning, my Queen, so not for a few hours."

That was good news; on the other hand, if he had nothing left in his stomach there was nothing to bring up. The shots and meds would help.

I bent. "Would you touch the blade of my sword, please, General."

He gave me a puzzled look.

"A Celtic custom, for good luck, my Lord." I drew it from its scabbard and laid it beside him. It glowed.

He nervously laid his hand on the blade, "Why does it glow like that?" Agricola asked.

'It was probably just sunlight catching the blade as I laid it down, General."

"Odd, there is little sun today. But to please you and your customs, my Queen. Centurion," Agricola called. "Be sure our honoured guests are shown full Roman hospitality, bring food and wine. Show them to a room near me where they can stay. I may need to get up briefly."

"If you're getting up for what I think you are, my Lord, please keep some, I need to see it."

He gave a dissatisfied look. Perhaps he thought it demeaning?

"If I am to cure you, it is vital. I am sorry, but I am discreet, General."

Even feeling awful, he still managed a smile. "Very well, Queen Lauren, if you say so."

A lot of chest thumping went on and we were ushered into

an adjoining room. Putting Celts right next to the top Roman General meant we had their complete trust. Refreshments appeared, brought by servants who placed them on the table. They stared at us as if we had come from another planet. The room was again, spacious, but had only one bed to one side and a table with fruit on it and chairs in the middle. Loungers lay at various places.

Squirrel stood looking at the exotic fruit, dates, cherries, apples and many more.

"You're allowed to eat some if you want to, Squirrel. They are to consume, you'll like them. Apples are nice and good for you." I heard scuffling in the next room, that probably meant the General had been to the toilet.

Ligarius popped his head in. "Do you wish to see, Highness?"

It was loose with what looked like streaks of blood. I wondered if he had an ulcer, it was possible, although a General would eat well. Cancer was a concern, it certainly existed in Roman times. There was nothing I could do about that unless I had Godly aid, but an ulcer was treatable. "Ligarius, can you obtain apples for baking and fish to be steamed. How long since the General has eaten?"

"Several days, Highness. He was sick each time."

"Bake some apples well and get the fish steamed. Only small amounts, and I need Meadowsweet and Comfrey as well as Willow herb. Squirrel will make teas out of those. Give the General a cupful three or four times a day. Is there any Peppermint stored here? Let me know, please. If possible, get him fresh spring water."

"We have some of those in the bags, Lauren," Squirrel volunteered. "Would you like me to infuse them?"

"Yes please, Squirrel, for 5 minutes in boiled water, then let the brew cool. Ligarius, May Squirrel go to your kitchen, please?"

He nodded. "Come with me, young lady."

They helped her make the teas and took them into the General's room.

She looked tired when she returned. It had been a hectic day.

"Well done, Squirrel, you're a great help. Everything that can be done, has been. Let's go to the General and administer a couple of painkillers."

I felt his brow. Perhaps a little cooler. "No wine, General, and only the food I allow. Drink plenty of water though and the teas Squirrel brings in. Goodnight my Lord."

"Goodnight, Queen Lauren. Thank you. I feel a little better."

We left him to Ligarius' care.

Squirrel stood looking forlorn back in our room. With just a single bed, she may have thought she had to sleep on the floor.

"Come on, tuck in with me. I'm used to cuddling someone all night, so you'll have to do."

She laughed. "I hope I do well, Lauren."

We had blankets instead of furs, so different from our beds. Squirrel really came close, backing onto me.

I slipped an arm over her waist and pulled her tight. "This is how we cuddle, Squirrel, it helps us sleep."

Her head turned enough for me to see the smile on her face. She seemed happy for a change.

Chapter Twenty Two

Peace

Noises in the villa woke me, I expected from the kitchen, it must be early. Squirrel was still sleeping soundly so I slid out of bed, got dressed and went to see the General.

He called for me to enter.

"How are you, my Lord?"

"A little better. Am I still to only eat fish and apples?"

"For now, to settle your stomach. Once we have that calm you can begin eating normally, but small meals. I need to take your temperature, so pop this under your tongue and don't bite it, otherwise it will break."

"Have I just been told off," he said, a smile on his face.

"That's more than even a Goddess would dare do, my Lord."

That amused him. "I am beginning to believe you are, you do amazing things, my Queen."

"Your temperature has dropped, General, that is very good. But stay in bed, please."

"I shall do what you command. I can take orders as well as give them."

"You have a sense of humour, my Lord, so you must be getting better."

Squirrel and I stayed for five more days. General Agricola improved daily and began eating again, much to his relief. My red-headed companion enjoyed her nightly cuddles. I guessed it would be hard for her when we returned. I found her very sweet and gentle, so why she couldn't find a partner of some sort, puzzled me. Admittedly, she had been a bit of a scatterbrain when we first met her at Germaine's domain but as time went on, she calmed down. I felt sorry for her, much like I had done for Sheelan. Both had been waifs of the storm in a way, a little downtrodden and without an aim in life. I had hoped Sheelan and her would have hit it off when Madeil and I introduced them, but they had both fallen in love with another, and the another was me. I sighed. What to do? I decided to take Squirrel as a Handmaiden, that would give her lots of company and be close to those she liked. I lifted the blanket to get back in bed for a while longer.

She woke. A loud sigh left her. "It's been wonderful having a person with me, Lauren, thank you. When are we going back to the fort?" The question was tinged with sadness.

"Soon, maybe today if the General feels well enough."

"Oh, so soon..." her face dropped.

"That made you sad, my sweet assistant."

Another sigh left her. "I'll be alone again, Lauren. I shall have to call you Highness again, won't I?"

I gave her a hug. "Squirrel, how would you like to be my personal Handmaiden?"

She sat up like a rocket. "Me? Wow, yes please Lauren, I would love that. When can I start?"

"Right now. We have Agneta, but she's really Alyssa's Handmaiden, but Sheelan and I haven't one. A Handmaiden isn't a slave, you will be a helper, as Agneta is to Queen Alyssa, so you remain free."

"Thank you, Lauren. Where would I live?"

"In the annex, with Agneta, Fallow and Selene, so you'll not be lonely ever again."

She flung her arms around my neck and kissed me passionately on my lips. Then realised what she'd done and didn't know what to do. "I... I'm so sorry, I was excited, I got carried away. Don't punish me, Highness, please." Fear showed in her eyes.

"Squirrel, if you find someone and kiss them like that, you will have a friend for life. You're a lovely person, my gorgeous Royal Handmaiden."

Ligarius entered after knocking. "General Agricola asks to see you, Highness."

"Lauren has made me her Handmaiden," Squirrel burst out, unable to retain her excitement.

"A great honour for you. Should you call your Queen by her name?"

"Should I," Squirrel asked, turning to me.

"As my Handmaiden it's a privileged I extend, so yes, you may, as Sheelan did."

"Come, Highness, and your cheeky Handmaiden."

Agricola sat at his table. There was a bright flush to his face, not of a temperature this time, of good health.

"You are well, my Lord?" I asked.

He stood and saluted. "You are a Goddess, I am sure of it. I feel better now than I did before I was ill." That charming smile took his face.

I wasn't surprised, he could have been suffering for some time. "I am pleased, my Lord is so much improved," I replied, bowing. "May we return to our fort now, General?"

"Of course, I shall attach an escort of a full cohort for you, it is the least I can do. My slaves will keep the toilet area much cleaner in future if you believe I might have picked something up from there. So, you and your charming red-headed companion must go back to your people, who are no doubt missing you terribly."

People came out to look at our large formation, bowed or saluted, which ever suited that particular person. Kids waved, so Squirrel and I waved back. At the barracks, a guard was formed outside, the whole mass saluted as one. A cheer went up. The news of Agricola's recovery must have spread quickly and plainly he was popular. That didn't surprise me, he was a fair and considerate man.

The whole fort turned out as we entered, warned of the approach by the sound of hundreds of feet moving in unison, wondering why and what for, then changed to cheers when they saw Squirrel and me on our horses.

Alyssa and Sheelan were waiting outside the palace. They

rushed forward when I slipped off my horse.

"Are you well, darling?" Alyssa asked, looking me over to see if I still had all my limbs.

"Yes, perfectly. Hello Sheelan, are you both well? May I introduce our new Handmaiden, Squirrel?"

"I have one," Alyssa replied quizzically.

"But Sheelan and I haven't. I thought it time we did, my love. Are you cross with me?"

"No, of course not. It's a lovely idea."

"She can move into the annex with Agneta and the others." I bent closer to Alyssa's ear. "To stop her being lonely, my love."

She laughed. "You're being kind again. By all means, as long as she doesn't get in bed with us for a cuddle, as she did in the General's home."

"I couldn't kick her out and there was just the one bed, she looked so unhappy, you should have seen the smile on her face when I put my arm around her waist. Now Squirrel is full of it and with the others there with her, maybe she'll learn to dance?"

Alyssa looked straight into my eyes. "I can imagine how she smiled, I would have, darling. True, with the other girls in company, Squirrel might settle down. I do hope so."

Peace reigned for several years, mainly due to Legate being considerate and helpful, which made life adorable for us all and the people's existence in and around the fort settled into a routine.

Agricola brought his family to Britannia and allowed us to meet them, a charming wife and children.

The period had been so pleasant under Agricola I lost track of time. I guessed it must be about Anno Domini late sixty something or other. Even so, Alyssa and Sheelan looked no older, I would say younger if anything, the long peace had calmed their individual fears of the Romans and the dreadful treatment they had received from the two other Legates, faded into distant memory.

A trumpet sounded. This event held no fear for us anymore.

We went to the palace frontage, watching as the hallowed ground was flanked by lines of legionaries. Agricola rode along the middle, a smile on his face.

We bowed. "Welcome my Lord," Alyssa greeted.

"Good day to you, my Queens. I have had a message from Rome. Our new Emperor is Vespasian. It has been a fluctuating year, four in one, so I am particularly pleased he has taken the throne. I came because there is a notation at the bottom in the Emperor's own hand addressed the Queen Lauren."

"To me!" I was astounded.

He opened the parchment. "Greetings, Queen Lauren. You are truly a remarkable person. Your prediction I would occupy this exalted post was made when I was stationed in Britannia. How you knew of it is beyond my powers to divine, but you were right. I salute you, my wonderful Queen, as I salute Queen Alyssa and the quiet red-headed young women with them." He paused to look up. "I am afraid our Emperor is unaware Queen Sheelan was given that status."

"Thank you, and your great Emperor," I replied. "I knew immediately he would lead your great country one day."

Agricola looked at me long and hard. "You know many things of the future, I must recognise you as a Goddess." He bowed low, stood and saluted. Turning, he made a signal, and every legionary and Centurion saluted as one. "I leave you now, duties at my villa demand my attention. A last salute, and they all left.

"You did say that to him, Lauren, I remember," Alyssa muttered. "How amazing."

This year's Winter Solstice came and went, it had been a cold, wet one, so people were invited to the palace for food and drink in celebration. Now the year had moved on into February and it was as cold, bitterly so.

One evening, while sitting closely around the fire trying to keep warm, Alyssa came out with a question.

"What of our swords?" she suddenly said, breaking the glum silence that permeated the palace.

"What *of* our swords?" Sheelan queried, puzzled by Alyssa's sudden outburst.

"The quest isn't complete yet, is it?" Alyssa pointed out. "We found them, but what of the power within them, we have no idea how they should be used or even what for, have we? The long peace here has meant they got forgotten."

"Against evil, the Voice said," Sheelan replied.

"What is evil?" Alyssa argued. "The Romans were evil once, but now we don't view them in that light, do we?"

"Only because they are kinder to us," I interjected. "But in the end, they are still invaders even though they have been in our land for so long, does that make them evil? And what of Caractacus and Venutius, they are attacking Queen Cartimandua, are they evil for doing that? Venutius was King of the Brigantians once, he isn't now because he and Cartimandua separated and he got deposed, while she was accepted as Queen by the people. She is a Queen in her own right anyway by birth, so her taking over the tribe is natural. I think her getting off with Venutius' armour bearer, Vellocatus, must have rubbed salt into his wounds. Is it right he should thrust his Kingship upon the populace when they don't want it, that's as bad as the last two Legates, a dictatorship."

"Should we wait until the threat shows itself?" Alyssa went on. "It's so confusing. The Romans are doing some good and some bad things, so not totally evil like Scapula and Veranius were. I think another force has yet to show itself."

"Perhaps, Alyssa, perhaps. The history of this land is

varied and violent and bad rulers do take control at times. But they are several years in the future. Are we to live that long? That possibility seems very far-fetched," I mused. "Although from what the Voice told us, it might be a possibility."

"We are Fairy Queens," Alyssa said. "We lived in the caverns and Fairymounds, so cannot die. But that may only have applied in our dimension, not this one. I have always thought it was possible to die of a fatal wound, but not of illness. Does that still apply after the Stones experience?"

I was about to reply when Shaila asked to enter.

"Good day, Shaila," Alyssa welcomed. "How can we help you?"

"Good day my Queens. We are low on furs and meat again, I am afraid. People use more in this cold weather, furs to keep warm and meat for energy."

"A hunt," Sheelan cried excitedly, jumping up. "We haven't done one for ages. Can we, pleeease..." she pleaded.

"Haven't you had enough excitement in your life?" Alyssa said, laughing. "We've been over half the country, captured and rescued twice, fought wild tribes and Romans, been hunted goodness knows how many times and you're still excited at the prospect?"

"I love hunting," Sheelan replied, a rapturous look in her lovely green eyes. "It's so... so... magical."

My return look was punitive. "It's been far *too* magical at times with bears, wolves, floods and fires, we don't need another one of those, thank you, Sheelan. A nice quiet peaceful hunt this time. We should savour them now the Romans have started cutting our forest down, there won't be any more one day."

"Will they cut them *all* down," Alyssa asked, horrified.

"No, my love, not all. There were some substantial ones left to hold adventures in later on in history, like Sherwood and Lincoln Forests, the New Forest down south, only it wasn't new at all, it was an ancient one, Wychwood and Chiddingfold forests and many more. They never succeeded in the end, I think they ran out of time. But the land wasn't

239

like this anymore, where we ride under the canopy for a week or more, it will be open country."

"Can we," Sheelan pressed. "All we've done is ride forever."

"What about all the hunting you did during that time? I would have thought you would be sick of it by now," I viewed.

"Mmm, you and me, Lauren, that would be heaven. Like in the southern forest when we were trying to free Alyssa, Alegia and the others."

"We can't go on a hunt on our own, you know that as well as I do, they were exceptional times. We'll need Ev... oh, no... Um, Bran then, and about twelve others, you know how many twelve is, don't you?"

"Yes, twelve," Sheelan replied with a cheeky grin. "This many," she added showing me twelve fingers.

"Good, you remembered. After all the lessons you have had you should be able to count to at least a hundred by now and read a little, too. I'm very proud of you, Okay, I'll choose Bran, Gannet, Mona and Addani, which means Artorius and Aulus will be coming, you can choose the rest. But leave Alyssa, Freda and Juna as her personal guards and Jeela for her guard group. Pick someone who can drive the wagon."

Sheelan pouted. "You've chosen the best ones. Let me think." She stuck her tongue out from one side of her mouth as her eyes wandered up into the roof. "Nianda then," she said clicking a finger against a thumb. "Squirrel, Greta, Kwail and Lark, oh and Uva and Widgeon. How's that?"

"Fine, fourteen in all. Greta can drive a wagon. I'll call Bran, or would you like to?"

Sheelan stared back. "Me, call somebody, like you and Alyssa can? Do you think that's possible?"

"That Voice said you had our powers and were one of us, so try, sweetheart."

She hunched her shoulders and giggled, then closed her eyes to concentrate. "I've done it," she muttered. "Do you think it worked?" she ended, unsure.

"You called me, Highness," Bran said, looking straight at Sheelan.

"Um... err, why, yes, I did Bran. Please organise a hunting patrol of these people." She closed her eyes again, I assumed to think of our list.

"Very well, Highness. I'll start immediately," Bran replied, and left.

Sheelan was standing in the middle of the room gaping at me. "I did it, Lauren, called her and told her who should go. I could never have done that before. Now I can, can't I." She yelled in delight and went spinning around the palace excitedly.

Alyssa laughed at her antics. "I hope I didn't behave like that the first time I did it," she said. "Well done, Sheelan, now you know for sure you're a fairy spirit."

Chapter Twenty Three

"What Can Go Wrong?"

Late February held little appeal for me to go on a hunting expedition. It was cold, often wet and foggy and there was still a distinct possibility of snow at any time. The ground could be slippery and treacherous underfoot and easily cause a horse to miss its fooling and break a leg. On top of all those things there was little cover, so tracking and sneaking up on animals was difficult. Apart from that, it was fine! My glum feeling must have shown on my face.

"Come on Lauren, cheer up. We're going on a hunt, that's all. I've done loads and you know I'm good. What can go wrong?"

"I wish you hadn't said that, sweetheart," I replied, shaking my head. "Okay, is the unit ready outside now?"

"Yes, all ready, your horse is being held by Verna."

"Verna! What's she doing in the patrol?"

"Taal asked if they could tag along, I said yes. Thought we could use an extra couple for the camps. You're not angry, are you?"

How could I be angry with Sheelan, she was lovely. "I'm sure she'll be okay, maybe even learn something if you can teach her."

Sheelan beamed back, delighted I had agreed without argument.

We assembled outside the palace ready to move. The day was slightly foggy, a haze of it hung in the air and that brought a chill with it. Horses scraped the ground with the hooves impatiently causing the harnesses to jangle, their breath vaporising as it was snorted from their nostrils to drift and mingle with the fog.

Bran was about to shout "Mount Up", or something similar

to get us sitting on horses, when Rheanna walked out of a house with Fane holding one of her hands. She had been keeping herself scarce for a long time, even Fane had begun growing up.

"Good morning, Highness. I am sorry for the fright I gave you a while back, nobody had told me not to call you by your title."

"They beat mummy for not telling them, they thought she knew you were in the fort and was helping hide you," Fane said. "I had to tend her wounds."

"I'm sorry you suffered, it wasn't your fault. Are you well now?"

"Yes, thank you my Queen. Shaila rubbed ointment on after cleaning the cuts. Fane and I found your lovely swords and brought them to your palace but you weren't there. So I hid them in the mattress. I was going to tell you that day but you all went running away. I'm sorry."

"It was you that saved them then? Alyssa, Sheelan and I all thank you from our hearts. It's such a relief having them back."

"I see you wear them now, Highnesses," Rheanna said. "They are so beautiful. We found them by accident while out looking for herbs. A glow came from under a bush and when we looked, there they were. I think they called us because they never glowed after that."

"Thank you again, Rheanna. How are you, Fane?"

"I like it here, Queen Lauren. I wish my father was with us."

"Where *is* Damarion, Rheanna?"

"We don't know, Highness. Caractacus came to ask his help a few years ago and they went off with a big group of Silurians. We've heard nothing since."

"Caractacus escaped after being beaten in battle and was going to the north for help, but I've not heard anything about Damarion. Agricola never mentioned him, so perhaps he's still free? Venutius is still fighting in the north, maybe he knows something? Have heart my dear woman. Look after

244

your mother, young man, you've grown since I last saw you. Goodbye to you both, I'll see you when we get back."

I went to Alyssa and hugged her. "Goodbye my love, we'll see you soon. Are you sure you'll be well with the guard left for you?"

"I would rather be coming with you, darling. You know what happened before when you left the fort, you never returned for most of a full seasons cycle, it was unbearable."

"We have our special swords, as you have, don't ever take it off while we're away A dozen or so deer should see us through until the spring." We kissed, and through it came her concerns, her fear of losing us as she had before.

I held her tightly. "We'll be extra careful and think of you all the time, my love, won't we, Sheelan." I kissed her eyes, once on each lid, then her lips.

"You haven't done that for a long time, thank you, darling. A very special way of bidding me goodbye. Now allow me to say my special goodbye." Her eyes opened wide, a strange aura enfolded them as they searched deep into my body. Her lips touched my heart and the world left my senses for a few brief moments.

A gasp left me. "That was amazing, Alyssa, something you have never done before. Thank you."

Alyssa took Sheelan into an embrace and bid her the same farewell. "Look after yourselves, both of you. I love you," Alyssa said through her tears.

We tore ourselves away. It felt as if my heart was being taken and hugged by Alyssa, which made my departure much harder. Sheelan must have felt the same.

The early morning mist clung to the ground, hiding it and the horse's hooves from sight. Tendrils swirled among us as our movements disturbed it. A horse snorted here and there, adding their brand of mist as their breath changed into diaphanous vapour. People spoke in hushed tones as suspense held the group in its grip.

Bran approached. "May I take the patrol out, Highnesses?"

For some reason my heart stayed heavy and I sighed. "Yes,

carry on, Leader." I turned as we rode out, waving back at Alyssa, who in turn blew a kiss after us. That sight reminded me of the last time I left her here, not to see her for months on end and then come back to find her desperately ill and aged. I wished she would have come along but there was a land dispute that had to be resolved urgently. I wasn't prepared to let Sheelan go off alone, I knew only too well how things can change very abruptly in a forest.

The mist hung on for ages. Bran called a halt for a lunch break at an area with forest both sides slightly above the track on rising ground, which meant the main group could stay away from the right-hand side and allow a hunting party to go off searching for prey.

"I'll take Greta, Kwail and Mona, Lauren," Sheelan said. "See you soon." She hugged me as she placed a kiss on each cheek, then turned calling names out.

The small group walked down the hillside and almost vanished into the mist that still hung in the hollow of the road. I realised they all had longbows. Having been in a trance of worry for them I felt at least one should have taken a cross bow. I called, but perhaps the mist prevented my voice reaching them, they disappeared into the trees.

Taal and Verna got a fire going and made tea. They began cooking a quick meal so I watched them with interest, mainly because I liked Taal and didn't want to see her used in some way. But they seemed to chat away and worked well together. I moved to the fire for a little warmth.

"The sky's got dark, Highness."

Taal's voice broke into my thoughts of Alyssa back at the fort.

"I hadn't noticed, Taal."

She indicated with an arm the heavy clouds coming in from the north. "Looks like it might snow, Majesty."

I nodded vaguely. We had hunted in snow many times so it wasn't a problem. My mind went to the night hunt with Germaine and her clan, how that had changed so quickly and how Madeil fought the pack of wolves that attacked us so well, of how Wolfy had helped barking or howling in the direction he knew an attack would manifest from. I wondered where he and his pack were now? Our unit had no such protection, Omen was too young and had stayed with Alyssa at the palace, A kiss on my cheek woke me from my wanderings, it was Squirrel.

"Here is some tea and warm soup in a bowl for you, Lauren."

I retuned her smile. "Thank you, Handmaiden Squirrel." I was teasing her, but she liked me to a little, I think she felt it made us closer.

"You looked so far away then, may I ask what you were thinking about?"

"That night hunt with Germaine, Madeil and Wolfy."

She sat next to me, so close her body touched mine. "I prefer it at the fort with you, Lauren. I've done lots of things I would never have with Germaine. She's a lovely woman, but never allowed me to go on hunts."

"That's because she thinks a lot of you, Squirrel, she didn't want you hurt."

"But you let me come?"

"That is so you can gain experience, not because I don't like you."

"Do you?"

"Do I what?"

"Like me..." She blushed red looking down at the ground, thinking she may have overstepped the mark.

"Of course I do, why do you think I made you my Handmaiden. I would hardly have chosen somebody I didn't like in your position, would I?"

She smiled and rested her head on my shoulder. "That was because you didn't want me to be alone, Lauren. It was kind of you." She cuddled closer.

The yell from the road caught my attention and fortunately broke Squirrel's course of action, whatever it might have been.

Sheelan and her group were returning. All seemed well and

two of them had deer across their shoulders.

She grinned as she let her load drop to the ground. "A quick hunt and two skins already. Are we staying here overnight, Lauren?"

"You decide, you're the boss. Tell Bran what you want to do so she can organise the camp."

"We will then. I'll take the same group with me in the morning. It's getting dark early, isn't it?"

"Taal said it looks like snow. But that shouldn't worry you, sweetheart. We've hunted in worse conditions."

"We've had a good few narrow squeaks as well because of bad weather. But for you, Lauren, we could have been in trouble."

I laughed. "What do you mean, could have been, we were! Go get you and your team some soup, it'll warm you up. Did you tell Bran to organise camp?"

"No, I haven't seen her."

"You don't need to, use your skill. Tell her by thought, go on, you need to learn to use that power given you."

She had that daft grin on her face. "I will then," she said with determination, screwing her face up and closing her eyes tightly, she thought deeply.

Bran appeared. "You wish us to stay overnight, Highness Sheelan. I'll get the camp set up in that case." Bran went around detailing individuals off for jobs, soon we were settled. She came back to Sheelan. "I've told a few people to mount guard but to change over or call either you or Queen Lauren, if anything of note occurs. Is that well, Majesty?"

"Oh... err... um, yes, of course, Leader, thank you." Sheelan blushed for some reason.

"Why did you blush?" I asked.

"It seems so wrong me ordering people about, that's all, sweetheart."

"You're Queen Sheelan now, but you didn't order, you asked very nicely, there's a lot of difference. Now to bed, I'll cuddle you tonight as you caught our food. Who is Squirrel sharing with?"

"Bran, Aulus never came. Now you don't have to worry and take her under your wing."

Camp settled. Sheelan was lovely and warm as she tucked her bottom into my tummy. My arm slid over her, she sighed and was soon asleep.

A wolf howled somewhere. It made me wonder if Omen was well. She was probably tucked up nice and warm in the palace.

A kiss on my shoulder woke me. It was Squirrel. "It snowed overnight, Lauren. Bran's gone on a hunt, said it would give Sheelan a break and let her lie in. I was cold on my own, so got up."

I wasn't really awake. "What time is it?" I asked, rubbing my eyes with my knuckles.

"Shortly after dawn, Lauren."

"Just after dawn. Is anybody else up?"

"Only two guards, I'm on my own."

What could I do with her? Why didn't she stay under the furs? "Come in and lie behind me then. Be quiet, try not to wake Sheelan, she had a busy day yesterday."

She was extremely cold.

"How long have you been outside?'

'Some time, Lauren. I was hoping they'd be quick, like Sheelan was on her hunt, but there's been so sign of them."

'How deep is the snow?" As I asked that question, her cheek rested on my shoulder blade. It was freezing.

"Deeper than my feet. I couldn't see the track at all." She was shivering violently.

"Get in between me and Sheelan, we'll warm you up."

She crawled over me a lot more slowly than she should have, I felt. "Should I cuddle Sheelan?"

"Of course, her body will warm you one side, mine the other."

Sheelan stirred as Squirrel's arm went over but didn't wake.

I pushed my body close and my arm pulled her in. I was surprised just how cold she was, Squirrel must have been alone out there for ages. "Is that better?"

"Mmm, yes, it's wonderful, Lauren. Thank you."

"I meant, is it warmer for you. I need you to stop shivering like this, it's a sign of hypothermia. You've worked in the hospital so know what it is."

If she had been hanging about in the snow and cold wind and hypothermia had set in, her organs could begin shutting down and Squirrel might die. My concern increased.

"Who's got hypowhatsits, and why is my back so cold?" Sheelan asked curiously.

"Squirrel, we must warm her up, sweetheart."

Sheelan rolled over, and I could see Squirrel thought she was in trouble. But Sheelan cuddled her closely. "You are, aren't you? Can't have you that cold, we'll warm you."

Squirrel, who had been as tense as a board, at last relaxed. A sigh passed her lips.

We must have gone to sleep. I awoke to shouting outside. The tent flaps erupted as Bran poked her head in. "Three deer, Highness, a good hunt. There are a lot of tracks in the snow."

"What of, Leader?" I asked.

"A mix of wolves and bears, mainly wolves though. I guess very many, too many to identify," She finished, worry lines on her face.

That could mean anything, even a super pack. It had happened before in a winter when food was hard to come by and wolves amalgamated for better results. But from our last two hunts there seemed to be plenty of deer about to keep them busy.

"I'll get Taal and the others up for breakfast, Highness." Tent flaps hung loose again.

My attention returned to Squirrel. She had stopped shivering at last, but I felt she would be better between us for a while longer. I noticed she had gone to sleep. "I wonder if she slept last night?" I whispered to Sheelan.

"She didn't even wake when Bran came in and she wasn't quiet. How does Bran sleep, Lauren?"

"Light, from my recollections in the southern forest, so she may move a lot and get up and down checking on things. I don't want Squirrel so tired she gets into danger, that's very easy to do out here. She got very cold waiting outside, can't have that either, she's a good helper and our Handmaiden now. Would you mind if she shared with us? We can take it in turns being in the middle."

"I think a lot of Squirrel, Lauren, so want her to be safe. She's welcome here while on this patrol. But what about Bran?"

"Lark can go in with her, let's see how they get on. Would you slip out and see what conditions are like, please?"

Sheelan wasn't gone long. "Thick snow, Lauren, and a cutting wind, no wonder she got frozen," she said, nodding at Squirrel. "One thing about it is we can see deer tracks easier and find them quicker. Bran's had the others process the deer."

"Get the offal well away from us. If there's a big pack around, we don't want to bring them into camp."

"Bran's sent Taal, Verna, Lark and Uva out already, all armed on horseback."

I popped outside to see the weather conditions for myself, they weren't good.

Nianda appeared with some porridge. "Here, have some hot breakfast to warm you up, Highness. Oh, I didn't realised Squirrel was with you," she said as she peered into the tent. "I'll get her one."

I went back in, gently shook her shoulder and whispered in her ear. "Squirrel, breakfast."

She rolled, put both arms around my neck and kissed me on my lips. "Oh, Highness... I mean Lauren... I mean... I'm sorry, I didn't realise it was you."

"It's okay, here's some warm porridge. Who did you think it was?"

"I was dreaming, I'm sorry. I should have brought you

251

your breakfast," she stammered.

"Did you sleep better with us?" I avoided asking who she was dreaming of, the reply might have embarrassed her.

She blushed full red. "Yes, thank you both. Bran's a terrible fidget."

"You'll stay with us from now on, in that case and at all times. If we hunt, you come along."

She grinned from ear to ear. "Thank you both again. I'll love that."

Bran called the mount up once the offal party were back and we set off for the next forest. I looked across Squirrel to Sheelan. "Bears, do you remember?"

"Only too well. Isn't this where Brevit saved you, Lauren?"

I nodded. "Yes, it is, and gave her life. What a woman she was."

Sheelan nodded. "Many would do the same, people admire you my love, Madeil did, too. She was lovely. I'm your bodyguard, so my life is dedicated to you, as I believe Alyssa's is. I liked Brevit, even though she was short on conversation," she ended, with a grin.

"She was a courageous woman, always led patrols, I don't know how she did it. I do miss them all."

"Make camp," came Bran's shouted command.

Chapter Twenty Four

Lost!

The next small forest hove into view, the one where the flood had occurred, so we were near the huge southern forest. That brought back memories of our journey through it to the Wolfa village, the fight with a raiding party, herb patrol and the disastrous journey back. Bran's run in with that enormous boar, her terrible injury and then the attack from the Babrani, who I named the Shield People, that cost most of the patrol their liberty, leaving Madeil, Bran and me free after we dashed into the trees. Even though we travelled a great distance through it, I knew little of what was in there. When we had to run from hunters it seemed never-ending, until we came out farther south into the mountainous area where Germaine's clan lived. However, that was only one direction, there were large tracts of it undiscovered in which to lose your way.

"You're in that mile place," Sheelan whispered very close to my ear.

It forced a smile from me, Madeil would have said exactly that. "Yes, memories of the southern forest."

"Bran told me a lot about that time, when you were trying to live and not doing very well. Madeil hunted then, didn't she?"

"Both her and Bran, once we found Lalena they could go together and I still had someone with me at camp. Until then, it was Maddy. You have so many of her ways, her character and even the things you say and way you look. You're a joy to me, Sheelan."

She gave a broad smile back. "Thank you, my love. I'll get a team together, might as well go as soon as possible."

"Add me to it, and Squirrel, it will give her experience and us a chance to see what she's like."

"Okay, six then, that's right, isn't it?" Sheelan asked.

I nodded. "I must get you counting higher than you twelve, try to make a hundred."

She vanished, I went and filled quivers. Checking my straddle bags and rifle were supplied, I mounted.

The team surrounded me. "We're ready, Lauren," Sheelan said. "We'll enter over there," she finished, indicating a gap between some fir trees.

We crossed the track, our horses sliding slightly in the deep snow, wary of their footing. Once under the canopy they found it easier, not much snow got through, although it did in patches.

I stopped beside one and was shocked at the number of wolf prints in it, and blood to one side where a deer had been taken down, dragged here and eaten.

Sheelan led, checking the ground and changing direction as needed. She held an arm up, so we stopped.

"Leave our horses here with Kwail and Uva to guard them. There is a small herd nearby we should be able to hit hard. Once we start, only hand signals, so watch me."

"Keep an arrow in your bows," I said to the two guards. "And stand your ground with a wolf, don't ever turn and run, they will kill you for sure."

Sheelan went stealthily on with Squirrel, Greta and me following as quietly as mice.

I was surprised at Squirrel, she copied Sheelan perfectly, she had a good grasp of a hunt.

Sheelan's forearm went vertically, meaning stop dead.

Had she seen the herd? There was nothing in sight.

Then the howl came drifting through the trees.

Wolves!

Goose bumps ran down my back causing an involuntary shiver.

A hand took one of mine, it was Squirrel.

Her eyes were wide open, any wider and her eyes may have popped out.

I gave it a squeeze and smiled. It was then I noticed she'd gone as white as the snow on the track.

Another howl from a different direction, then another on our right. They were all around us.

I suddenly wished I had brought the rifle instead of a longbow, but an arrow is silent and it's often possible to get another shot off for a second deer. But not with a gun, the first bang would scare the whole herd away and we would just see their tails scampering into the distance.

"We're surrounded," Sheelan said quietly. "Keep in a tight group and try to get back to the horses."

Steady progress for a while, but then howling began behind us and a line of around forty animals stood barring our way.

Looking over my shoulder I saw a further mass coming in from the rear, possible two or three hundred. "Keep tight," I said loudly, there was no point in being silent anymore.

Squirrel certainly did that, she was shaking like a leaf in fear. I had to do something, but what?

"Sheelan, go to the back, draw your sword. I'll go to the front and Squirrel and Greta must stay between us."

Two swords rasped out of their scabbards, glowing silently in our hands to warn us of danger.

The wolf packs had closed the gap, they were only about ten to fifteen feet away in either direction. A group of five moved nearer to me from the front pack. A large, black animal stepped forwards, quivering lips dragged back to display impressive sets of incisors and a few fangs. Red gums stayed moist with saliva as it ran down. Snarls became almost continuous.

I held my sword out in front of me, ready to plunge it into the beast's heart, a movement that brought even louder snarls and snapping teeth, it's evil eyes glaring in anticipation.

The animal too a few steps forward and my sword tip almost touched its head. I knew it would be impossible to kill every one, but Sheelan and I would take as many with us as possible.

Another snarl and snap. It jumped forwards, touching the sword blade as it cunningly ducked underneath to stand inside my guard, about a foot away.

The blade of my weapon began glowing, brighter and brighter until it appeared to be red hot. Yet the hilt was as cold as ice to my touch, even though it glowed as the sword did.

The wolf wasn't spared heat. It leaped upwards, swivelling and gyrating in pain, smoke issued from its fur as it began burning. Yelps echoed around our ears until finally, it lay at my feet, dead.

Another black wolf came on, but kept its distance, issuing snarls and an odd sneezing as its fury escalated.

"Come on then," I snapped back. "You're just cowards if this amount can't take just four of us." I heard Sheelan utter something similar behind me. "Stay close Squirrel."

She was so tight against me I think every time my body moved, hers did as well. Her fear came through the contact, a violent trembling, a quick glance at her face showed sheer terror in it.

"I... I will, Lauren. I'm frightened."

I released one hand from my sword, slipped the arm around her waist and cuddled her. "We'll be okay."

Our horses should have been in sight by now, but the place we left them in was empty.

"Where have they gone?" I called back to Sheelan. Then I saw the bloody mess a short distance farther on. My heart sank. I hoped it was a horse, but the trousers lying on the ground told a different story. Either Uva or Kwail had died here, or both, but there wasn't enough carnage for two humans and their horses.

"If they had any sense they would have got on the horses and galloped off," Sheelan called back.

She had to know. "One of them has been taken," I shouted back.

A silence hung between us for a few seconds. "Bloody wolves," Sheelan burst out. "Who?"

I couldn't answer, my fury was building up and anger captured my heart. There were plenty of deer here, why take a human? I couldn't control myself any longer and moving at a trot began slashing out across my front with my sword.

Cries and yelps rang in my ears. A backhanded swipe took out another dozen. Realising they were now the ones with fear in their hearts, I charged.

Wolves fled in all directions amid cries of pain. Many lay dead along my path of attack. Over a hundred animals disappeared into the trees to stop and glare at me, their eyes illuminating, ghastly, threatening.

Moving to Sheelan's side, I shot her a glance and nodded my head at the massive pack before her.

She bent and kissed me. "Lest we fall, I love you."

Kissing her cheek, I repeated, "Should we die this day. I love you, too."

Greta tugged my sleeve, a pleading look on her face.

I kissed her cheek, then Squirrels.

"In case we all die this day, but we won't, Sheelan and I are going to attack this time, so stay close behind us, but out of our sword's way."

They nodded rapidly. "Yes, Lauren," Squirrel said. "We will, won't we Greta?"

By the look on Greta's face, she had no idea what she was doing, abject terror shone from her eyes.

Sheelan stretched her sword arm, I copied her. "Ready, Lauren?"

A nod confirmed I was.

"Charge!" she bellowed.

Using our now glowing swords like scythes, which to all intents and purposes they had become, we ran into the throng.

Screams and howls of pain and fear erupted from the horde of grey and black as we rampaged through it. Turning around the other side showed how effective our weapons had been.

Heaps of bodies lay strewn about. Some went limping off whimpering, others yelping in pitiful tones. It was a sad sound, like a puppy makes when hurt or in fear. But many more stood their ground, although visibly shaken by our actions. Now they were very uncertain of us.

"Again?" Sheelan asked.

"Yes, we must scare them off as far as possible. Now!"

As we ran I felt the sword trembling, the heat from its blade singeing fur, their ears or noses, anything it came near, got burned.

This time the whole mass retreated, but only as far as the gloom of the forest hid them from view.

"Which way, Lauren?" Sheelan asked.

"We can't go east or west, so maybe south to try and skirt around them." My heart was grieving for whoever had been killed and hoped the other had managed to get the horses back to camp safely. Slipping my sword back into its scabbard, I viewed the scene.

"Do you think the rest will try to find us?" Squirrel asked, a quaver in her voice.

"I have no idea, Squirrel. They may have been attacked as well. We have no idea how large this pack is, big by the look of it. Stay close to me, Greta can stay beside Sheelan, that way you'll both have a sword for protection."

"They glowed, Lauren," Squirrel said in a hushed, reverential voice pointing at our swords. "As if they are magic. Yours killed that first wolf without touching it. Is that because you're a Goddess?"

"More likely due to our weapons being empowered by the Gods. We had an incident at the Stones Altar. It gave Sheelan greater powers, like Alyssa's and mine. At least we do have a defence."

"South then," Sheelan said, and we began walking.

Our group tried several times to go east, but every instance was blocked by wolves who were tracking along with us.

"Will they come again?" Greta asked.

258

"They're keeping their distance at the moment, not being sure of us makes them wary. We have defeated them twice and they may not understand why. If the pack decides we are too hard a nut to crack they could leave for easier pickings," I replied. My knowledge of wolves told me it's best to face them out, it makes them wonder why we do that, instead of running, like their usual prey does, our boldness makes them uncertain.

"We have no water," Sheelan pointed out. "Where was that stream?"

I huffed out. "Westwards I think, but I've no idea where we are, I've never been in this part of the forest before. The packs are keeping us on this heading which is worrying, are they leading us into a trap, perhaps an even bigger pack?"

Sheelan stared upwards. "It's gone midday. We can't walk forever, Lauren. Any ideas?"

"We could charge them again, but the gain will be small, they reform. I wonder where our horses went?"

"To gallop out?" Greta said, hopefully.

Her voice surprised me, it was almost the first time she had spoken since the debacle began. "Mine has my firestick on it, Greta. I might be able to shoot our way out. We have full quivers, but they won't last long if we're cut off, we need food, so must hunt, which means we must conserve our arrows."

"We can't do that with wolves all around," Sheelan pointed out.

"Listen," I replied. "What do you hear?"

Sheelan gaped at me. "Nothing, Lauren."

"Exactly. Especially west of us. That section of the pack seems to have moved off. I wonder what for?"

"The camp," Squirrel stated flatly.

"That's east somewhere?" Sheelan said. "We've walked for ages, the forest has even changed, it's much denser here, the wolves can get nearer."

"I haven't heard them for a while. They often snap at each other but there's been none of that. Let's move west a little, see what's over there."

"I'm not sure where west is, Lauren. The sun's hidden by clouds, so we could be anywhere."

By mid-afternoon trees had thinned so that bracken and grass grew. "We're not going to make the camp today, even without wolves in the way," I said. "We'll have to make a shelter."

The group looked blankly back.

"I'll show you. Find a forked tree with two trunks from ground level. Cut long branches to form a lean-to, use daggers to cut vines stems for rope to tie them with, then cover that with evergreen branches with the outer end facing down, that keeps rain off. Collect bracken and fern leaves for inside and to cover us with. Sheelan, would you collect pine needles and acorns, if there are any left after the animals have foraged and any other leaves with moisture in them, I'll get some mould and dirt. We need to cover our scent, so they have to be crushed with a stone or chunk of tree, then rubbed on us. If they can't smell us, they won't come looking."

"How do we cut branches down, Lauren, we have no saw?" Greta piped up.

"Like this," I replied, drawing my sword and taking a swipe at one. The weapon cut it clean through. Another swipe at the cut end gave us something to crush our leaves with. "Sheelan will hunt after that, maybe take Squirrel or Greta with her."

"I'll go." Greta volunteered.

"Sheelan will teach you well, Greta, go and learn. Now Squirrel, it's just you and me. Our job is to make a home, bed it out, set up a cooking frame and wait for them to come back."

She came close and put her arms around my waist. "I'm frightened, Lauren. What will happen to us?"

My arms enclosed her to me. "We'll make out, you'll see. When I was in here before with Madeil, Bran and Lalena we got into tighter scrapes than this and survived." We hadn't furs, which was a concern, it can get cold at night. "Come on, let's start work."

Squirrel was good, she got on with things, whipped the tree branches together well with creeper stems. The hut frame got erected quickly, as did our cooking frame ready for when the other two came back. And that was a point, they had been away ages, far longer than I expected. A worrying feeling began forming in the pit of my stomach. Sheelan had her sword, so unless something terrible had occurred they ought to be fine. But our situation was one none of us had been in before, so anything might crop up. I didn't mention that to Squirrel. We would survive for a day without food and water at a pinch.

"Where is Sheelan?" Squirrel asked. "It will be night soon."

"Sheelan is very capable of looking after herself, Squirrel. She'll make a camp like this and camouflage it, as we have ours. She'll also have one on watch all night, take it in turns, although knowing her, she'll do a Brevit and take it all on her shoulders."

"We have no food or water."

"I know, but going without food for a little while won't hurt us. We must find water tomorrow though, otherwise we'll dehydrate."

"What's that, Lauren?"

"When our bodies get too short on water, that causes organ shut down and we don't want that. Get into the shelter, I'll give you a cuddle."

"I'm ever so thirsty."

I sorted around the ground and found two round pebbles. Using my tunic to clean them, gave her one. "Suck that, it will help sweetheart. I won't light a fire until we're all together again, then we will make our scent inhibitor juice."

Poor Squirrel looked totally dejected. This had turned into a very dangerous hunting patrol, us all split up and one possibly killed. I hoped the other guard had escaped back to camp, and Sheelan away with Greta was looking after them both.

Chapter Twenty Five

The Power of Thought

"Where is Sheelan and Greta, shouldn't they be back by now, it's night time."

A sigh left me. "I don't know, Squirrel. I'll try to make contact." Closing my eyes, the vision of Sheelan came into my mind. What was she doing up a tree? I wondered.

"We were attacked by a pack, Lauren. I fought off several but there are too many. Greta's okay, she's up in the tree with me but we can't get down, they are lying on the ground below waiting. What can I do, my love?"

"It's almost dark, you're better off staying where you are. Try to get some sleep and we'll sort something out after dawn. I love you."

"I'll call you when we're ready. Goodnight my love. Are you two safe?"

"We have the shelter made so will sleep in it. We do need water urgently though. Goodnight, be safe."

"What did she say, Lauren?"

"They're up a tree, so off the ground. There are wolves hanging about so they are best off staying there, it's safer, Squirrel."

Squirrel got into the shelter, I followed. Neither us seemed sleepy after the events of the day, so I propped myself up against a tree trunk. Squirrel came tight next to me.

"May I stay close, Lauren?" She sounded terrified still.

"Lie down, rest your head in my lap. I'll pull some bracken over us, it will help keep our body's warm."

It was totally dark now, I couldn't see much farther than the entrance of our shelter. I drew my sword and lay it beside

263

me, ready.

A noise woke me. I must have dozed off so took a hold of the sword hilt ready to defend us. It didn't glow, which was odd if an enemy was near. "Who is it?"

Silence.

Another slight sound, then a huge nose entered the shelter.

"Ahh," I cried out, then realised what it was. A horse.

"Whe.. wher.. what is it," Squirrel stuttered.

"A horse, I wonder where that came from?" I squeezed out to check. It was mine, the rifle was along its side. "How the hell..." I mused.

"What's hell?"

"A place in the future, Squirrel, an expression. What I meant was, how did it get over here and find us. I'm pleased it did though, now we have transport, my lovely little Handmaiden. I'll tie it to this tree lightly, if a wolf comes along it can break free and escape. Now we should get some sleep, or you should at least. Lay down again, is that comfortable?"

A soft sigh left her. "Yes Lauren, thank you."

A whinny woke me, it was daylight outside and plainly no wolves had been near because the horse was still tethered. Sheelan hadn't been in touch so maybe they were walking back.

Then another whinny from further away. My horse returned it and out of the trees came two more. "Our horses are back, some of them, anyway, there's one missing, assuming the other was ridden back."

Squirrel emerged from the shelter. She smiled at me. "Thank you, Lauren, for letting me sleep in your lap. I don't feel so afraid when you're beside me."

I gave her a cuddle. "You've done well, Squirrel. Now, we'll tie a horse to the one you'll ride and I'll take mine. Let's go find Sheelan."

My mind tried to connect, but failed, so I hoped they were okay and not in trouble. A sigh left me, although I didn't have a feeling of foreboding.

"We're awake and still up the tree," Sheelan's thoughts came through. *"The wolves are still below waiting, maybe hoping to starve us out."*

"Is it a good solid tree?"

"Not bad, why?"

"I'll send a high wind. Can you try to find out if the Voice gave you a power, like Alyssa's and mine?"

"I'll try," Sheelan replied. *"There's a big wolf just below us, a black one, they seem to be worse than the others, maybe the leader. Ouch!"*

"Why did you say ouch?"

"A streak of something shot out of my fingers and hit it. It made me jump, but the wolf yelped and ran away."

"I think you have the power to eject electricity, do it again."

There was a pause.

"It worked. Wow, that's brilliant. We're not far away. I killed a small deer, it's up the tree with us. Send your wind please, I'll use that electriywhatsits and see if we can get back."

My vision went into the cavern, there to find the swirling wind, turning it into a vortex. Faster and faster it spun, widening at the top, picking up the floor dust as its strength increased. I flipped my head forwards, the whirlwind shot out of the cavern.

Squirrel and I sat quietly on our horses, then a cheer came through the trees and they were walking towards us. Sheelan, as promised, with a deer across her shoulders. She dropped it at her feet and dashed to hug me.

"It worked, my love, the wind and those Nodens things, the wolves fled. There is a river farther over, it's where I got the deer. And where did you find horses?"

"They found us. You can either have one each and Squirrel can ride behind me, or you and Greta can share."

"I'll ride behind you, Lauren," Squirrel said as quick as lightning.

I smiled to myself.

There was a small river. Squirrel got a mug out of my straddle bags while Sheelan and me made a frame to cook the meat over. Greta sliced it up.

"We won't get dehyberated now, will we, Lauren," Squirrel stated.

It brought a smile to my face. "No, we won't, Squirrel. We should drink our fill though, as much as possible, before we move off."

"We must backtrack, Lauren," Sheelan said. "I hope the camp is well?"

I nodded agreement. Following our meal and another drink, our group began the journey back. It didn't seem so far on a horse, soon that patch of bloody tissue lay before us. I slid off my mount.

"May the Gods of Otherworld care for our fallen companion. She is a good soul, please welcome her, mend her injuries as only you, our Gods, can. Now I ask you to guide us to our camp and hope in my heart it is safe and our friends well. Thank you, my Gods."

The day had brightened, a weak sun filtered down.

"This way," Sheelan said.

At a guess, it took us half an hour's steady ride before the forest suddenly cleared and our horses stood on the track ankle deep in snow.

A cry went up and many ran towards us. Bran was first.

"What happened, Highness? I've been worried and was going in with a patrol today. Thank the Gods you're well."

"We're fine if a little shaken up. Did you have any problems with the wolf pack?"

She looked blankly back. "No, Highness, it's been quiet, apart from some howling in the forest."

It had to be said. "I have to report one of us was eaten by the wolf pack during a fight we had with them. It was either Kwail or Uva. Did one or the other make it back?"

"Highness?" Bran queried, she sounded puzzled

"We had to fight, but when we got back to where we had left guards with our horses, they weren't there and bones and a pair of trousers littered the ground. Our horses must have bolted, they came back to us last night, Leader."

"They are both here, my Queen," Bran replied, indicating with an arm. "They came back both riding a horse late yesterday, so we knew you had a fight, they said they heard it. But it was too late to go out searching by then."

I stared at Bran. "Both here! Then what was that mess on the ground?"

Uva and Kwail walked to us. "We saw them coming so mounted up. Kwail killed one with a single sword blow, but one grabbed onto her trouser leg so she calmly took them off, she was impressive, Highness. They immediately set upon the one she killed, that must have been what you saw."

I leaped off my horse and hugged the pair. "Thank the Gods for that, I am so pleased you're both well. There's what's left of a deer on that horse, we only had a little, so why not cook it."

Bran put her arms on my shoulders. "You look exhausted, Highness, go and have a sleep, go on, you and Queen Sheelan, Squirrel looks worn out as well."

"Thank you, Leader, we will. I leave the camp in your very safe hands. I think Greta should sleep as well, we'll take her in with us."

Bran let us sleep. It was dark when I woke. Squirrel was tucked in between us and she and Sheelan were still asleep Greta was being cuddled by Sheelan. Shouting outside got me up, I squeezed out from behind Squirrel so as not to wake her.

There was a big fire in the camp. Walking up the gentle slope towards it was Bran and a few others, each had a deer.

She grinned as she dropped her load. "A good late hunt, Highness, three more. Another hunt after a move in the morning should do it, then we can return to the fort."

"I can't say I'll be sorry, Leader. It's been an interesting patrol."

"You all got back, that's the main thing."

A howling rang through the night air. "Watch your backs tonight, Bran," I said.

Waking, I rubbed my eyes, sat up, realising it seemed very bright. Peering out of the tent I saw why. To my horror, it was thick snow. As I moved, Squirrel woke.

"I'll get your breakfast, Lauren," she muttered, still groggy with sleep.

Touching her arm, I kept her lying. "Let one of the others bring it, there is heavy snow outside."

Tent flaps opened to reveal Bran's face. She wasn't smiling, which was unusual. "The wolves are back, Highness."

Damn it. "Thank you, Leader. What measures have you taken?"

"I've set up a perimeter, but there aren't many of us to do that. Also getting a fire lit and something to eat. Taal and Verna are doing the fire, Nianda and I have begun breaking camp and all the rest guarding. I'm thinking of taking Kwail out and pairing her with Nianda, she's a lot to do. That means this many," Bran finished, holding eight fingers up.

"We'll all help, Leader, tell us what you need."

"You, Highness? Are you sure?"

"We're all in this together, so of course. Perhaps we could be a roving guard unit?"

Bran nodded. A good idea, Highness." She left, shouting out "Kwail."

Shortly afterwards, the diminutive woman looked through our tent flaps. "Leader told me to bring you all porridge, Highness. Here, nice and warm."

"Thank you, Kwail, and well done for getting away from the wolves. I thought you had been killed, that made me very sad."

"'Squirrel said you gave an appeasement for me, that was kind, Highness."

I smiled back. "You're a lovely person, of course I would make a verbal offering if it ever happened. I am very pleased it didn't, though."

"Good morning Squirrel. How are you today?"

"Me? Oh... err... I'm well, thank you Kwail."

"We should have a chat soon, you can tell me what it's like being the Queen's Handmaiden."

Squirrel grinned. "We should, very soon, and I will. Thank you, Kwail."

"You may have found a friend, Squirrel. Don't let her offer pass. Go now if you like, she's helping Nianda."

"May I? Thank you, Lauren." She disappeared out of the tent.

"We need to get up and on guard duty, sweetheart," I whispered in Sheelan's ear.

She moaned a bit, but got up, slipped sandals on and we left the tent. Nianda, Kwail and Squirrel began packing it.

"On horseback, my love, we can get to any point of guard quicker." As my mount circled around the outside perimeter, I noticed the multitude of wolf prints in the snow, but there were no wolves in sight now. A howl came from within the trees.

"Mount Up!" Bran yelled, and within a few minutes we left the scene and close calls. "I'll stop beside the next forest where Queen Sheelan hunted, might get another couple there, Highness."

It took less than five minutes to lose sight of the track. Horses began stumbling, slipping and sliding all over. The trouble was the track, wherever it was, had been badly rutted and when our mounts did find it, the ground was very uneven. That situation begged for a broken leg, a false move and a horse would be down.

Sheelan called a halt. "This is terrible, Lauren. We might as well stop as go on before we have an accident."

"We can't stop here, sweetheart. There's little shelter from the wind. Why don't you use one of your powers?"

"Powers! What powers, Lauren?"

"Your power over trees."

"You want me to ask the trees to move?" Sheelan replied, giggling. "They won't do that, will they?" She wasn't sure.

"I don't think so, but something simpler perhaps?"

"Like what? For some to grow right beside us?"

"What lives on trees?"

Her face it up. "Squirrels. But how can they help?"

"What else, think, sweetheart."

"Birds?" It was an uncertain question with an upward lilt at the end of the word.

"Don't you remember Alyssa calling for help when we hit these conditions once?"

A smile slowly enveloped her face. "Ravens. Yes, I do remember." Her eyes closed, she sat perfectly still on her horse.

A loud Caw came from some high branches, then another and another. Four Ravens flew down to land a few feet in front of her.

Sheelan must have heard their wings flapping. Her eyes opened, her face changed into an expression of disbelief. "Did I call those, Lauren?"

I nodded. "Nobody else did. Now tell them what you want."

"Oh... err, yes, what do I want?"

"A safe passage might be good."

"Yes, right, safe passage. Kind Ravens of the trees and caverns, would you please guide our horses along the track to the next forest, Thank you all." She looked at me, a daft grin on her face. "I feel a fool talking to birds, my love."

A bird flew up, along a bit farther, then settled on the ground flapping its wings. Another followed, going on more, so setting up a route. Then another and more even, all prancing and flapping about on what we assumed, was the line of track.

"Well I never," Bran said, "I never thought Queen Sheelan

could do that. Forward patrol, follow those birds."

"It worked, Lauren, I did it," Sheelan gasped in amazement. "I have the power of Alyssa, how wonderful."

"You're the one that's wonderful and yes, I guessed you had been given them at the Stones. It took a little encouragement to get you using them, that's all."

In no time we were beside the forest, stopped and dismounted.

"Thank you, kind Ravens," Sheelan said. Then, to her utter surprise, one flew onto her shoulder to rub its beak on her cheek as a kind of kiss. She giggled. "Go now, back to your flock and home. Farewell my friends."

The bird hopped along her arm and took off with a great flapping of wings, cawing back at Sheelan.

She sat on her horse with that delightful daft grin on her face. "It kissed me, Lauren."

"They are our friends, why shouldn't it. Such noble birds."

The group camped, Bran taking over to organised workloads. Taal and Verna got a fire going ready to cook as before, Addani and Artorius took up guard duties with Nianda and Kwail. Greta, Squirrel and Lark got the tents up and prepared for the night, which left Uva, Gannet and Mona at a loose end.

"I'll take them on a hunt, my love, before it gets dark. With luck we might get enough to return. We've been longer than planned, Alyssa will be concerned," Sheelan stated. "Come on, hunters, Uva, you use a crossbow, the rest longbows. See you soon, Lauren."

With that, they walked across the snow-covered track and disappeared into the trees.

Chapter Twenty Six

Uva

I relaxed in the tent. Sheelan was well capable of looking after her novice hunters, although I felt she should have taken Addani. Maybe she didn't want Artorius along, he was even less qualified at the art, for an art it most certainly was, and someone like him fumbling about would easily spook the prey.

Squirrels head appeared. "May I come in, Lauren?" She had tears in her eyes.

"Of course, you're my Handmaiden, you have no need to ask, you stay with me. What's the matter?"

As she sat next to me it came flooding out, tears galore.

I put my arms around her. "Tell me what's wrong, Squirrel, please."

"Ler... Ler... Lark said she didn't want me near her and I should stop talking to Kwail. I hadn't done anything, Lauren, just general chatter."

That was unfair and I wasn't going to have bullying in a small group, it could destroy our cohesion. "Would you go and chat to Taal and Verna please, I need to have words." I embraced the poor young woman and gave her a kiss on her cheek, she was plainly distraught. "Let me wipe your tears away. There, Squirrel, now go and find Taal, please."

She smiled weakly back. "Thank you."

Once she'd gone I went in search of Lark. She was sitting with Kwail, making up to her, so I could see why she didn't want Squirrel anywhere near. "Lark, go to my tent, immediately." I purposely snapped it out so she knew she was in hot water.

She stood, eyes wide open waiting for what I had to say.

"I will not tolerate bullying or rudeness in a patrol, not even in the fort," I said, once we had privacy. "Squirrel is my Handmaiden and I am not having her upset by petty disputes, especially about romances. You will go and apologise to her, straight after leaving me. What is wrong with her that you should decide who she should talk to and who she shouldn't? Has anybody given you that authority?"

"No, Highness."

"Everybody is free here, even I do not tell people what they should do in their personal lives so you should definitely not. If I find out it's happened again, you will be punished and ejected from the fort, because that kind of behaviour sows the seeds of dissent and that is intolerable. Do I make myself perfectly clear, Lark?"

Tears came. "I wanted Kwail to myself, Highness, and Squirrel kept butting in."

"She told me she was just talking. What you must understand, is Squirrel has been very lonely. It's one reason I made her my Handmaiden, so she had my company at least. Have you ever been totally alone, without friends? It's a horrible thing. She was just trying to make a friend or two, I told her to go and talk to people which she plainly did, so your attitude undermined my directive, a Royal Directive in fact, it means you disobeyed me. You cannot decide a person has to be yours and yours alone, that is slavery, especially if they don't want it. If you are attractive to Kwail then she'll accept you, if not, then leave her alone to choose her own friends, it's that simple. I have warned you, there will be no other. Heed my words, I mean them. Now get out of this tent and do what I told you. I am very displeased with you, Lark."

"Yes Highness, I will. Where is Squirrel now?"

"With Taal and Verna. Go and say sorry and mean it, not just a simple "I'm sorry", that would not be enough to mend hurt feelings and a heart."

She left. In a way I hated doing it but left to continue, it was an attitude that could catch on, and then many more would be throwing their weight around and telling others not

274

to speak to whoever they had the hots for.

Squirrel poked her head in. "Lark said she was very sorry, Lauren. I can speak to Kwail if I like."

I patted the space next to me. "What did you say?"

"That I thought she looked nice and was a pleasant person, and she does and is, I meant it as a compliment. I hoped it would get her talking to me. I'm still lonely, Lauren, not many do."

She looked totally miserable. I cuddled her. "I'm pleased you told me, I am very fond of you, Squirrel and don't like seeing you hurt. When we get home, you'll take up your duties to me and Sheelan again and live with the girls. Do they talk to you?"

She nodded. "I like it at the fort, both Selene and Fallow talk, and Agneta. I was only trying to be friendly, Lauren." Tears came again. The incident had gone deep.

I held her close. "I think you're lovely. If I wasn't Vowed to Alyssa and Sheelan, I would snap you up," I whispered, pulling her in tightly.

Two large eyes looked up at me. "Would you, wow, that's amazing, and you being a Goddess, too. Thank you, I feel a lot better now."

Someone was yelling. It was Sheelan.

I dashed out the tent, to see her waving her arms frantically. "Squirrel, get two longbows and quivers, quickly sweetheart."

The remainder of the camp ran over to find out what Sheelan was yelling about as Squirrel handed me the bows.

"One for me, one for you," I said, grinning. "Whatever is the matter, you're going to help me. Stay close, come on."

As we arrived at Sheelan I could see blood all down her front. "What's happened?" I asked, dread in my heart at the likely reply. I looked Sheelan over, but she had no wounds.

"It's Uva, Lauren. She's been attacked by two boars, she's badly hurt."

I turned and yelled at the mass the other side of the track. "Lark, bring two furs, quickly. Take me there, my love," I said to Sheelan.

"We were trying to get out to pick up the deer when those two monsters came charging out. Uva wasn't quick enough, she got tossed. Here she is."

Lark arrived. "Oh, by the Gods, look at her," she muttered, putting a hand over her mouth in horror.

Uva lay in the recovery position, put there by Sheelan, I guessed. She was smothered in blood that poured from two long gashes, one in a thigh, the other across her torso. She was a mess, that was no mistake.

"Get her onto the fur and back to the camp, Gannet will help you, Lark."

"Yes Highness, straight away."

"Where are the deer?"

"Over there, Lauren," Sheelan said, indicating with an arm. "The boars are still there."

"Mona and Squirrel, come with me, we're going to get the deer out as quickly as possible."

Mona gave me a look of fear. "But the boars, Highness...?" her voice trailed out.

"Let me and Sheelan worry about those, you two take a deer each."

Walking forward, the noise of the boars came to our ears, loud snuffling and snorting, a disgusting sound. The river lay about ten yards away which is where the deer were, they must have been drinking when taken down.

"Get in between Sheelan and me," I said to Squirrel and Mona. "Track along with us." I drew my sword the same moment as Sheelan did hers. They began glowing, so were aware of danger. I noticed Mona's eyes fixed on mine.

"Your sword is getting hot, Majesty," she gasped. "Why?"

At that instant both boars turned at the sound of Mona's voice, scratching the ground a few times with a front hoof, dropped their heads a little and took off like express trains, straight at us.

"Oh no you don't," I muttered through gritted teeth. "Ready Sheelan."

There was no time for her reply. We held our weapons out in front of us so they would hit the oncoming masses of muscle. As each boar touched the tips, there was a blaze of light preventing us from seeing what happened. Once that dissipated, there were two stone dead boar lying before us.

Sheelan's face was a delight to see. Total amazement and shock. "They're dead, Lauren, and I didn't feel a thing."

Mona was on her knees before Sheelan. "You are a Goddess, Sheelan. How incredible."

"Get up, Mona, I'm nothing of the sort. Go and fetch more of the unit in, we can't waste good boar skins and meat."

"I must get back to camp, can you manage here?"

"Yes, go see the Uva, Lauren. I'll get our people to move the carcasses."

Uva was in a bad way. She was still losing blood, that had to be stopped. "Verna, is there any linen in the wagon?"

"I'll look, Highness." She was quickly back. "Here, we packed some in case of an emergency."

"Come here and help, please. Is there warm water, Taal?"

"Yes, Majesty, I'll bring some."

Verna gave a hand wash the mess off of Uva, then we could identify where blood was still oozing from and get her cleaner. Using the linen, I held pressure pads on Uva's wounds. "Here, Verna, you do this, I must go to my straddle bags." I needed some antibiotics and painkillers.

The rest soon got back and began processing the animals. That relieved us of an audience so I could work easier. I realised at that moment, I should have asked Stan for pain relief fluid that I could inject locally. But Uva had passed out so I was able to use suture on her without her knowing. Now the blood had stopped, I could concentrate on the woman more. Her brow was hot, she had acquired a temperature quickly. That spelt trouble.

Sheelan tapped my arm. "We should get her back to the hospital as soon as we can, Lauren. We nearly have our target amount of deer, but we're still over a day away, so another camp."

277

"Get us fed, call Bran, she'll see to that. I can't move Uva yet, it will open her wounds up again and they may already be infected, boar must carry a lot of bacteria on their tusks."

Sheelan's face showed the question that was about to come.

"Don't ask," I said, holding a hand up, "I'll explain another time."

A grin lit her face. "You knew, Lauren," Sheelan said, more than a bit surprised.

Uva was moved to a tent. She slowly began to regain consciousness, crying out in pain as feeling also returned.

Lark comforted her, wetting her lips with water now and then until Uva swallowed, then bathing her forehead to cool her. She looked up as I stood over her. "I'll look after her, Highness, I promise."

"Good, I leave Uva in your care in that case. Call me immediately if her condition changes."

"I will, Majesty. Thank you for trusting me."

I patted her shoulder. "We have to be a team, Lark."

Next morning, we were all up very early. Addani and Artorius moved Uva to the wagon and made her as comfortable as possible. Luckily it was a milder day and the snow melted a little along the track, but steadfastly remained elsewhere. It made the aid of Ravens unnecessary, much to Sheelan's disappointment. I think she had enjoyed that experience. The day passed slowly, mainly because the wagon's speed had to be kept low so Uva wasn't bounced around. As evening wore on, Bran searched ahead for a camp site. She found one beside a stream with trees on the weather side which afforded us protection from the cold wind. It was soon organised, Uva removed and put in a tent so I could look her over.

Lark was good, stayed with her continuously, even travelling in the wagon in case Uva needed anything.

I examined her wounds. They were redder and weeping lymphatic fluid and of more concern, she was getting hotter all the time.

"Lark, get some help and move Uva to the snow bank in that dip of land. We're going to cover her in it to reduce her temperature."

"Won't she freeze?" Lark looked horrified.

"I hope so. We must get her cooler. Then, I'll work some real magic."

"Will you? I... I mean... you will, Highness, of course you will."

I smiled to myself. Lark had no idea what I intended doing.

After fifteen minutes I checked Uva's body heat. She was a lot cooler. "Take her back to the tent, please." As they moved, I drew my sword. If ever a good person needed help right now, Uva did.

I laid it upon her body, it began to glow. Looking up to the sky above, I called upon the Gods. "Oh, great Gods of the Fairymounds and Otherworld, I charge you with the power invested in me to cure this honest woman known as Uva who has served you faithfully for many years. Now she needs your help to recover from the fever she is in. Please come down and touch her heart. Thank you, Great Ones. I am your true servant, the Goddess Queen Lauren." I had intended it as a little melodrama, to take the curative powers of my sword away from me and place them squarely at the feet of the Gods.

I had barely put ten paces between me and Uva's tent, when there was an almighty crash of thunder as a bolt of lightning ripped down from the clouds to trike the tent Uva lay in. It lit up and shone like a beacon.

Nobody was more surprised than me! Well, that's an exaggeration, the others fled to the track twenty yards away to stand looking back in fear.

Had the Gods killed her? Lightning is enormously powerful, she might be burnt to a cinder in there. Worse, Lark had been with her, had I slain two of our patrol with a stupid incantation? Yet the tent was still intact, not a burn or scorch mark upon it.

Lark's smiling face came out. "She sleeping now. Thank you, Goddess Highness."

I stood looking at her with my mouth open. Snapping it shut, I rushed forwards to see for myself what had happened. Sure enough, Uva was sleeping peacefully. A touch of her brow told me the fever had vanished, just like that. "Her temperature has gone, how amazing," I said to Sheelan as she stared over my shoulder.

"That Voice said you were a Goddess now and you've just proved it, my Love. You must be able to do incredible things."

I had serious doubts about that. My request to the Gods was rewarded, I didn't do it.

Chapter Twenty Seven

"I'm a mess."

At last the fort came in sight. I think every one of us gave a sigh of relief that this patrol was over. It had certainly been different to any other we had been on.

I noticed the gates were closed, unusual for this time of day. "Sheelan, would you give them a wakeup call please?"

"Hello at the fort," she bellowed. "It's Queens Lauren and Sheelan returning with the hunting patrol."

Nothing happened. "They must have heard that, my love, you have the loudest voice I have ever heard."

A head appeared above the palisade by the gate. Someone shouted down to open them and slowly, they swung inwards just enough for our party to pass through.

Haff was there, looking from one to another closely as if expecting half the patrol to be missing.

"Thank goodness you're all here and back safely, Highness," she breathed with relief.

I looked at her questioningly. "Why shouldn't we be, Haff?"

"They came, hordes of them. Rheanna is hurt and in the hospital, you should go and see her, your Majesty."

"Hordes of who, Haff, you're not making any sense?"

"Wolves, Highness. She was coming up the slope to the fort when they attacked. Queen Alyssa sent Nodens after them and saved her. We got her into the fort and shut the gates after that, they've been closed ever since."

"Squirrel, we must go and see how she is immediately and get Uva there as well. Sheelan can explain to Alyssa where we are."

"Yes, go. I'll attend Alyssa in the palace. Is the Queen well, Haff?" Sheelan asked.

Haff nodded. "Yes Highness. She used a Nodens stick, the wolves ran away long enough for us to get Rheanna in."

"Well done, Haff, that was brave. Thank you. You surprise me at times," I added.

Haff smiled shyly. "I do things for you, Highness."

We galloped to the other end of the fort, jumping from our mounts in haste. The wagon lumbered along behind us. Several women came out of their house to help with Uva.

Rheanna had been put to bed, Shaila was by her side. She rose when we entered.

"Thank goodness you're back, Highness," Shaila said with relief. "Rheanna has been badly mauled."

"Where, let me see please? Would you get Uva into a bed as well, please."

"What happened to her?"

"A nasty accident, she'll be fine now."

"Rheanna's legs, Majesty, look," Shaila finished, carefully lifting a sheet away. A smile flickered across her lips at my enquiring look.

"I had our women try making this out of linen, like the Romans have. It's lighter than furs or a woollen blanket, so less painful on her wounds."

"You have done well, please make some more, one for each bed if possible." I examined Rheanna. Her lower legs were a mess, plainly there had been a tug of war between our people and the wolves, long gashes still bled. "When did this happen, Shaila?"

"Two moons ago, Highness. I washed with garlic, as you do and used some of the cream too, but they are bad cuts."

"Have you used the needle?"

"No, I didn't know how to, Majesty."

"Squirrel, anti-tetanus and the needles please."

"Here Lauren, a fresh needle like you always use."

Shaila gave her a stern look.

"She's my Handmaiden, Shaila, so it's a privilege I allow anyone in that position. Squirrel, roll Rheanna's sleeve up please. This may hurt a little, Rheanna, try to remain relaxed.

Now take a couple of these little pills, they will ease the pain." I felt her brow, she was hot. "There's an old custom, Rheanna, when a cure is administered, that you should touch my sword. Do that now please." I withdrew it from the scabbard across my back, it began to glow.

Rheanna became fearful of it. "Ber... but it's hot, Highness, I will be burnt."

"I am holding the sword as well, yet my hands are cool. It will be fine, but you must trust me and touch it."

Her hand went nervously out. First a finger dabbed the blade momentarily, then when that didn't hurt, the rest of her hand gradually took hold. She smiled. "It wasn't hot at all, Highness. Why does it glow?"

"To give you strength to recover, my dear woman. Now Squirrel and I must see Uva and be sure she's comfortable."

As we walked over, a smile lit her sweet face. "Thank you, Highness, for helping me. I'm a mess, aren't I? Nobody will want me now with my leg covered in such terrible scars." The smile dropped away to be replaced by a look of despair.

"Don't be silly, Uva, you're going to be fine, try not to worry."

"But there will be big scars, Highness," she insisted, "I've seen them before on other people, they look awful."

"They never had me looking after them, did they? Let me see your wounds." Both gashes had begun healing already, I was surprised, but pleased. "I think you will be okay, Uva."

Her head went at an angle. "What does okay mean, Highness?"

"That everything is well. Try to sleep now, I'll return later. I must go and see the Queen. Shaila will care for you. Where's Hahn, Shaila?"

"In the women's house playing a game with the Princess, I think. Thank you, Highness."

"Are they getting on well?"

"Yes, your Majesty, and Willon. They seem to have made a threesome up, wherever one goes, so the other two follow."

Alyssa stood as I entered the palace. "Our daughter is

making firm friends. I am so pleased. They'll end up like us, Lauren."

"Why should they?" I asked, puzzled at her analogy.

"Inseparable, as we three are."

A chuckle passed my lips. "Alegia is too good at the games. I told her to let them win sometimes."

"She has powers the boys don't understand. But they'll forgive her, she's a charming young woman."

"She seems to hold court over them," I replied, a smile lit my lips at the thought.

Next day I walked to the hospital. Squirrel was by my side, as she always was as soon as I moved. Sheelan wanted to stay with Alyssa.

Rheanna's cuts were much improved, it wasn't even possible to see where any of the wolf bites had been.

"Thank you, Highness," she said, 'You must be a true Goddess to cure me this quickly."

I patted her arm. "Perhaps I was just lucky."

Squirrel had already gone to see Uva. "Lauren, you had better come quickly, please. Something has happened."

Uva's torn and bloody leg was perfect, as was the gash across her body, not a mark showed. "There, Uva, I told you it would be okay, and it is."

She went on both knees to kiss my ring. "Thank you, my wonderful Goddess. I can't believe they healed completely and so fast Highness. Rheanna is right, you are from the Gods. Not even Shoelr could have done this."

"It's amazing what rest and sleep will do, Uva. I am pleased for you. Nobody will shun you, as you feared. Squirrel helped you as well."

Squirrel stood so close I was sure I could hear her heart beating. "That was no accident Lauren, nor an overnight sleep. You worked magic on Uva, didn't you?"

"Maybe, but it's our secret, alright my lovely Handmaiden?"

She giggled. "Yes, Lauren, our secret. I am so proud to be with you, I was nothing when you came to Germaine's' lands, now I am with you, a Goddess." She put her arms around me in a hug.

A few days went by quietly. Uva was discharged and sent back into the fort's community. Rheanna stayed in bed for a few more days, I wanted to be sure no ill effects from wolf bites manifested themselves.

It was on the fourth day as we were just waking, when the commotion began outside.

Thinking the worst, I shot out of bed, grabbed clothes and dashed onto the palace frontage, to be greeted by Shaila and Squirrel in excited states. "What on earth's the matter with you two?" I asked.

"Please come at once, Highness," Shaila blurted out, at the same time grabbing my arm to try and pull me along. It was most unusual behaviour for her.

"Please calm down and stop tugging my sleeve off, Shaila. Tell me what's happened."

"There's a strange man begging for help, Highness, he's badly wounded. He said you know him."

"Didn't you ask his name?"

"He collapsed by the gate after saying those few words, Highness. So, we got him onto a bed and came here."

"Okay, let's go and see who this mysterious person is."

The shutters were closed so it was a little gloomy. "Open the windows please, Shaila, then we can see what we're doing."

The man lying before me was absolutely filthy, plainly wounded and obviously having been in a battle somewhere. Mud, grim and blood streaked his body and had hardened on him, hair matted and unruly and there was a sandal missing, so I guessed he had travelled several days after the fight to get here.

"A sword wound, Highness," Shaila said, "Here, on his left side."

I didn't recognise him under the filth. "Fetch some warm water and linen, please Shaila. Squirrel, we'll have to cut his tunic off, I dare not risk trying to lift it over his head."

Shaila returned quickly, standing the bowl on a bedside table.

We all got to work, dabbing, teasing, soaking and any other trick we could use to clean him.

"Why, it's Chief Damarion!" I exclaimed, as his features appeared from beneath the muck. "Something dreadful must have occurred. Get the wound cleaned, Squirrel, I'll give him a shot. When he comes around he can have a couple of painkillers." I sent a message to Alyssa so she knew what was going on and wouldn't worry if we failed to return.

Rheanna tried to get out of her bed, but Shaila refused her. "Queen Lauren wants you to rest a little longer, Rheanna. Let the Goddess tend your husband first."

Damarion must have been exhausted, it too ages before his eyelids flicked as he returned to consciousness. He grasped my arm. "Thank the gods it's you, Queen Lauren. I've struggled for days to get here for help."

"I noticed that, Chief. Squirrel and Shaila have looked after your wounds and cleaned the grime of battle away. Can you tell me what happened?"

He pointed to his throat.

"Shaila, please bring some water."

He drank deeply, eventually putting the mug down. There was a haunted look in his eyes, one I had never seen in him before. "It was Caractacus, Highness, he never learned from the first battle. We were many strong, far larger a force than the Romans that faced us at the bottom of the hill. Caractacus had our army up on a craggy, large rough hill strewn with boulders and claimed no army would dare try to take us off, it was an impossible slope to climb."

I waited while he took another drink.

"The Romans formed up as usual in big blocks of men, so

286

we began loosing arrows. But our bows aren't as powerful as yours, Highness, and they had little to no effect. Suddenly, from a shouted command, all the shields were brought up above their heads, the side ones moving to cover their flanks. They simply advance under them in perfect order, like a huge iron clad monster and there was nothing we could do about it. As they marched up, they loosed ballista machines and those rock throwers you have here, our lines were decimated. Once close enough, the shields were used normally and many short spears were hurled at us, killing very many Celts. Close-hand fighting was with the sword, but by then our numbers had been reduced to the extent we couldn't defend ourselves and they came in with those short swords they use. Most Celts fled, making their way farther north. Caractacus fled north, said he was going to see Cartimandua. It was a terrible slaughter, my Queen." He collapsed back on the bed, to lie staring vacantly at the ceiling.

"Your wife is here in the hospital, Chief, over there in a bed. I'll have Shaila move her next to you. You can see your son, as well. The battle must have been ages ago, Caractacus was captured by the Queen and handed to the Romans." I turned to Squirrel. "Look after him please, I must go and talk to the Queen."

Alyssa was waiting on the palace forecourt. She had worry lines on her face. "Is there an army coming here?" she asked, nervously.

"From what Damarion told me, they were defeated and moved northwards, my love. Most of his tribe may have been wiped out or fled in other directions. The Romans are following them so are not coming here, they have no reason to."

Her shoulders dropped slightly with relief. "Thank the Gods for that, darling. How is the Chief?"

"He was filthy from the battle and has a nasty sword strike on his left side. I gave him a shot and pills and he's with his family."

At that moment, a trumpet sounded. Legate was paying a

visit.

Chapter Twenty Eight

Northwards Bound

"I wonder what he wants?" Sheelan muttered. She was still very wary of them after the last two, even though General Agricola had so far been very reasonable and afforded us privileges most clans were not allowed.

His short horse slowly made its way along between his guard, stopping opposite us." He smiled and saluted.

"Welcome, my Lord," Alyssa said, bowing slightly.

"Good day, my dear Queens. Please, you do not need to bow to me, a Queen or king has higher rank than a General. You all show me respect and that is sufficient."

Wow! That was a revelation. But my mind wondered why he was being so lenient towards us and I had suspicions there was an ulterior motive.

He looked around, for what, nobody was sure. There was a long pause before Agricola spoke again. "A big battle has been fought in the west in which we took the day. Many rebels were killed when they stupidly tried to hold off our army, the rest retreated in total disorder somewhere north. Their leader, a rebel called Caractacus, fled to Queen Cartimandua asking for refuge. She is loyal to Rome and handed him over to us. He is now on his way to Rome in chains. We think his remaining people may combine with Venutius' rebel band and try to evict the Queen from her lands in the north-east. Our other legions are engaged even further north, fighting wild men in pleated skirts, I shall be joining them soon, so we are sparse on aid for her. I wondered if you and your warriors would accompany half a legion to try and help her? I am aware she is known to you and that it is a lot to ask, it may even mean you being in combat with your own Celtic people. If the realm cannot be saved, then the best course of action is to bring her here for safety."

Alyssa and I stared at each other. The implications could be far reaching.

Sheelan came and put an arm around our waists. "Fighting our own would be awful," she muttered, her head hung low. "But we are already if Venutius is challenging Queen Cartimandua, they are both Celts, so if we are forced to defend ourselves there can be no fault or recriminations directed at us, can there?"

Sheelan was right. I turned to Alyssa. "While Celts fought Romans everything balanced out, but not when native Britons began squabbling among ourselves, that places a different complexion on everything. Yet in fact, Celts had been doing exactly that for years, each trying to take something or other from the nearest clan or tribe, as we know only too well. What do you think?"

Alyssa held her head high. "If we have to fight, we fight as brave and fearless Celts should fight. An injustice is being done and that can't be right. How large a force is half a legion, my Lord?"

"About a thousand five hundred men, Highness," Agricola replied.

Again, Alyssa looked at me for guidance, she had no idea how many that was. "Now I ask you, Lauren, what do you think?"

"That isn't many, my Lord. We could come up against a Celtic army of a hundred thousand. What is the situation like there?"

He nodded slowly as he thought about it. "I can only spare another cohort, my Queens. I'm sorry, I must take several in support of other operations farther on, so I am short of manpower. Caractacus is out of the fight now and Venutius was soundly defeated in the far western mountains so his force is seriously depleted, perhaps no more than half that number of untrained warriors. Our legionaries will stand their ground, they are well trained. Will you help us, please?"

I gazed into Alyssa's blue eyes. "That evens the odds, but they are still heavily in Venutius' favour by a large margin, possibly ten of them to each of us."

She wavered, there was indecision in her eyes.

Agricola sensed it. "I shall give you my aide, Ligarius Manimus and his personal guard of a hundred men as well. He is reliable. Will that help?"

"I think that is a very kind offer, my Lord. But Queen Alyssa must have the last say, she is by far the most senior Queen here." I knew it was pushing the final burden onto her shoulders but both Sheelan and I weren't as well qualified in the way of governing Celts as she was. It had to be her choice.

"I liked Queen Cartimandua, she was a pleasant person and cared deeply about her people. Yes, my Lord, my Celts will support your Roman troops. We need two days to gather our force, is that well with you?"

A broad smile took his face. "Thank you all, I wasn't sure you would agree, but am greatly pleased you have. Your participation is beyond praise and value, there's so much we still don't know of your race of people that you can guide us with. Two days is ideal, giving us time to prepare a convoy and victual it, a supply that will take into account your people as well. How many are there likely to be?"

"We think about a hundred, perhaps a hundred and fifty, but no more, my Lord. We cannot ask farmers to fight in this kind of situation, only our warriors will be included," I answered.

"Then I'll load supplies for the greater amount. Thank you all again, I hope the patrol goes well, my lovely Queens. I shall tell of you all to my wonderful wife, I hope you will meet soon, she will be thrilled." He gave a thumping salute, mounted, called his escort together and left.

I was still in a sort of shock. Alyssa broke me from it.

"It doesn't seem possible the mighty Roman army came

and asked us for help, my love. It shows the trust General Agricola has in us."

"I've called Bran, she needs to know about this, it's a very long journey. I wonder if Artorius and Aulus will come with us, seeing as Bran and Addani may well be?"

Bran arrived. Alyssa and I explained the idea behind this patrol.

"We will be aiding the Roman army and possibly fending off a rogue Celtic one," Alyssa said, pointedly.

"From what I've heard, Highnesses, Venutius has been causing trouble and getting our people killed to suit his own ends. I'll go and get the wagons ready as well."

Next was Addani; she looked me straight in the eyes and smiled. "Where you go, Highness, so do I. Artorius will come,"

Alyssa thanked her for showing such loyalty. "I expect there'll be losses, Lauren, my love."

"Yes, I expect there will be, darling. This is a very dangerous patrol and with Romans. Celts may not understand our reasons for doing it and turn on us. There will probably be a battle, we have a large contingent of Romans with us and Celts attack them all the time. None of us will ever forget what happened during one particular battle when we sustained losses, that was very unexpected and could easily occur again."

"All three of us must visit the Stones and ask the Gods for protection for us and our people, that rightful punishment be done to those who transgress both human and Godly laws, Lauren," Alyssa stated."

"I agree. While the wagons are being prepared we have time to go. Let us wear full robes and swords, the Stones will expect it of us."

The day was chilly, it was still early in the year, so we were glad our attire was full length and warm. Down the south gate slope, across the stepping stones and into the small forest that had taken Eva away from us. The Stones looked forbidding, grey, cold and I thought, lifeless. Over the ditch that surrounded them and into the circle itself. There, the wind stopped as if an invisible hand had closed a door. It was eerie.

Alyssa moved to the Altar, indicating Sheelan and I should stand either side of her. Once we were in a line she held her arms up to the sky. "Oh, great Stones, we come in honour of you, of your power and care for our people, of your undying love for the Queens of this land and of the many gifts and aid offered to us. We three sovereigns come to ask for your protection on this dangerous mission to save Queen Cartimandua from rape and pillage that is being thrust upon her by rebel Celtic forces. We beseech you, mighty Gods, to watch over our warriors at all times, for their safekeeping during moments of strife. We Queens will do our best to aid them, not put them into danger if at all possible, for we dearly love our subjects and would wish them no ill. We march with Romans, but honest and fair Romans who are also trying to offer their protection so the northern Queen may keep control of her rightful realm. We draw our swords you gave special power to in respect, oh Gods of Here and Otherworld."

To my surprise, Alyssa knelt and kissed the Altar Stone. As her lips made contact the sky rumbled and a streak of lightning swept down to gently touch her head, lightly dancing around it as if stroking her beautiful hair.

A deep resonant voice spoke. *"Go, my Queens, fear nought and do your duty to another Royal. The Gods will be with you and judge your decisions and movements as you choose them. We are with you, your Leader is an honest man, take heed of his warnings. The Roman Agricola will go farther north to quell an uprising that is causing more loss of life. He will be near, so call upon his forces if you must if in dire need."*

With that gem of information, I assumed the meeting between the God and humans was at an end. As Sheelan and I went to aid Alyssa to her feet, the lightning returned to envelop us all in its folds.

I felt an elation, as though I was in the air instead of having my feet firmly on Terra Firma and a light headedness, too, one of confidence and courage and an overwhelming urge to do my duty to humankind. The others must have experienced identical feelings, especially when I looked at Sheelan standing with her mouth agape, a startled, yet deeply satisfied expression on her face.

Alyssa turned to us. "We have the Gods permission for this expedition into the unknown, my loves. We may go forward with a confident step and meet our Fates, whatever they may be."

We embraced, turned back to bow to the Stones, then made our way back to the fort.

Two days passed quickly. Bran was a tower of strength and patience. She and Aulus really had their fingers on the pulse.

That gave us time to talk through our options.

"What if Venutius attacked us as we approach Queen Cartimandua's settlement? That army must be in the area, the Queen is under siege according to General Agricola, we have to work out a way of rescuing her. Obviously, we must defend ourselves, but perhaps not to the extent of going over to the offensive. Would that act betray us as Celts?" Alyssa asked.

Sheelan put her opinion. "They have already attacked us, Alyssa, you had to fight to save the fort only a few years ago, so why shouldn't we?"

Alyssa nodded agreement. "Sheelan is right. If pressed, we fight, but only if we have no alternative. Retreat can save lives and that should be our main aim, yet, pressing a fight can do exactly the same thing. It all depends on the circumstances at that moment, as the Stone's Gods said. They will help guide us."

A trumpet sounded.

"Legate is here. Let us meet him," I suggested.

We gathered on the palace forecourt as General Agricola stopped his horse beside us.

He saluted in the Roman way, then dismounted to walk and stand in front of us. "I see you're prepared as you promised, my Queens. It's important to keep your word, and I hope I have at all times. Ligarius Manimus has his small force waiting by your northern gate, they are ready to serve you, as are the three cohorts I promised. They are amassed on the road waiting for you. My small force in the barracks at Sarum will keep an eye on your fort and its occupants. If they need anything at all, please tell them to ask immediately and it will be done if within their powers. Perhaps the elder, Shaila, would do that? You have my utmost respect. I bid you a safe journey but be on your guard at all times, the rebels attack without warning. Whatever you decide to do, you have my support. I shall be taking the other half of my Legio Augusta and part of the Legio XIV Gemina. We may meet at some point. We also have a new overall Commander in Britannia, Publius Petronius Turpilianus, who is sympathetic to your tribes. Farewell." He saluted again, mounted, waved a hand and departed.

Our farewells were far more emotional.

Shaila was in tears. "Please be careful, my Queens. Return to us soon."

Alyssa thanked her. "Legate said for you to ask for anything you need. Their soldiers will be looking over you all. Farewell, faithful Shaila, until we meet again."

Our daughters both came and cuddled us. "Don't get hurt, mummies, I want you back here again with us." Alegia leaped into my arms and hugged hard.

"We will, try not to worry. There are many Romans coming with us that can fight very well, so will keep us safe."

Eventually we tore ourselves away.

The spectacle of our departure, escorted as we were by a hundred legionaries of Ligarius Manimus's personal guard, caused a great deal of excitement. We wore tunic and trousers, crowns and swords, items that glistened in the cold morning sunlight. Out of the north gate and into the forest that held the mysterious mist, fortunately not due to manifest itself today, we will stay in this era in that case. Alyssa indicated with a nod of her head as we passed the boulder on our right and smiled wistfully.

"Not today," I replied, "Thank goodness."

Chapter Twenty Nine

The Ritual

The wood was not so extensive now after the Romans had begun clearing the far side. There we found a road, the same road that ran near my home in the future. I had always wondered why it was so straight, now I knew.

Ligarius indicated we turn left, and there before us were masses of legionaries and their Centurions, standing waiting in perfect order. Something was shouted out and the whole mass snapped to attention as we moved along one side to attain the head of the column. Many heads turned to see who it was demanding that much respect, and I think surprised to find it was a large band of Celts.

"How amazing," Alyssa called over. "So many Romans coming to help us."

"I think the idea is that we help them, Alyssa. They are the larger force and will hopefully do most of the fighting. Our mission is to get Queen Cartimandua out if she wishes or if the Romans are unable to beat Venutius. This is a relatively small Roman contingent, we will be vastly outnumbered."

At the head of the column we met the Legion Commander, Marcus Cerilius. He slapped his fist to his chest in salute. "Welcome, my Queens, to this punitive expedition to the north east of this land. May I ask your contingent to take place behind the first block of legionaries. It is for your safely, Legate Agricola was most insistent."

Ligarius motioned us to wait until the legion moved off so we could file in between units. "The second unit will pause for your people to take their place, Highnesses."

Most of the legionaries had to march, so we had to restrain our horses to keep a slower pace. On twisting to look back, I could see a substantial dust cloud being thrown up.

There always seemed to be mounted Romans dashing up and down the huge formation, perhaps conveying orders or keeping the rear in touch with the front.

Ligarius' Personal Guard was marching behind us, so he came to check we were all well every so often. He smiled, looked us over, then returned to his men repeatedly, carrying out an order given him by Agricola.

A halt was called. Once stationary, each unit was dismissed to sit and rest while the victualling unit got a meal ready. Everything was typically organised.

"Do we need to get our food?" Alyssa asked.

A group of Romans came with trays of food. "We will attend to your needs, my Queens," Ligarius explained. "If anybody needs anything at all, please ask. I shall have water flasks issued to you all."

After lunch the legion formed up and began to march north again. This process continued for three days, camping each night under canvas.

On this day our legion must have been near Lincoln, known to the Romans as Lindum Colonia. Small villages sprang up in a variety of shapes and sizes, some tradition roundhouses, others had tried to copy the Roman model, built square with windows that could be closed at night by shutters. The inhabitants came out to watch us pass, subjugation on their faces after the Iceni had risen and been crushed by General Gaius Suetonius Paulinus, so looked at us with indifference. The fight had been knocked out of them. A few stared at us, some bowed respectfully while others gave us looks of hate for siding with the invaders. The main thing was, they were beginning to integrate and live beside those that now governed them. I knew it would happen many more times in the future but the Britons are a hardy race and would always rise above invasion.

We had progressed well. The air was chillier here so plainly farther north, at a guess our next destination would be Doncaster, in this era called Danum. There was plentiful cover everywhere due to the amount of thick tree growth that abounded here still, parts of Sherwood and Lincoln forests still extended across vast areas. Our route had followed Roman roads as much as possible. Although not exactly straight, they weren't far off it, which made the march pretty easy and fast. It also meant the trees had been cut back away from the road, a counter-measure against people leaping out at them in close proximity.

I felt uneasy, this part of our journey reminded me of our own forests and how easily we had ambushed part of a legion in them. "Arm yourselves," I called back at our warriors. "Bring longbows ready for use."

A soft voice whispered in my ear. *"Be careful, my love, there is a trap laid ahead."*

"Is that you, Maddy?"

"Yes darling," she giggled as always. *"Tell the Roman with you."*

Pulling my mount out of column I waited for Ligarius to catch up. "I have a feeling there is an ambush ahead, Centurion. Your legionaries should be prepared."

He stared at me for a few moments, thumped his chest and went galloping forward to Marcus Cerilius.

Soon a slight difference in formation began filtering back along the legion, nothing obvious, a subtle change.

Suddenly, a loud screaming war cry emitted from the undergrowth either side as many Britons leaped out to attack. They were a typically unruly and disorganised rabble, faces painted in a variety of colours, some had their hair shaved off or wore nothing at all other than Woad, their bodies having turned blue with it.

Within an instant, Roman shields slammed down and a wall was formed, their gladii poking through. Pilum were hurled at the mass before them, cutting them down by the dozen. If a soldier was injured or killed, another stepped into his place and kept the shield wall solid. It was an exercise in perfection, facilitated by knowledge of the impending attack.

We drew our swords but were reluctant to strike at Celts.

But we had no shield protection as the Romans, those huge oblong highly decorated objects that kept them safe once formed and interlocked.

The Celts did not differentiate however, and as soon as Kwail got hit our swords came into action. Drawing them in a long flourish, they were swiped sideways like a scythe as we turned from defensive to attack mode in the blink of an eye. We had no option, being outnumbered so badly.

Blood spurted from jagged rips across their bodies, arms lopped off to fall on the roadway, the limb's owner collapsing in their death throes. Our weapons glowed brightly, putting fear into the faces of out attackers.

It was soon over.

Ligarius brought his horse to us. He bowed and slapped his chest. "Thank you, my Queen, your warning saved us from an ambush. Most are dead, there are a few Celts left if you wish to question them."

Alyssa nodded, went to where the surviving few being held by Roman guards.

"Who are you?" she demanded.

Looking across the group it was plain they were a scruffy, warlike lot of individuals. Sullen faces stared back resentfully at me. There were no women in their numbers, which was odd. Celtic women normally fought alongside the men and just as fiercely.

The man spat at her. "You fight with the enemy."

A Roman Centurion hit him round the face with his shield. "Speak politely to a Queen, barbarian."

"I ask again, who are you?" Alyssa repeated.

He was squatted, glowering at her. "Who are you to come into my lands issuing orders and invading us?"

"These are your lands?" Alyssa snorted. "They are a wreck. Where is your agriculture?"

"We need none, we are hunter warriors, we kill what we want, our slaves do the rest."

Addani stepped behind him, gripped his hair and twisted his head sideways to face her. "You say your Majesty to my

Queens."

"I have no interest in women," he snapped. "They are only good for simple tasks and satisfying brave men, like us."

"What is the name of your tribe?" Somehow Alyssa was remaining calm.

"The Partisea, a separate part of the Parisi, who we reject because of their weak ways."

"Weak ways?" I asked.

"They farm and do women's work. We fight and hunt."

I didn't like the sound of any of this. They had no fields, just forest, so I expected a meat diet. And what where these tasks of satisfying men? His offhand concern for the female gender niggled at my heart. "Take us to your village?" I said.

"We need no more women, let Cernunnos take your hearts and burn them."

Addani gave his head another tweak as she carefully drew her long dagger and placed it across his throat. "I told you once how to address my Queens, another slip and my hand will as well, across your miserable throat." She cast a disparaging look at the other few men left. "Each of you will follow if you fail to show respect."

He glared at her. Plainly he wasn't used to being spoken to by a woman in that manner. After a pause, the nod of acceptance came.

Addani hoisted him up onto his feet. "One false move and my dagger will be planted in your back, is that clear. I will not hesitate."

"I'll detach ten men from my bodyguard to go with you, Highness," Ligarius said. "They have been ordered to kill without mercy. What is your name, barbarian?"

Another sullen look.

Ligarius drew his gladius.

"Chief Barbalus."

"This wretch is yours to judge, Great Queen," Ligarius said, and bowed.

The rebel Chief looked puzzled, not understanding why a Roman Centurion would bow and show respect to a woman.

Alyssa bowed her head. "Thank you, Centurion Ligarius. Lead on."

The Chief took us through the forest for some distance until a small village came into view and to say it was unity did it justice, it was a jumble of disorganisation.

As we entered I noticed many women cowering to one side, dirty, unwashed and unkempt, grime and dirt with blood streaked in the mess that covered them. The look of subjugation shone in their eyes staring wide open at us in fear and confusion. Walking to one I smiled. "What is your name, my good woman?"

She gaped at the Chief, bound and a prisoner, but didn't reply.

"Is this your Chief?" Alyssa asked as softly as she could.

The woman nodded, still with a look of terror.

I knew Alyssa had the same uneasy feeling about these women and their plight. They had been sorely used by some terrible regime, that was obvious by the bruises and cuts that covered them. What that was, we needed to discover. My thoughts went to her. Why were they so afraid? Why so unkempt and why huddled together like this?

Alyssa spoke my thoughts, pushing the Chief onto his knees. "Why are these women in this state, don't you allow them to wash?"

"They are our women, we do with them as we please."

"Not any more you don't," I snapped back. "Why are there no youngsters here? Where are the babies of this clan, your next generation? After all, it seems to me you have used these poor slaves freely for sex and little else other than menial tasks."

Alyssa took the woman we had spoken to by a hand and led her away from our prisoners, the women looking back at the men.

"Whatever has been happening her, will stop, right now. You may have no fear of us, we travel north to aid another Queen who is being subject to threats and invasion. These two women are Queens Lauren and Sheelan, I am Queen

Alyssa. The others are women warriors from a fort far to the south. Tell me, what did the Chief mean by "used as they pleased?"

"For sex, my Queen." She spoke at last.

"What if you refused?"

"If we were unwilling, we were severely beaten and forcibly raped by them."

I cast the Chief a derogatory look. "By their own admission they felt it was their right to do whatever they liked with these women, Alyssa. But I still don't understand where the children are. Where are they Chief Barbalus?"

Silence.

A tweak on his bound arms by Addani loosened his tongue. "We discard them," he retorted with disinterest.

"Discard?" I asked.

He shrugged his shoulders and looked back blankly.

Alyssa went to another of the women, "You are free now, you don't have to be slaves anymore. We now know you were all subject to rape or forced to do things you didn't want to. Did any of you have children?"

She broke down in tears, flinging herself at our feet. "Thanks to Gods you were sent to help us. We all offered ourselves to Them if They would free us from this dreadful enslavement. Yes, many women did, we weren't allowed to keep them. I would have loved to keep one of mine, they were so cute."

The truth had come flooding out.

"What is your name?" I asked.

"Alicia, your Highness." She fingered her torn tunic in anguish.

"Nobody is going to hurt you anymore, believe me." I hugged her.

Tears of relief flowed. "Thank you, Highness, thank you so much."

"One of yours?" Alyssa questioned apprehensively. "How many did you have?"

"We were raped over and over, there were many children,

my Queen. The Chief disposed of them at the ritual."

"Ritual, what ritual, and how?" Alyssa asked, tension growing in her voice as she looked in my direction. "Something debased has occurred her, Lauren."

"At the gorge, Majesty," Alicia replied.

"Show us?" Alyssa said tersely.

Alicia took us to a stone outcrop. Looking over the edge there was a drop of about fifty feet straight down into a gorge. At the bottom were massive rocks and between those, lots of little bodies all mixed up in an unholy jumble of death.

"Are these your children?"

"Yes Highness."

"How did they die?"

A vague look took Alicia's face, she shrugged her shoulders. "The Chieftain threw them in at the end of the ritual."

"What is this ritual?" Alyssa asked. "Explain, please."

"Yes Majesty. The Chief claimed our children were illicit fruits because we were such wicked women and we must be cleansed and punished of our crimes. Because of us, they had to be offered to the Gods to appease their anger. Each child was brought here and laid on that slab of stone over there. He sprinkled water on them, saying water purified its soul and our shame. Sometimes he would stab them with his long dagger, letting the blood ran over and down the stone, but more often they had to be cast over alive. He claimed that had greater meaning to the Gods. Some women objected and fought for the offspring they had borne, they were beaten and thrown into the chasm as well. We were unable to save our children, Highness."

"You mean they were simply thrown in alive and left to die of exposure and starvation and this bastard blamed you for it?" I felt sick in my stomach at the thought.

The woman nodded. "It was the way, your Highness."

Alyssa turned to me. There was a look of horror on her face. "**Bloody barbarians**," she swung and shouted at the prisoners. "It's not our way! They were precious children to continue your line, yet were cast over these rocks to land down there and be just left? I can't believe anybody would be that brutal and callous. Send some of ours down to see if any still live, Lauren."

"Bran, see to that please."

Soon her group return shaking their heads.

My attention returned to Alicia. "Many men are indifferent to young life, they are too much trouble and would interfere with their warrior lifestyle. You poor women have been used and put through absolute misery. Worse, your children were taken away in the most disgusting way, leaving you knowing what the mite's fate was, to die a wasting death in this eruption of evil. That must have been almost impossible to bear."

"Bring me the Chief and his remain warriors," Alyssa almost snarled. She was angry and about to emotionally explode.

I knew that look, those ice blue eyes as hard as granite and without empathy or interest in the person about to be placed before her. There would be no mercy.

Addani and Magda dragged them forward two at a time, trussed up tightly, arms and elbows behind their backs, feet bound at the ankles and forced to their knees.

"Bring all the women these swine enslaved to witness my judgement of the prisoner's crimes."

The men's eyes were wide with fear as they looked up at Alyssa standing tall before them, her crown tilted slightly on her beautiful hair and bejewelled sword and dagger denoting her status, those cold blue eyes casting disdaining glances across the prisoner's heads.

"Come here Alicia, stand beside me please," I encouraged. You shall witness what my Queen does to those that transgress human dignity and behaviour. Have no fear."

"You have all gone far beyond common decency towards other human beings. These women and their children have the same hearts and feelings as you, fortunately, not the same

305

minds or mentality. You have consistently abused, raped and murdered on such a scale as it is impossible to imagine. You are worthless wretches without compassion, as I am without compassion towards all of you. Now you shall be on the receiving end of punishment to suit your crimes. You shall be cast into the pit as all those before you were. Don't believe I will allow you to crawl or climb out, there will be no such escape for you, your legs and arms will be broken before you are sent over the clifftop, there to stay until you all die a long and slow death."

Gasps went around the gathered warriors. But they all knew what had to be carried out here, acts to free people from dreadfully cruel slavery of the very worst kind. Yes, we knew the Romans had slaves, but they were treated with a modicum of decency and many even managed to buy their freedom and become Roman citizens.

"I choose Magda and Addani to fulfil my decree," Alyssa called. "Warriors, please do your duty, carry out the executions."

Large boughs were brought. Both our women had no problems wielding them, bringing each down with such force onto the selected limbs the sound of them cracking was heard by all.

Screams came from the men, pleas for mercy and vague promises of finding a new way of life. Some tried to crawl away, even though bound and were dragged back and dealt with. After each had their limbs broken, Magda and Addani cast them into the ravine to drop with a sickening thud on boulders at the bottom.

Some women clapped, many jeered their tormentors as they fell victim, shouting vile accusations at them or of the righteousness of the retribution being meted out. Others stayed silently watching the proceeds with expressionless faces, their eyes showing the emptiness that lived inside their hearts.

Eventually it was done. A few went and looked over the edge, but showed no compassion or depth of feelings, then turned and walked back into the fold of the remaining clan.

Alicia approached us. "We thank you, Highness, for freeing us from this terrible life. There is nothing here for us now, only dreadful memories and suffering. May we join you, please?"

Alyssa's eyes had softened. "What do you wish to do?"

"I was secretly elected as our leader under this oppression but we could do little to aid ourselves. Now you have come, lifted our joyous hearts and freed us from the iron cloud that hung over us. We cannot thank you enough, oh three great Queens."

"We are going to help a northern Queen who is under siege, so there is a good possibility we shall be in battle. It might be far too dangerous for you to join us."

"We secretly trained to fight with a sword and shield, Highness. Not real swords or shields, we were never allowed weapons, we used what we had, wood usually. We had hoped one day, to overthrow those brutes and free ourselves, that day had not arrived yet. Our small clan may be of help."

Alyssa gazed at her for a long time, her mind running through the situation. Women who were half starved might not be strong enough to fight and would they understand our way of life? "Bran, Addani, test these women out with the sword please."

Weapons were willingly loaned and shields offered by our warriors who were keen to see how Alicia and her friends made out.

They were good, even in their present condition. Food would cure that. Each of our warrior's thrusts were parried and counter thrusts made, many would have been lethal had they been in anger.

Alyssa held her arms up. "I have seen enough. How long have you been practising?"

"A few years, Highness. We had to be careful not to be seen, which meant going somewhere away from our village when the men were out hunting."

A warm smile took Alyssa's face. "Welcome to my clan,

you are all brave and resourceful women. We have no slaves, all our warriors are free to choose what they wish to do, as are all others in and around our fort. This is the Goddess Queen Lauren and here is Queen Sheelan, they govern my land alongside me in equal status. Bran is our Fighting Leader, so look to her for guidance. Please feel free to ask any of us for help or advice."

Alicia knelt and kissed Alyssa's ring. "Thank you for allowing us to merge with you, your great Highness. May I kiss the Goddesses ring as well?" Her eyes cast my way, perhaps they had fear in them of the power of a Goddess?

I held my hand out. "I embrace you Alicia, and all your women, you are most welcome. Our warriors will also make you feel at home within our ranks. Now we must move on our way under protective escort of this Roman formation."

Our units turned and left that place of suffering, the wails of the injured still in our ears. Not one of our clan gave them a second glance.

Chapter Thirty

A Queen's Plight

"You acted correctly, Highness," Ligarius said as we arrived back with the legion. "We would have crucified them all for such vile deeds. I hope the women integrate into your society quickly."

"Thank you, Centurion. Bringing an extra group of people in may upset your supply numbers though. We couldn't leave them there as they were, many are traumatised and need support, and we can give them that."

He smiled. "We always over supply, in case of unforeseen circumstances your Majesty. It is not a problem. It must have been very upsetting for you, all those children..." his voice trailed off.

"It's at an end now, Centurion, their suffering is over."

The Legion reformed to begin the march north to Eboracum, York as I knew it in my other life. This was the land of the Parisi, the tribe that the Partisea had split from. I leant to Alyssa. "We should be on our guard, this is where that last abhorrent tribe came from. I wonder if these are the same?"

"Can two tribes be that bad? I hope not, we will take action if they are, darling."

As the forest faded the landscape changed to a patchwork of small fields, each with a roundhouse near them. People worked with oxen or tending crops, some in workshops creating barter goods, much as at our fort. It seemed promising.

A man bowed at seeing our crowns, smiling warmly.

"Welcome, Queens, have a safe journey," he called.

We acknowledged his politeness, returning his greeting.

Passing on, the countryside proved to be under cultivation by an industrious tribe who at the same time waved at our Roman escort. This was a peaceful folk, much to our relief.

In the distance lay a town made of modern structures in the Roman style. "That is probably Ebocarum," I called to Alyssa.

Ligarius rode to us. "We shall stop here overnight, Highnesses. It is a Roman town, so secure. Riders were sent ahead to arrange shelter for you and your warriors. Our contingent will use the barracks. My Personal Guard will escort you in." He bowed and saluted.

I had to admit the place was impressive. Our people were allotted a large villa, complete with beds, some servants and a pool. It seemed luxurious after so long on the trail.

"It's like Justinus' villa," Sheelan cried excitedly. "Look Alyssa, a pool, we can swim."

"We can all swim, it will be very refreshing. Bran, please organise beds for our people."

She and Addani were as efficient as usual and while a little cramped, all were accommodated, even our new members who went around wide eyed looking at all the rooms.

"Please bring the new women in to see me, Bran. I want to give them an examination to see if they need any healing."

"Yes, Majesty. I'll set a room aside until you're finished."

"Squirrel, will you get some hot water please, look for the kitchen, there will be a bowl or something there."

The women began filing in. This was the first time in their lives anybody had cared for them, shown them compassion or was interested in their health, so they were afraid of what might happen.

"Sit here, Alicia. Have you any pains anywhere?" I asked, as I began from her feet, working slowly along her legs.

"No Highness. Why are you looking at me all over?"

I laughed. "To see if you're well. Your feet are cut or split, as are your hands. I'm going to put some cream on them both to heal and soften."

She shied away. "Will it hurt?"

Sheelan walked in. "Lauren is a healer as well as a Queen. She's also a Goddess so can cure you, she's even brought people back to life after they drowned. Let her tend you, Alicia, she's wonderful." She came and kissed me.

Alicia looked from one to the other "Are we allowed to kiss a Goddess?"

"Lauren is Vowed to me, as she and I am to Alyssa, so yes, we kiss and love each other. Many of our women are Vowed, they are very happy. Addani, the tall warrior, has Artorius as a partner and Bran has Aulus, the two Roman soldiers who joined us. We have a very open community."

"We were never allowed to love each other. If the men found out we would be beaten, some were killed for it. That cream is so soothing, Goddess."

"You must all try to put that behind you now. You are part of the Atrebates clan, so can act and behave as we do. If anything troubles you, ask any of us, Bran, Addani, or any of the warriors. Don't be afraid to speak up, we all want to help you."

There were tears forming in her eyes, she looked distraught at their sudden change of fortune.

Standing, I put my arms around her shoulders. "You are all free women now. You can choose what you want to do. See how I ask people to do things for me? That is being polite and I thank them when they do it. Squirrel here, is mine and Sheelan's Handmaiden, she wants to do it, but I don't expect her to. Our warriors want to fight for our fort and protect our people, we don't make them. That applies to you and your people, Alicia. You don't have to fight if you don't wish to, something else may be better for you, there are many jobs to be done in a fort."

"I love being Lauren's Handmaiden," Squirrel said. "She's very kind and brave and saves people."

"Now, let my helpers wash your faces and bodies, get you clean and show us what you really look like. Then we are all going for a swim."

"All, Majesty?" Alicia asked uncertainly. "The same time as you?"

"Yes, all of us, even the two men among us."

Squirrel worked wonders, working with Kwail, Lark and Greta, they soon had the women clean and fresh looking.

Most were young, and that brought another point to mind; where were the elders? I asked Alicia.

"They were killed once they got old and unable to work or looked nice. The men didn't want them."

A sigh left me. It was the reply I expected, but that didn't make it any better.

The pool became very full with about two hundred in it. Alicia's people had never been in water before and splashed about madly, loving every minute, calling and yelling to each other. But it was cold and we got out and towelled each other down, much to Alyssa's delight.

"The last time I asked you to do this, you said I was a big girl."

"I also said you were very tempting," I laughed back.

When night fell people paired off. Alyssa and Sheelan with me, Agneta with Squirrel, and many more found somebody to hug and keep them warm.

It took several more days to reach the next town, which Ligarius said was Pons Aelius. From college memory, I believed that to be the area of Newcastle. That was well into Brigantian territory, in which case extra patrols were sent out both sides and ahead. Our Roman Commander had his wits about him. However, no attack materialised and we made our destination safety.

Alyssa kind of collapsed with weariness once we were shown to our villa. Again, it was cramped, but vastly better than under canvas here in the north of Britannia with a colder climate.

Ligarius asked to see us. He entered with a thump of his chest. "My Queens, our scouts have found the site of Queen Cartimandua's stronghold a considerable distance to the west. It is a fort like yours, has a ditch around the outside and palisades for protection against arrows. She is under siege by Venutius. He has not made an attempt to attack as far as we know but is amassing forces the other side. He is unaware of our presence here, that knowledge will be his as soon as we get near. We need to have the Legion move immediately. I apologise for the short notice, Majesty, I have only just heard."

We looked at each other. This was it, the reason we had come here.

"I hope the Queen can hold out until your men arrive, Ligarius. What does the Commander think?" Alyssa asked.

"If we force march he thinks about eight or so hours, Majesty. Can your warriors manage that pace?"

"We have never tried," Alyssa mused. "What do you think, Lauren?"

"Force marching is a high pace. We have never trained for it, we have never needed to because we are mounted warriors. So yes, on horseback we can maintain the pace."

Sheelan came close. "We will be in battle again soon, my loves. I hate it, the risk for both of you increases so much, I might lose you." Her face was wet, tears had flowed.

Alyssa and I held her. I stroked a finger down her nose and lightly tapped the end. "You are in just as much danger, darling. We all need to watch each other's backs, then we will survive. Let's get ready, tunic and trousers are best for movement."

"Crowns and of course, our swords," Alyssa added. "I should address our fighters, Lauren," she said.

Nodding the wisdom of that, I helped her onto a wagon.

"We are about to defend the Queen. There is no definite outcome of this battle, only that there is a great possibility we will be directly involved. Our target is to get Queen Cartimandua out of danger, not fight Celts if we can avoid it. Their dispute is not ours, that has to be resolved in another way. Fight if you have to, defend yourselves. Queen Lauren will decide our method when she has seen the situation there. Go and prepare to ride."

Our position was near the rear, one cohort in. Commander Marcus Cerilius wanted a Roman force at the from to absorb any charge by Celtic warriors.

The people came out to watch us leave, baleful looks in their eyes. They knew what was happening, Cartimandua was their Queen and it seemed, had been popular. Venutius was a wild card, his strength was an unknown quantity while we, as a Roman Legion, were considerably under strength. This legion was not named because it had been quickly assembled from two and several hundred auxiliaries, plus us.

A woman ran forward with flowers. "For luck and the protection of the deity I got them from, your Majesties. Save our Queen for us please."

It was a touching act. I handed them to Alyssa, who smiled with delight and thanked the woman.

When Romans said a forced march, they really meant it. Now I understood how Vespasian had returned so quickly to our fort after we had been flogged. They set up a cracking pace kicking up a large dust cloud behind us.

Night fell but they kept going, legionaries placed at the outsides with embers to light the way. I couldn't see the aquila now, as I could from our previous position, the bravest man in the Legion. I assumed that when line of battle was formed he would be in the centre somewhere.

Alyssa began nodding off so I took my mount close alongside and asked Sheelan to go the other. That way we kept her upright between us.

"We shall be too tired to fight at this rate," Sheelan pointed out. Will they expect us to go straight into battle?"

A shrug of my shoulders was her reply. "I've no idea, sweetheart, I've never fought with Romans before, only against them."

Sheelan burst out laughing. "We slaughtered them, didn't we Lauren?"

"Yes, it was a massacre. I am very thirsty, I wonder if they're going to stop for a short break soon?" I noticed the greyness of dawn slowly appearing above trees in the east behind us.

Orders were shouted and the column stopped dead. Shields bottoms hit the ground, I guessed they must be heavy so each legionary was only too pleased to take the weight off.

"We're taking a break," Ligarius informed us. "Send your warriors to the kitchen wagons to get water for your flasks, Highness."

We slid off our horses, it was nice to be on solid ground for a while.

Before we knew it, Squirrel and Agneta were holding out large drinking vessels to us. Squirrel grinned. "We thought you would like a lot, Highnesses."

Sheelan cuddled her. "Thank you Squirrel. We shall be fighting soon, I want to say goodbye in case either of us isn't here afterwards."

"Thank you Sheelan, that's a lovely thought. I wish the same to you."

We said our goodbyes in case events overtook us quickly.

Alicia asked us what we were doing, I explained.

"May we all wish you the same, my Queens. If it hadn't been for you none of us would have tasted freedom. I hope you all remain safe. Thank you."

The order to get into column came down the line, we mounted. The pace was slower this time, so we must be nearing our objective.

Centurion Ligarius informed us of events. "We shall be stopping shortly while scouts are sent out. Commander Cerilius wants to know the enemy's dispositions. Rest for a while. Get some food if you wish, my Queens."

"Thank you, Centurion, we will," I replied.

The whole legion sat or lay by the roadside and waited. It

was a tense time, although many of the legionaries seemed very relaxed. Perhaps they had seen many such battles.

"How do you feel?" I asked Alyssa, knowing she had been weary.

"I am well, my love. Just being near you is enough."

I rolled over and kissed her. "That was a lovely thing to say. I love you." I noticed movement up ahead. "They are falling in again, sweet one."

That coy smile played around her mouth. "Sweet one," she whispered.

Ligarius galloped up, reigning in sharply. "The Queen's fortification is just over that rise, Highness. She is within its walls with a few of her personal guard. Venutius is barely the other side of it and about to charge in. Our force is going to split into two and go out and round, to come in on his flanks forming into half cohort blocks. He may think there are more of us than there are. Our scouts estimate them at about twenty thousand. Will your group go and rescue the Queen, please?"

"Yes, I'll make our dispositions when we get closer and I can see how the land is set out."

Ligarius slapped his chest, then went to his unit.

"What are we doing." Alyssa asked.

"We shall also split in two. Let's creep closer without being seen, we can all do that, can't we. Verna, stay very close to Taal and do what she tells you and only that. I am trusting you to be sensible."

She seemed shocked that I should trust her to do anything, so warily nodded.

"I selected a group of warriors. Go with Addani, she's taking half the new women with her. Alyssa's unit will comprise the other half. Move in low and slow, use any cover that's possible. Once we have a solution I shall light a firestick, then you all get out as fast as you can. Right, go."

They quickly disappeared.

I led our group entering the fort over the ditch, through a few roundhouses, then I held a hand up. Indicating Sheelan to me, not that I needed to, she was almost in my pocket. We moved a house on. Then on again. It was very still.

Aloud scream rent the air as a charge developed from the other side. People began running all ways, diving under carts, in houses or chicken sheds, anywhere to escape the fury of the onslaught.

"Come on," I yelled at the top of my voice, and before we realised it we were standing in the middle of a square of houses.

Somebody called. "Queen Lauren, what are you doing here?"

"Come with us, my Queen, to safety." I replied. We came with the Romans. Are you hurt?"

"A cut arm. There are rebels coming in fast, you should get out before you're surrounded."

Alyssa touched my arm. "Over there, Lauren, look."

A group of rough men were coming our way in a semicircle, behind another mass of Celts from Venutius' force, surrounding us. At their head, a huge individual walked wielding a sword as large as Brevit's. It was impressive.

"It's Agar, my husband's personal bodyguard. He has never been beaten in battle." Cartimandua sounded defeated at the sight of him.

"Get behind us and ward off any attack for a few moments," I shouted to my band. "Come, us three Queens, let us face this giant of a man."

"It will take only moments, you'll all be killed, he is an ignorant oaf and shows no mercy," Cartimandua wailed.

Alyssa, Sheelan and me lined up side by side, facing the oncoming mob.

Agar stopped and roared with laughter. "What do you three weak women hope to do against me, the mighty Agar? I have many men surrounding you and have slain countless opponents, now and I shall slaughter you." He began walking forwards, closely followed by a dozen others.

Behind I heard the shuffling of feet as the mob approached Addani and Bran's warriors. Three swords were drawn at the same instant, held vertically in front of us. They glowed bright red.

Agar stopped, a puzzled look on his face. It was momentary, he continued coming on. At sword range he swung his mighty blade backwards ready to strike, then brought it round in a powerful sweep.

It hit mine with a resounding **Clang**, so loudly everybody jumped about a foot off the ground.

Agar stood rock solid, still holding the hilt of his sword staring at me. His only problem was that was all he had left, the rest had gone spinning away into the distance. His mouth sagged open staring at the remnants of his pride and joy, smashed and jagged in his fist. "Wha... what happened?" Anger took his face and drawing a long dagger from its sheath, lunged at me.

My sword swung with a loud whistling noise. I had had enough of this bullying over confident brute. That odd loud whistling sound accompanying it as the weapon struck his body at waist level, and kept going, slicing him neatly in half. The lower part dropped to the ground while the upper section fell sideways with the force of my blade. His shattered remnants lay rapidly oozing blood and gore into an ever-expanding pool on the ground, Agar's intestines spread across the top of that mess before the eyes of his villainous friends.

I took a step forward, as did Alyssa and Sheelan next to me.

"Who is next?" I enquired.

They looked at our swords, at Agar's remains, then every person turned and fled the field of battle.

Grabbing Cartimandua's wrist, I pulled her to us. "Now will you come?"

She nodded, gaping at the mess lying before her, too stunned to speak or resist.

I pulled the grenade out and lit it, throwing with all my might. It exploded in the centre of the square. Bang!

There had been a band of rebels walking into it, they bolted back out again.

Backing out, we met our other warriors.

Addani was grinning all over her face. "I saw that lot run away as fast as their legs would carry them, they were terrified, Highness."

"Good, it gives us time to get clear and away from here. The Romans can catch up."

As we left, the sounds of battle came drifting across the village. Our Romans had attacked.

Chapter Thirty One

The Defile

Behind us the battle raged on the far side of the village. Every now and then a loud thud would permeate the air as Roman shields were slammed down or at somebody. Our job was done, Cartimandua was moderately safe. All we had to do now was get all the way back to our own fort. Problems might arise if Venutius broke off the engagement once he discovered his ex-wife had fled. I guessed he would send scouts out looking for her, or who she was with.

Alyssa came close alongside. "Should we stop and check our people and the Queen's arm, Lauren?"

"Yes, now we have a sufficient gap between us."

Cartimandua had a slash across her right upper arm. Squirrel got cream and dressings from my straddle bags so it could be bound and keep it clean.

She watched Squirrel as she worked. "They are strange dressings, young lady. Where did you get them?" On arrival the

"Lauren got them, Highness."

The Queen glanced at me. "She calls you by your given name?"

"Squirrel is my Handmaiden, so I allow it."

"Squirrel, that's an odd name."

"I lived in a mountain village but left with Lauren to join her. I was a lot wilder than now, Highness, I think they called me it for a joke."

Cartimandua smiled. "You have the right coloured hair for one. What was that thing that went bang so loudly, Lauren?"

"It's what I call a grenade. They won't be invented for a long time yet."

"A long time yet?" Cartimandua muttered under her breath. "What can that mean?"

I didn't try to explain, curiosity would in her heart.

Everybody else was fine so our group made its way to our start point. It was fairly easy to find; the road was dead straight. People looked us over as we arrived, expecting casualties. They bowed at us and their Queen.

"What do you think Venutius is going to do?" I asked.

Cartimandua casually looked over her shoulder as if she expected to see him there. "He'll probably want to kill me. He won't be happy with simply claiming my rightful Queendom." There was no fear of death, she was a Queen and accepted that as her duty to her people if it came to it. The injustice was hurting her more than anything else.

"Here, Jeela made some tea. Try to relax a little, you're safe here."

She gave me a soft smile in return. "You have amazing swords, my Queens, I have never seen anybody do such a thing before. Do they come from the future?"

"From the Gods at the Stones," Alyssa replied. "They are very special."

"Yes, very special..." Her words trailed off.

It was nearing evening when we heard the tramp of marching feet.

"Addani, go along the road and check who it is, please."

She sped off, to return quickly.

"The Romans Highness. I wonder if they have wounded?"

Cohorts dispersed into units on arrival to settle and make food for everyone. It seemed chaotic, yet out of the mass of moving people came order.

Ligarius walked over. "We have wounded, Highness. Can you help please?"

"Yes, of course. Take me there."

A couple of dozen lay in a separate area. Mainly sword gashes when I examined them, one or two had spears thrusts in their sides as well, which were the worst injuries.

"Squirrel, bring my straddle bags please." Then to

322

Ligarius. "How many Celts were slain?"

"Many, Highness. They rushed our cohorts and fell to our pilums. Those that made it to the shield lines were cut down. Why do they keep running at us like that in disorganised waves?"

"It's the way Celts have always fought each other, two armies clashing headlong and the one with the most left, wins. It's a wasteful way, and not what I would do."

"You are a Goddess, Highness, everybody says that and I witnessed you cure the General Agricola and Laenius, we all thought him as good as dead."

I smiled back. "Thank you, Centurion. What is going to happen?"

"We rest tonight and begin the return tomorrow morning. Commander Marcus Cerilius has chosen a different way back, he feels it might put any pursuers off our track."

I had serious doubts about that. This mass of people would leave a trail a five-year-old could follow. But it mattered not, Fate would decide what happened.

"If we may, I would prefer to have Queen Cartimandua in the centre of our unit. She'll be safe with our Queens and in Celtic company."

Ligarius saluted. "That would be well with the Commander, Highness."

There were about thirty wounded. It was obvious we needed every one because our retreat, which is basically what it would be, was certain to be attacked.

While Squirrel went around cleaning and dressing their wounds, I had them touch my sword, explaining it was a Celtic custom.

We all rose very early. It was a foggy morning, tendrils snatched at our ankles and wove themselves among us. Horses whinnied, nervous because they couldn't see far, the chink of weapons and noise of armour and shields banging wafted about, combined with shouted orders. The column could be heard for miles.

We had been told to position ourselves in the centre of the cohorts. Perhaps the Commander felt we were well protected with legionaries in front and behind. I would have preferred them either side, but this was how the Roman army marched.

Ligarius appeared out of the haze. "Good morning Highness." He saluted. "I have checked all our wounded and every single one is cured. Whatever that cream was is truly amazing." He bowed. "I thought I had better let you know. I must return to my post now."

Orders were shouted and the column moved away from our camp onto the road. After half a day it bore right to go farther inland. This road was wider, meaning the cohorts could space out better and place guards either side.

"Will Venutius try attacking?" Alyssa asked, casting around both sides of us.

"He may, sweet one. We can only wait and see. Best we stay in a cohesive unit, we can get to any part of it quickly then."

She smiled back. "Sweet one. Thank you, Lauren."

Screams and yells came from behind us, followed by the clash of swords. The column halted immediately, reforming to face the threat.

I thought that a bad idea, it exposed the rear to forest behind us. Stay facing forwards. Cartimandua, come with me," I shouted.

Within a second or two another horde appeared out of that forest.

There was a slight gap between the first Celts and the front cohorts. We needed to get out quickly. "Follow me," I shouted again, drawing my sword and pushing my mount towards the opening.

It meant our people getting into single file and galloping as fast as their steeds would go. We went thundering past the forward cohorts who were in the process of deploying back. If they did that they might get caught if Veranius had another mass in the trees ahead, it would be a classic trap.

Out in the open now and on along the road. But where to? We needed to hole up somewhere, a place protected on all sides where it would be impossible to outflank us.

"This way, Highness," Alicia called as she rode to me. "I know the place to go."

I looked at her steadily for a few moments. Should I take her advice? She had lived near here so knew the land a lot better than me. I nodded. "Lead on."

She grinned back, pleased I had trusted her and excited at fighting, something they had practised doing for a long time.

Through the trees, deeper in forest. I was starting to wonder if I had done the right thing.

Our horses broke out at the bottom of a deep defile, the cliffs high above us, sheer faces that would be impossible to climb.

Alicia thundered on, right between the cliff faces until it began to open out. Then, and only then, did she halt. "Here Highness, you can defend this for as long as you want."

"Well done Alicia, this is perfect. Dismount, get the horses through the defile and clear of us. Addani, take half of our people and lodge them along the left side, Bran, take the rest and hide on the right. Alicia and your people, stay with us, we are going to bar the way."

She spun her horse, waving the sword Sheelan had given her high in the air. "Now we fight, my women, and help those that saved us."

We were secure and waited. The Romans were too far away to hear the sound of fighting, which meant we had no idea if they had prevailed.

"Light a fire please, Greta," I said. "Let's all have some tea and something to eat. Sheelan is going the other side of the defile to hunt."

"Am I?" she looked puzzled.

"The Romans have our food, so it means catching some, sweetheart. You'll be safe that side, take Jeela and Squirrel if you like, but no more, don't want to spook a deer, do you?"

They departed. Sheelan had her sword and a longbow. Jeela had a cross bow, so a spread of weapons. Squirrel I sent to get her out of the way in case an attack began.

It was getting into dusk by the time the trio came back. Sheelan had a deer across her shoulders, Jeela a doe.

"We killed the mother before I realise she had young, so had to kill it as well."

I knew she didn't like doing that, but things happen. "It was the best thing, sweetheart, it would have died a slow death otherwise."

Greta and Lark started the meal. We needed nourishment for to coming fight. It was obvious there could have been a draw in the ambush, although the Romans didn't know where we were. They might be pursued all along the road with attack after attack until too weak to defend themselves.

We ate and night fell. Lookouts were posted part-way up the start of the defile in case the Celts tried to sneak in. But it remained peaceful. People slept where they could, mostly very uncomfortably on this rocky ground.

The new women took it in turns with watches, Alicia having organised them into pairs. She was a good unit commander, I was impressed and thought it best to keep them all together for now. We could integrate them once back at the fort.

Cartimandua paced about for ages.

"What's the matter?" I asked.

"Venutius," she whispered, as if he might hear her.

"He has to get into this defile and can only do that from the ground, we have lookouts posted. We cannot be surprised. Try to get rest, tomorrow might be a lot busier."

Chapter Thirty Two

Retreat

Dawn broke. It seemed very quiet to me, unnaturally so. Yesterday birds had been singing along the walls of the defile. Now, nothing.

"It's quiet, Lauren," Sheelan said stating the obvious, as Madeil would have.

I smiled. "Perhaps because it's early in the morning sweetheart?"

"I have a funny feeling," she replied.

That made me sit up and take notice. Sheelan was like Maddy in practically every way and had feelings about upcoming events, just as she had.

"What sort of feeling, Sheelan?"

"Something's going to happen soon, my love. We should prepare."

"Addani, Bran," I yelled.

"Yes Highness?

"Sheelan has a feeling. Ready your people please."

Both Leaders knew exactly what that meant, bowed and went to their posts to shout orders.

We went about a hundred yards or so along the defile and marked the spot. It gave us a range for the first loosing. After that was completed, we waited ages for any signs of activity. An owl hoot came back from Addani, followed by another from Bran. They had seen the enemy.

I heard arrows loosed, the fallowing sound clear in the brisk morning air. Shouts went up near the start of the defile.

Jeela came running back. "Highness, they wish to talk."

"I'll come. Alyssa, Sheelan, let's go see who wants to talk."

A tall slim man with a dark beard and unruly mop of hair stood in the centre of the track leading into our protective zone. He had been halted by Bran and Addani.

Bran walked to us. "It's Venutius, Highness. He claims he wants to negotiate."

"You are a Queen?" the individual asked, almost demanded as he looked at our crowns.

Our appearance surprised him, Cartimandua wore a torc.

He was abrupt, confident and with what I thought, an overbearing attitude. It wasn't the best way to open any form of communications with what ostensibly, was an enemy.

"We are all Queens. What do you wish to discuss?"

"Hand over Cartimandua."

"That is a demand, not a discussion," I answered testily.

"I have an army behind me. I want her handed over, now."

"You are still not discussing anything. Do not threaten us, it will be the worse for you."

He laughed in my face. "Simple Queens. You might wear fancy crowns and carry gilded swords, that doesn't mean you can use them."

"You say "Your Highness" to my Queen," Bran snapped.

Venutius drew his sword and went to strike her, anger in his violent eyes.

Mine seemed to leap into my hand and blocked the blow. As his sword hit mine a loud **Clang** rang out.

Venutius stood looking at his shattered weapon in shock.

"You dare to come under a peace discussion and then make demands and attack my Warrior Leader. Go, you have destroyed any likelihood of negotiation. If you attach, you will find us a very hard nut to crack, harder than the Romans."

He backed away a few paces. "What is that sword?"

"Your doom," I replied. "This interview is at an end."

I turned to walk away, motioning Alyssa and Sheelan to come with me. I felt the movement behind rather than saw it. My right hand was lifted up, placing my sword behind my back.

The ring of iron echoed off the defile walls.

Turning, I discovered Venutius holding a slashed arm and a dagger on the ground. "You tried to sneak a blow at me. You are a stupid man. You cannot best a Goddess. Come my Queens, we return to our lines."

A cheer went up around us. "Hooray for our Queens."

I guessed it was Addani and Bran, and that Venutius had slunk away to nurse his wound. I had to wonder myself at those two incidents. It was as if my sword had a mind of its own. Perhaps it was Madeil or the Gods that had protected me, whoever it was could read his mind as if he had told them what he intended doing.

Sheelan grabbed me. "He tried to kill you Lauren."

Alyssa laughed. "I think that might be more difficult than he ever realises, Sheelan."

We waited for the inevitable charge, or whatever Venutius had in his devious mind. Perhaps they were talking options over, they were a long time about it?

Noises came from Addani's position, shouts and the clash of weapons. It lasted only a few minutes.

Jeela came running back. "They tried climbing along the side of the defile, Highness. Our group beat them off. Addani sent me to let you know."

"Give Addani my compliments, tell her well done."

Another pause. Alyssa and Sheelan squeezed up close. There was concern on their faces.

More yelling drifted along the gorge, so they had tried again. "They are probing our defences."

This time Greta came, panting from her run. "Bran drove them away, Majesty."

"Okay Greta. Return to your post." Where would the next push come? They had tested both sides, hoping to get around us, but outflanking here was impossible. Celts normally charged so I guessed that was their only option now.

It soon came. A screaming war cry echoed off the walls of the defile as a mass of humans came running down, swords waving it the air, their blue bodies looking ugly in the light reflecting off them. The closeness of the defile sides prevented a mass charge as they no doubt would have liked, to overwhelm us, forcing them into a width of five or six people.

"Steady, loose when at the first outcrop we marked." I nocked an arrow and drew my longbow to full extent.

The mark was met, arrows went off in a cloud, albeit a small one from our hundred or so warriors. But a second and a third volley followed quickly.

The enemy stopped dead in their tracks, the force of arrows alone pushing men backwards. Many lay dead or dying, their Woad no protection against a longbow.

Venutius tried to rally them, standing as he was, in a multitude of twisted corpses. But even wild Celts have limits and must give ground under such a bombardment of missiles. They began moving backwards, then came under fire from either side as their retreat came level with our two forward hillside units. More fell.

"How many are there?" Alyssa asked.

"I have no idea. The Romans may have killed many at the village and then on the road so their numbers could be severely reduced. Each time they charge us they'll lose more, there is no way they can get along this defile to us."

"Maybe they'll go away," Sheelan mumbled.

"I doubt that, sweetheart." Then an incident came to mind from history, Thermopylae. The Spartans had held that pass successfully against the Persians but were outflanked when a Greek traitor showed them a barely known mountain track which the Persians used to get behind and defeat the defenders. "Alicia, would you take your women back and see if you can find any way of getting along the top of the defile. Look both sides please. Take longbows with you, can you use a bow?"

"Yes, Majesty, we all can. See you soon."

Another wait ensued. None of us had thought of looking to see if the cliffs could be scaled somehow, if they could, then an enemy could climb down as well as up. I didn't want Venutius coming on our rear and so surrounding us.

Loud yells came from above. A man came tumbling down hitting the ground with a thud. He lay very still, an arrow sticking from his chest.

"Lark, Kwail, pick this many," I said showing them six fingers, "up to help Alicia. They are fighting on the left side above us. Go girls, quickly!"

Moments went by without a sound.

A hellish scream bounced off the defile walls as another body tumbled down the side of the rock face, bouncing evey time it struck until it too, lay higgledy piggledy in a jumbled mess. There was no arrow.

Kwail appeared running back towards us. "We found a patrol up there, Highness. They must of have a job climbing because their hands and legs are all cut. Alicia had beaten them back; the track is very narrow on a ledge. The last one slipped and fell. She said her women can hold it all day, just a handful, she's sending the rest back down. Is that well with you?"

"Yes, and well done. I don't think Venutius will try that again. Take this many and check the other side, please, Kwail." I felt four would be sufficient.

"Me lead a unit, wow! Thank you, Highness." She went off calling names.

"How did you know they would do that?" Alyssa asked.

"College, remember, sweet one."

She laughed. "Yes, I remember. It must have been a wonderful place."

"Can't sit here forever, although it is perfectly defensible. Our fort needs us, as do our people, Alyssa," I pointed out. "We also need to find the Roman legion, they'll be on the road."

"But if we leave this place, Venutius will be able to surround us," Sheelan said. "We can't keep a large force at bay for long, Lauren."

"Come on Sheelan, you and me, up onto that ledge and

work our way along until we can see how many Venutius has now. It's important we know."

Her look was uncertain. "Is it wise, my love?"

"We have to disengage from him somehow. You take a couple of grenades, I'll have my rifle. Let's see if we can frighten them enough to run back to their village."

A wicked grin spread across her face. "Okay, let's."

A kiss for Alyssa each, loaded our weapons, swords, grenades and rifle, no bows, they were bulky if on a ledge. Lark showed us where they climbed up, plenty of hand and footholds, the climb began. It was a stiff one and needed care to avoid jagged rocks.

Alicia waved as we stepped onto the track. "Here, Highness. See how narrow it is, we can keep them from coming along here all day."

"I need to see their numbers. We're going along that ledge, watch our backs please."

Moving along meant one hand for us, one for the rock wall on our left. The path was made up from broken rocks and stones and hardly wide enough for a person, no wonder one had fallen. It was possible to see Addani and her team the other side lower down, tucked into nooks and crannies. Then the path opened up a little, sufficient for us to squat and peer over the edge.

Below lay Venutius' camp. At a guess I thought about thirty men. Whether or not this was all that was left of the force that attacked the village or was a part of it or even all that remained after their encounter with the Romans, I had no idea.

"Not many, Lauren," Sheelan said. "Can I send Nodens down?"

"Let my firestick speak first, that should make them wonder how I can strike men down without a bow." Flipping rounds into the magazine, I took careful aim. It might have been best to take out their leader, but they all looked the same from here so I had no idea which one it was. The morality of doing it at all entered my mind. But they had attacked us, we had been prepared to talk, only he wouldn't. If Venutius had his way I would be dead by now with his sword in my back. Taking aim, I squeezed the trigger.

Bang!

A reload, click clack.

Panic ensued below. They were searching around for the source of the noise; the explosion having bounced around the defile.

I stood, aimed and fired again.

Bang!

Someone was pointing up at us. Voices were bandied about in terror.

"Return to your village before my Goddess strikes every one of your dead," Sheelan hollered, and wow, could she holler.

"Never," a voice came back. Shaking fists were aimed at us.

Taking another bead, I fired.

Bang! Another man dropped.

"Use a Nodens Sheelan."

A huge grin took her face. She lit the wick and casually tossed it over.

Somebody laughed and shouted that throwing sticks would make no difference.

Bang!

Screams and yells drifted up. People fled in all directions, some hiding, some still running.

"I am a Goddess and shall send Nodens down again. Go back to your village at once. Be satisfied, Venutius, that you may still be allowed to keep it. If I come there I shall destroy the houses and you with them."

This time no shaking fists were waved, no caustic comments thrown up at us. There still persisted an unwillingness to move though.

"Another, please sweetheart."

Bang!

Now weapons were gathered and they moved away

towards their home, sullen and defeated.

"Let's go find our Roman escort, shall we?" I said, with a grin at Sheelan. "I can't see them wishing to take on a Goddess in battle, can you?"

Chapter Thirty Three

Venutíus

Within an hour or two we saw the Roman column ahead.

Ligarius was surprised to see us all still intact. "I heard the fight, Highness. Very loud bangs, what were they?"

"Lauren is a Goddess," Sheelan cut in. "She controls Nodens."

"Who is Nodens, Majesty?"

"Our God of thunder and lightning, Ligarius. Venutius has, we hope, retreated to his village now."

"Lauren said she would go and destroy it if he didn't," Sheelan giggled.

"I'm sure you're capable, your Majesty. I have seen you do amazing things." He saluted. "Would you return to your position in the centre of our column, please?"

I nodded. "Have you any wounded?"

"A few, my Queen. We are due to stop soon, would you kindly look at them then?"

"Of course."

The units fell out eventually beside a stream. Horses were watered, some Centurions and Commanders rode them. All of us did, we had given the men's mounts taken at that terrible village to Alicia and her women. Once or two had to double, so we rotated those as much as possible.

Ligarius had all wounded assemble in one place, it was faster. Most were sword cuts. Field dressings were used on those. Only one thrust in a side, which was more awkward. And he had to go into a wagon, it was too severe to walk.

He looked miserable. "We have an old Celtic custom, young man," I explained. "that all wounded warriors should touch one of their Queens swords. Which one do you wish to choose?"

His eyes went from one to the other. "The one with short red haired, please Highness."

"Her name is Queen Sheelan, do as she commands."

Sheelan had that daft grin on her face. She had never used her sword before like this, only I had done so. She slowly unsheathed it from her back scabbard, it began glowing slightly.

"It glows like the sun on a dull day, Highness," he said unsure. "Will it burn me?"

"I'm holding it," Sheelan replied. "I'm not burned."

He slowly touched the blade, then grinned. "It was cold, Majesty. You must be a Goddess too."

Sheelan blushed.

"You have hair the colour of fire, Goddess Sheelan, like the evening sun shining down on us in glory."

She blushed even more.

"The Goddess Sheelan is a very shy Goddess," I explained. "She is Vowed to me and Queen Alyssa."

His face dropped. Then brightened. "That would be correct, three Goddesses together. Our Gods would agree with that, my Queen."

Alyssa patted his shoulder. "Just get well young man."

The next few days were uneventful. The column stopped many times now there was no dreadful urgency to get anywhere, although Alyssa, Sheelan and me wanted desperately to see the fort again. We however, had to move at the speed of the Romans, which in truth was fairly fast, their marching pace was high.

At this particular stop I have taken my horse to the river and was standing idly wondering what Venutius might be doing.

"He's in his village," a voice said.

And there stood Madeil.

My mouth dropped open. Gathering my emotions together, I put my arms around her. "How wonderful to see you again, darling. How is Eva?"

"She's here..."

As her words faded, Eva appeared standing beside her. "Hello Highness, thank you for what you did and the dreadful chances you all took. I cried, it was so lovely. And here you are fighting again, risking that precious life of yours."

"I wanted you sent properly, Eva. If anybody should, it was you."

She clasped me to her. "I was hurting for so long, but that has gone now, I wanted to come but wasn't sure how so Madeil helped me. Wasn't that kind of her?"

My voice choked up. Tears fell. "Yes," I croaked, "she is very kind, I love you all."

"Venutius is thinking about attacking again. He believes you use a trick in the defile and thinks you can't do it if away from those rocks. Be careful darling, he's already on his way. I'll keep an eye on him. We must go now, a Roman is coming." they slowly dissolved into thin air.

Ligarius came with Marcus Cerilius. They both saluted.

"Thank you for your support, my Queen. You seem to be able to do things we cannot and Centurion Ligarius Manimus has told me of some wonders you performed recently. General Gnaeus Julius Agricola is making his way back to Sarum, I received a runner yesterday. I am sure he'll be pleased to hear of your help and successful outcome." He saluted again and was about to turn and leave.

"Commander, I advise you Venutius has left his village and is intending to mount an ambush soon." I bowed.

Cerilius looked blankly back.

"Queen Lauren is known as a Goddess among her people, Commander." Ligarius Manimus slapped his chest.

"She can see into the future?" Cerilius said it, unbelieving.

"Yes, Commander, she can, and uses cures from the future

on our men."

Cerilius hesitated for several moments, looking at Ligarius' deadpan face weighing up his statement. "I will accept your advice, my Queen, but am uncertain of it. However, I have ignored such information in the past and regretted it. Thank you." He saluted and left.

I huffed out. At least he wasn't too proud to accept my word.

Alyssa was by my side. "You look..." she paused... "odd Lauren. What is it?"

"Madeil and Eva came. "Eva thanked us all for sending her away so well. Then Maddy told me Venutius is heading our way hoping to set an ambush. He's still intent on capturing Cartimandua. She must stay in our midst at all times, sweet one."

Alyssa nodded knowingly. "I'll set a guard around her, my Personal Guard is best, they'll protect her with their lives, as they would us. Did Madeil say when this might happen?"

"No, but I think soon. We are almost at those big forests halfway back, that is the most likely place."

Cerilius ordered the column on. Forest rapidly increased, although the Romans had maintained open areas either side of the road along which we travelled. He had also moved a single column of legionaries to march both sides of us. It was a slim line of defence and I didn't give much hope for it withstanding a massed attack.

I was getting an uneasy feeling and told Alyssa.

"It seems quiet enough," she replied.

"That's the trouble, sweet one, it is too quiet. That usually means humans are in among the trees that are not hunting. A trap towards the road will only be hidden from that side, ambushers wouldn't worry about the rear. Fauna would see them and run away. I'll warn our leaders."

Bran and Addani nodded acceptance and went to alert our warriors. We were as prepared as we possibly could be.

The war cry came suddenly and so loudly I think everybody jumped. Dozens of painted tribesmen flooded out of the forest on either side aiming their charge at our section and the legionaries.

Their huge oblong shields swung off their shoulders, displaying the brightly emblazoned fronts of red overlaid with a golden wing radiating out to the four corners, a golden twisted horn horizontally across the centre with added jagged lightning in between all those. Spears bounced off, javelins hardly made any penetration, the legionaries remaining safe behind them. Then they threw their pilums, iron javelins, heavy and lethal to any unprotected person, such as the Celtic warriors are.

Many fell before reaching halfway across the gap, the impetus taken away from the wild charge. They finally clashed with the shield wall and many more fell victims to the Roman gladius before being able to strike a blow.

Some Romans did fall, and Celts broke through to us.

"Swords," I shouted as loud as I could, drawing mine the same instant as Alyssa and Sheelan.

A Celt grabbed my right leg, trying to pull me off my horse. My downward sword stroke cleaved his head in two, brains and blood spilling out as he fell. The next seeing his comrade's fate, hesitated long enough for Alyssa to stab him through.

Two tried to dismount Sheelan; her riposte was a sideways swipe that decapitated both, their bodies slumping to the ground.

The remainder stepped back after witnessing the power of our weapons.

Not so Venutius. He had come to capture Cartimandua and plainly felt this was the moment. To his confused mind, there was no chance of our tricks on the defile, no little bangs that were magnified by the surrounding rock faces. His ugly face was beside Cartimandua, having got through our warriors as they fought off the rush. He made a grab, took hold of an arm and dragged her to her feet. It was easy enough to pull a person from a horse, we had no saddles.

I jumped from mine to face him. "Let her go," I demanded.

Venutius laughed. "You have no tricks here, woman."

"True, but I have my sword so need nothing else."

He pulled the Queen in front of him. "She dies if you try to stop our escape."

I bowed to him.

He seemed surprised. "Well it is, that you recognised my superior standing, woman."

My bow had been to pluck a dagger from my calf sheath, which I promptly threw at his face.

He screamed in agony, letting go of Cartimandua to clutch at my weapon that stuck out just below his left eye.

Three Queens surrounded him at sword point. "Get away from this place of ambush, a trick that has failed you. Leave the Queen alone to a life of peace. You have enough injuries, depart and nurse them." Realisation dawned that the battle had stopped.

Venutius walked out of our lines, back to his followers. "You win this time, woman, but the next time we meet I shall stand victorious."

It was a stupid and conceited statement, having lost to us three times already.

"You will surely die then, Venutius."

He glared at me, casting a look at the dagger he had flung on the ground in anger. Then walked away into the folds of his men again.

It wasn't for long. Ten or so ran back screaming like madmen at us in an attempt to instil fear.

They reached within fifteen feet when the fallowing sound of arrows filled the air.

Every man fell, mostly lifted off their feet to be thrown backward several feet.

I turned to find the new women standing with spent longbows. Alicia bowed. "They attacked again, Highness, we had the right."

"Addani, Bran, check them please."

"Only one lives, my Queen, Venutius. But he is badly wounded. Shall we dispatch him?"

I walked to the figure lying on the ground, an arrow sticking out of his left shoulder. "You now know the power of our bows. Don't ever try to foil them again because one of my archers will loose the next and they are much better shots. Go to your fort and stay there, your life will not be spared again if I ever see you near our fort."

Cartimandua stood in shock. She had almost been taken and that meant no leniency, only humiliation and possibly death after torture.

Cerilius stood beside me. "Are you uninjured, my Queen?"

"Yes, my Lord, we all are, thank you for asking."

"They are formidable bows, my Queen. You have allowed the rebel to live again?"

"If he ever shows his face near any of my warriors they have strict instructions to kill immediately." I said it loud enough for Venutius to hear where he lay as some of his tribesmen tried to drag his away.

"Very well, we resume our march south."

Chapter Thirty Four

A New Way

Another four days saw us in friendly territory. I was aware Alyssa desperately wanted to be back in our fort and get back to running it as she had for so long.

We had a new Queen as well. What would happen to her? She was used to governing and that could be awkward, we already had three queens here as it was. How would we manage to integrate her in a compassionate way? We needed to find out how she felt now after such a traumatic experience and ordeal. She might be in shock, she had said very little other than thank us for saving her life. I felt her aim was to stay in her stronghold, but that would have been impossible with Venutius on the warpath and determined to take her life. My reverie was broken by Ligarius speaking to me.

"We are at the forest leading to your fort, Highness," he said, saluting us as one with a smile. "The General has instructed me to detach a cohort to escort you all back safely."

"Inform the General he is most kind and considerate. We hope he is received with due honour at Sarum."

"General Agricola will arrive soon, as well. Our barracks will be to strength again. Our losses shall be made up from the deplete Twentieth Legion after its battle in the far south, my Queen."

There had been an uprising near Exeter, known now as Isca Dumnonoirum. Romans had odd names for places I thought.

"Are all your warriors well?" Ligarius asked.

"They are, Centurion, thank you again for your concern."

He saluted and left us with our escort.

"Home," Alyssa sighed. She looked tired, it had been a long campaign and with many fights. "How wonderful to be back. I wonder if Shaila has had problems, although I feel nothing amiss."

The ground began to rise as we started onto the short climb to the north gates and into the fort. Everybody was aware of a visit from some sizeable unit and had flocked to the gates to see who it was. A wild cheer went up as our people entered, but eyes were cast about our numbers looking for any missing warriors.

Shaila dashed up beaming all over her face. "Highnesses, you are back safely?"

Alyssa acknowledged. "Yes Shaila, we all are. We have more women who need looking after until they decide what they wish to do. They've had a hard and brutal life so care for them well, please. Ask for Alicia, she seems to be their leader."

The convoy halted outside the palace. The cohort Centurion saluted. "I leave you at your fort, my Queens. We return to Sarum barracks now." He saluted again as was the Roman way.

"Thank you, Centurion. Have a safe journey," Alyssa replied.

It suddenly hit us; we were back home in our own palace after all the trials and tribulations we had suffered.

Alyssa slumped onto the bed to lie and relax. "How wonderful to sleep on a comfortable bed tonight, darlings. We should make it a special night, don't you feel? I have missed your tender touches far too long."

Sheelan had a broad grin on her face. "It would be like Hod Hill."

Alyssa's warm smile came through then as she recalled that experience. "What a beautiful idea, Hod Hill, yes, that was really special." She reached into a small box beside the bed, stood and walked to the fire. Her hand moved across the top of the flames, opened and what looked like ashes fell.

344

A misty haziness quickly began to fill the room and begged us to breath it in. It was intoxicating, delirious, welcoming of our senses, asking them to join each other in a blissful union.

I felt light, as I had last time as the room became blurred.

Sheelan drifted to me, putting her arms around my neck to plant the gentlest of kisses upon my lips. The pulse of fire she created within me by such a simple action became indescribably exciting. I knew Alyssa was with us, her warm body touched me in a myriad of sensuous emotions. Yet another two came close as well, their tender hands seeking out secret places that tempted us further, to cry out in the joy of our intimacy.

A strange feeling of desire ran across my back and down my spine to end between my legs. My mind turned into a kaleidoscope of want, to have my body answer the call of theirs, a call that turned into a demand that was impossible to deny. I called their names loudly, felt their bodies upon mine, their touches that sent me to a higher plane of feelings so Intense, I screamed.

The enveloping mist had cleared in the room. All three of us were naked in bed, furs a rumpled mess of untidiness. My consort's faces swam into focus and looking at the door, I saw Agneta watching us with eyes wide open. She bowed hastily and ran back into the annex blushing.

Alyssa and Sheelan had returned to their beautiful youthful appearance, so perfect and charming. "You are both incredible, I do so hope you will stay this way for all time."

A radiant smile was returned. "That was worth waiting for, Lauren darling. How I love you both so deeply."

Sheelan just giggled and had that daft expression that made her look so like Madeil. My heart smiled too.

It must have been early next morning when Agneta finally returned. I sensed her presence rather than saw her, the room was dark still. "Is that you, Agneta?"

"Yes Highness. You called out again a short while ago. Did you want something?"

"I must have been asleep. Where is Squirrel?"

"I let her sleep on, Majesty. She is a lovely person, we cuddled all night."

A secret smile flitted across my lips. "Squirrel is a very special woman. Look after her and treasure all the moments together life might allow you."

"Agneta?" a voice called. "I missed you, were have you gone to?" Squirrel stepped into the palace, her vision beginning to adapt.

"Come here, Squirrel," I asked softly.

"Lauren, I apologise if I woke you," she said.

"I was awake. Step closer so I can see you please."

She was naked. "I beg your pardon Lauren, I have just left our bed... I mean my bed... I mean..." her words trailed off.

"You have at least found Agneta, my lovely Handmaiden. I am very pleased for you both. Don't ever be afraid to show affection to each other no matter where you are. Love is a beautiful emotion, you are both young and should enjoy it to the full. Would you get us some porridge please, I'm afraid I have woken my loves up?"

Agneta and Squirrel looked at each other in surprise at my statement, then turned and almost skipped out happily.

"Squirrel won't keep kissing you now, at least," Alyssa said laughing. "Sheelan and me can have you all to ourselves."

We ate our bowls of breakfast avidly. "I think we used a lot of energy up last night," I commented.

A trumpet sounded.

"Legate is early," Alyssa muttered. "What on earth has got into him. I hope it isn't another request for help."

We hurriedly dressed in gowns, crowns and swords. The air had a morning chill in it as we walked onto the palace frontage.

General Agricola had already dismounted. "Did I wake you? My apologies if that is so."

"No, my Lord," Alyssa replied. "Would you take refreshment with us?"

"Willingly, my Queens." He entered, taking a chair. "I wondered how you all were after that adventure?" he asked, looking around us.

"Well, General, thank you. How did your deployment go?"

"Very satisfactory, thank you Queen Lauren. I have a question." He paused, licked his lips to moisten them, then looked into each of our faces.

I began wondering what was coming. It was peculiar behaviour for a Roman, to say the least. He seemed nervous, unsure how to phrase his point.

"When you returned, did you notice anything different about the fort?"

"No, I did not, my Lord. Should we have?"

"You are very observant, Queen Lauren, but then you had only just got back from time away and I expect wanted to relax in your palace."

I nodded. "We had a welcome from some people who cheered us in. Then we came here to rest, General."

"I thought so. It's just that many moved to Sarum while we were all farther north. Some have remained, as you saw, but many haven't. Will that be upsetting for you?"

I knew it would for Alyssa. Her heart lived for the fort and her people. To have so many leave and turn their backs on the old ways would be a terrible blow. I put and arm around her shoulders.

"Gone away," she almost whispered. Her face showed confusion, of having to swallow such a bitter pill that her subjects should desert her while away for such a short time. Tears began trickling down her lovely cheeks. She was lost.

"I thought it better coming from a friend, your Highness," Agricola said as kindly as he could. "Rome and the Romans are greatly indebted to you, to all of you and your warriors.

347

The services given so freely to us touched our hearts and minds. We think of you as Romans, respect and admire you. All through the problems you and your people suffered under unfair Legates, yet you still supported my legions, and even me," he added with a rueful smile.

"You never harmed us once, my Lord, we respect you for that," I replied.

"Perhaps this mode of life is ending, my Queens. People want to live more comfortably in better houses. You should all live in a grander palace, one that is light and airy the same as your hospital but larger. It is my great pleasure to be able to offer you such a place, a large villa on the outskirts of Sarum not far from my own. I beseech you all, come and join us, allow us to protect and show you our ways. Queen Lauren already knows of them I am sure, she knows how the future will develop and will move on. I will even have a hospital made for her near to your villa. Your slaves, oh, I mean servants, can also join you, as ours live with us. You need to decide what place Queen Cartimandua will play in your hierarchy, too."

I huffed out. That was a bombshell and completely unexpected. "Thank you General. Would you give us a moment please?"

Alyssa's beautiful blue eyes seemed empty. "Our people gone?" she groaned dejectedly. "That was so quick. Why Lauren, why?"

"For the same reason the tradesmen and women will, slowly but surely. The fort will fall into disuse. With no population to care for life will get lonely. Some will stay, those that till the land, farmers must have a farm after all. I hadn't taken much notice when we came back, although the crowds weren't as large as usual. I am afraid it is the future, sweet one. Why not accept the Genera's offer? You can still be Queen Alyssa in Sarum as well as here, that won't change. You will have a pool as well, so can swim to your hearts content."

The smile back was weak. "I suppose I can still be my

people's Leader, can't I, darling? still solve their problems and have them visit for whatever reason?"

"Yes, that is exactly what you can do, be a Queen somewhere else., but still the Queen."

She gave the deepest sigh I think I have ever heard in my life. "What of Cartimandua, my Lord?"

"I leave that up to you, Highness. After the trouble of rescuing her, perhaps you might prefer her to move with you, but have her own villa. She is a Queen in her own tight."

Alyssa nodded. "Very well, I submit. When would you wish us to move, General?"

He gave a broad grin. "Now, Highnesses. Behind me are wagons and men to assist. All you need to do is ride there. Your women in the house near the north gate will be moved as well and housed near you. I know you respect the elders of your clan."

And so it was. The Roman army moved us lock, stock and lots of barrels, all that lived in the fort including Toler and Bod. Our warriors were to be house as well, so Alyssa would still keep her ever faithful Guard. Bran and Addani were to be placed a couple of houses from us so would still be on call.

As we rode slowly out of the north gate, Alyssa pulled her mount to the gatepost, pausing to allow her hand to touch and linger on the wood. ""

I went to her, a lonely figure that needed a loved one beside them now. My hand rested on hers. "Never forget you are still a Queen, my love. And will be forever.

Her face was streaked with tears when she turned to face me. An attempt at a smile held her face momentarily like a moving shadow. "Thank you, my sweet Lauren. Now let us leave this sad place." Then, tapping its side with her heels, her horse moved down the slope into the forest, passing the boulder where so many momentous events had taken place.

A cohort stood formed on the road to escort us to our new home and way of life, a new world and new challenges. The column moved off, passing the small village we had stopped at when searching for our swords. People came and waved, many cheered us, some came to hand flowers to our warriors. A short distance on, a large villa appeared on our left.

Ligarius rode beside me. "Here is your permanent home, my Highnesses. The General had much Roman furniture installed, but your amazing bed has been brought here for you. Settle and enjoy your new status."

I bowed on Alyssa's behalf. She was in no state to reply. What would this new status be? Not as it was at the fort, I was under no allusions about that. Romans ruled here, not Celtic Queens.

Walking between the gate cut into the high surrounding wall we traversed a garden, then the house and the atrium, finding that spacious and bright. White walls everywhere reflected daylight to illuminate the place, so different from the darker rooms of a roundhouse, even with the white walls of the palace. The villa was large, as Agricola had promised with reception, dining, several bedrooms and relaxation rooms. There was even a bath section. Outside we discovered a large garden with a pool, much as at Ligarius' villa that had pleased Alyssa so much.

She seemed to cheer up. "It's so wonderful, darling. I think I can rule my people here as well as at the fort."

Sheelan and I cuddled her. The change had been tricky, Alyssa might have been a fish completely out of water in Sarum. But whatever she might be, she was also a realist. Living conditions would be far better, not only for us but for all her subjects and in the final analysis, that is who the Queen cared for more than anything else. She knew, that with no occupied fort there would be nothing to attack. The Romans would keep order, any such rising would be dealt with ferociously, as we would have. Far better Romans died attaining peace than our warriors.

We lived a life of relative luxury for several years. Our warriors kept themselves fit for our protection, should the need ever arise.

Chapter Thirty Five

Departing

A sunny day dawned, much like many other sunny days had. Yet there seemed to me to be an unanswered question in the air. What was our purpose here now?

The Gods made us almost immortal. Our warriors and us had fought battles against repression and injustice and won. We also knew Venutius had died of an illness, so his regime was gone to be replaced by a more lenient Brigantian one, although it still fought Roman occupation.

Other tribes in the south and west were pacified having lost too many of their numbers during wars with a greater unstoppable force. Occasional squabbles broke out and a legion was sent to repress it, which they invariably did efficiently.

Alyssa had settled and was happy, which is all I ever wanted for her. She remained youthful, rarely dared wrinkles or stress lines appear on her lovely features. In fact, all our lives were blissful, the Romans saw to that. Agricola never forget his promises and our support for him and his men.

Queen Cartimandua stayed at the fort for a considerable time as the sovereign, much as Alyssa had. In the end however, there was little left to govern and she too, moved to Sarum, the Romans again keeping their agreement to support her, only in a different way, to ensure her comfort.

So, the point came back again; what of us? Both Sheelan and Alyssa appeared distracted, uneasy, as though expecting an event, yet wasn't sure what it might be.

"I have an odd feeling, Lauren," Sheelan said, breaking the silence that had hung in the room nearly all morning. That was unusual too, both Alyssa and Sheelan were normally chatterboxes so silence was oppressive. They looked downcast as well, unhappy about what might lie ahead.

"What of, sweetheart?" I asked nervously, knowing how very odd her feelings could be from bitter experience.

"As if all this, our home, friends and everything we hold dear, will fade," she replied, a melancholy note in her voice.

"Fade? In what way?" Alyssa almost whispered. "I have to admit, I have a similar feeling. Do you, Lauren?"

For some reason my foresight had left me, I had no vision of the future. Yet I had studied it, knew of it and what would occur to this lovely land in years to come. But now that vision had gone blank.

"I feel nothing and I don't understand."

Alyssa stood and motioned us together in the centre of the room. "We must hold each other tightly, I have been instructed," she said. Yet her statement made no sense.

"Instructed? By whom?" I asked.

"By the Gods I believe, darling. I heard a voice."

I certainly hadn't. Perhaps, as Alyssa was the "senior" Queen, the Gods were telling her first.

Meeting the others, we linked arms. The warmth of their flesh touched me, so hot were they the sensation surprised me, transmitting from them to me in a cascade of power.

Then I heard it.

"Great Queens," the deep resonant Voice came, "You have completed your objectives and tasks for this period of time. Your work is at an end until your skills will be needed again to help a new people survive invasion and integration. That time will come, but not yet. There is a special place where such people as you reside between such tasks, now is the time for the Gods to take you there."

We looked at each other stupefied. What special place? What tasks? The room became indistinct, hazy, out of focus, losing solidity, become distant. Perhaps the Lords and Gods felt we had done enough for now, peace reigned in the land and forts were no longer inhabited after people moved nearer towns and made villages. The Britons had become independent so three Queens were no longer necessary. As our environment changed another vision began forming around us, a large Cavern with a vast table along its centre piled high for a feast. Lights glistened off the walls as Elven Pipes played enchanting music that echoed around and enfolded us. We were still hugging each other as we had in the villa, Sheelan on my right, Alyssa to the left.

Alyssa, her red hair flowing down her back and around her shoulders like a heavenly cloak, broke tenderly from my grasp, to stand resplendent in a long, beautiful blue gown. Brushing the front of it smooth with her hands, a movement that altered the angle of the crown she wore so it glistened like a million stars. I recognised that action, bringing back a memory of a hill fort where this beautiful Queen once lived and ruled. Sheelan still stood on my right holding my waist, the warmth of her arm reassuring during this strange event. On her right Madeil and Evelyn slowly appeared as if from nowhere, and behind them, upright and strong, Brevit and all our other brave warriors who had come to welcome us.

We were home, where such Queens as us should be and live. That is, until our abilities would be needed again in the vastness of time...

Chapter Thirty Six

The Museum

Stan had walked to the site of the hill fort where a small museum had been built, an annex to the hospital research section. As he entered and saw the artefacts displayed for public viewing, his mind drifted back to earlier times and fond memories of those he had met and his friend Fran Bromyard.

Yes, Fran. During her excavations she had looked farther afield to the woods behind Alegia's old home and found a low barrow that had been covered from view by bushes and soil. Inside were the remains of several women, their bodies had been carefully laid side-by-side, skeletal hands holding some of the weapons used during their lives.

Fran had realised they were some of the forts warriors and had remove them to safety. While she knew they would prefer to be left, the wood was going to be felled and couldn't allow these women she had known, spent time with and held in her arms, to be destroyed with it. She had them taken to Stan's unit and persevered there. But time had enforced a change of director and all remains had been transferred to public display.

Should that be prevented Stan mused? They represented the fight for freedom of all ancient Britons at that time, the struggle against Romano subjugation and oppression, of self-sacrifice and honour, extreme bravery and courage in the face of overwhelming odds.

Professor Stan Slater had tried to oppose it but had been outvoted. Skeletons had been placed in airtight glass boxes as they were found, holding hands. Scans are taken of the skulls so facial reproductions could be made to show these iron age Warriors to every visitor how they looked during their brief lifetimes. Now they will gaze out onto the world again and perhaps for all time, in fact Stan thought, Forever, and Until Eternity.

There had been a mystery too; what had happened to Fran? This centre had been her idea and inspiration, but once built she had suddenly disappeared. Perhaps she had gone back in time, she had been strongly influenced by the era when they had taken the plunge and used the portal. Had she used it again?

A young girl stood beside the glass cases, her mother and father behind her. The youngster seemed fascinated.

"They were great warriors, it says on this plague, in AD 60 odd. They fought Romans, then amalgamated and helped them. There were many battles and they often came close to getting killed. Dangers existed when hunting, it says, Alegia," the man finished, addressing his daughter.

"I know," Alegia replied." I can see their faces. There are some missing though, three Queens. One had long red hair, another other shorter blonde and the other even shorter red hair. I wonder why they're not here?"

"How do you know that," her father snapped with a deriding laugh. "You're making it up."

"I just do, that one spoke to me. Her name is Brevit, she was the Fighting Leader and gave her life for the Queen called Lauren. The Queens had two young daughters they adopted because of battles and a raid. One had the same name as me. She was very pretty and brave too."

Stan, from his position nearby had overheard everything the girl said. He went and looked at her for a while.

"What do you want?" the man asked, hostility in his tone.

"I was the curator here and can't believe what you daughter just said. You can see that, young lady?"

She nodded. "I think her name was Brevit and saved Lauren. She whispered to me. The other Queens were Alyssa and Sheelan. One girl had my name, the other was called Betany. Is that right?"

"I am amazed, yes, that is exactly right."

"How can you know that?" argued her father. "It says here that was two thousand years ago. They never left any records."

"I'll tell you a story that you may find unbelievable but it is absolutely true. One day the local police picked up two women and when questioned, they claimed to have come from the Iron Age. Nobody believed of course, a natural reaction. I was a psychiatric professor at a nearby hospital. I was called in to check them over, the police thought they were probably mad. Their clothes were the first thing that struck me, woollen tunic and short trousers, the blonde woman's were dyed red, very unusual. As I talked to them it began to dawn on me the blonde one known as Lauren, might be telling the truth because of the things she said and that she couldn't have possibly have known otherwise. I had some of their objects and clothing radiocarbon dated and sure enough, they were that old. The police released them to my hospital for observation. I asked them if they would help my friend Fran Bromyard, an archaeologist, to find the fort they lived on, and they did. I knew the pair wanted to return, there had been a battle and were worried about the other Queen and their friends. I arranged that, letting them use a time portal they claimed existed and never saw them for ages. I knew their medicine was very primitive and as Lauren had been a modern woman and was trying to heal people from illness and wounds, sent a box of stuff to them through it. That portal appeared at specific times in the large wood that used to be just over there," Stan said indicating the place with an arm.

"Fran wanted to go through it and see what it was like back then. She said if they could walk through it to here, we could do the opposite. And we did, spending a few weeks there. So I met and knew all these people. It was my job here to preserve bodies found in the barrows near here. But I wouldn't put them on display. Then I had to bow to pressure from the board, I hated doing it. They never asked me anything about them so their faces aren't quite right and as you rightly say, Alegia, the Queens are missing. That's because we never found them. Lauren lived near here once but got drawn into that strange mist and found herself in the Iron Age. Me and Fran are the only people who know of that portal and exactly where it is. I keep it a close secret because it would be very dangerous to go there. They did have two daughters, one called Alegia, like you, and Betany, as you say, young lady. Poor Fran nearly got eaten by a bear while we visited, those and wolves still lived here back then. Fran loved it. She gave up her job here as an archaeologist and disappeared. I never heard from her again, nor any of the Queens. I don't know how you know about them, Alegia, maybe you're the same Alegia reincarnated? You plainly feel a very strong connection."

"Would you show me where the portal is, please?"

"No, I dare not do that. You may go back at another time when everything is different." Stan bent and whispered in the girl's ear. "They were fairy Queens, so could live forever and that is why we never found their remains. Alyssa told me they would return to the Fairymounds when they died or their time here was up and live in the Caverns. Would you like to do that?"

"Didn't they get old?" Alegia asked.

"Never. They looked old at times when they were unhappy, but when their lives were filled with joy they were incredibly beautiful, more than you can ever imagine. I know, I saw them."

"I will come back again one day. Will you be here?"

"I might Alegia. Go to reception and ask for Professor Stan, they all know me. I think you will find them as beautiful as ever. You have a unique gift if you can see them as they were, I envy you. But I know what they looked like from memory and in my heart. They were really kind and the people loved Queen Lauren, she cared for them all deeply.

358

They all called her a Goddess because she used modern medicine and recovery practices. However, most of the women that lived in the fort were warriors so could fight with bows, swords and shields to protect them or hunt wild animals. Goodbye Alegia, you do look like her. Perhaps we'll meet again one day soon."

Alegia turned and waved as her parents took her away. "Goodbye Stan."

Yes, Stan thought, she's the spitting image.

The End

Forever, and until Eternity

The Quest

Book Eight in the series; Abandoning the Hill Fort after the Romans come and flog them on frames, the Queens realise it is unfair on their population living in the forest; they tell them to return and merge into the Roman way of life to survive. But the Queens must find the magical swords, empowered at the Standing Stones, but hidden under a bush as Legate Veranius arrived. Alyssa is imprisoned in the cell and left to die. A subterfuge is invented to save her. Their daughters are taken with them for fear of execution. Damarion finds them, and with his followers and Gramm's village, they fight part of a Roman legion. Will Quintus Veranius try to take revenge? They are outlawed and begin the Quest for their lost swords, taken by an unknown person from their hiding place.

Forever, and Until Eternity
Book One
The Hill Fort

Forever, and Until Eternity
Book Two
Bravery of the Soul

Forever, and Until Eternity
Book Three
Proof of Innocence

Forever, and Until Eternity
Book Four
Into Destiny

Forever, and Until Eternity
Book Five
Tragedy of the Heart

Forever, and Until Eternity
Book Six
Maiden Castle

Forever, and Until Eternity
Book Seven
Freedom Fighters

Forever, and Until Eternity
Book Eight
The Quest

About the Author

This is a recent picture of me. I spent a good few years holding a naval commission. On leaving the Service I spent three years retraining in horticulture, then went on the bring several large estate gardens to an acceptable condition from wrecks over twenty years. From Surrey and Hampshire, I moved to west London, England and began writing. The journey has been an interesting one, partly from research of the period but mainly from what has been described as an overactive imagination. It has been great fun, but at the same time very sad, but seriously researched. And just in case you wondered; yes, I've been a warrior (don't be fooled by my soft, cuddly exterior) have used both the cross and longbows and enjoy archery. I also took martial arts lessons, shoot guns, play golf and simply love ancient history. Oh, and climbed trees too. When I get time, I write.

eBooks

My series Forever, and until Eternity is available from Amazon and other outlets.

Angela Jane Halliday

website http://www.angelahalliday.co.uk

Angela Halliday on Facebook

Angela Halliday on Twitter

Proof

Made in the USA
Columbia, SC
01 June 2018